Among Australian writers and writers on Australian subjects the reputation of Ion Idriess stands high. He has travelled many thousands of miles throughout the practically unknown country of Central Australia and the far North, and speaks with authority on many phases of life unknown to most of us.

This writer can find charm and romance in unlikely places. Whether he is walking through a pandanus thicket or exploring a water-lily lagoon he sees always the beauties of his surroundings, the strange vegetation and the unusual things.

"In Crocodile Land" is principally the story of travels by lugger through northern waters and into slimy creeks where the huge crocodiles abound. The author took part in many hunting expeditions and enlightens us on the various methods adopted for catching these fearsome creatures. The party had more than a little success, to the great glee of the blackfellows who accompanied them.

We journey next into the country of the buffaloes. Here on sunlit clearings through thickets of pandanus palms the buffaloes were to be found in hundreds. The author describes the scene. "Around its green edges were big red kangaroos cropping the grass while giant jabirus and smaller cranes fished the lagoon edges, buffaloes staring at us solemnly.'" There is plenty of risk in hunting the buffalo. A man must have a fine horse, intelligent and sure-footed: he must be a perfect shot, for there is only one sure way of killing a buffalo with the first shot-a bullet into the backbone where the hide is thin. Once the shooting starts, the horse must continue his gallop, faster than the buffaloes and alongside them, keeping them going. One stumble and the end is near for horse and rider.

Western Mail, Perth 1946

Skinning on board.

In Crocodile Land

Wandering in Northern Australia

ION IDRIESS

Introduced by Tony McKenna

ETT IMPRINT
Exile Bay

This 9th edition published by ETT Imprint, Exile Bay 2022

ETT IMPRINT
PO Box R1906
Royal Exchange NSW 1225 Australia

First published by Angus & Robertson in 1946. Reprinted 1947, 1948, 1950, 1951, 1952, 1966, 1969.
First electronic edition by ETT Imprint 2022

Copyright © Idriess Enterprises Pty Ltd, 2022
Introduction copyright © Tony McKenna 2022

ISBN 9781922698-29-2 (pbk)
ISBN 9781922698-31-5 (ebk)

Cover: Crocodile hunting on the Daly River, 1934.

Designed by Tom Thompson

CONTENTS

CHAPTER   PAGE

Chapter	Title	Page
I.	UP SAIL FOR CROCODILE LAND	9
II.	THE CREW	14
III.	THE CREEK	20
IV.	IN THE HOME OF THE CROCODILES	26
V.	"LITTLE FELLER" CROCODILE	34
VI.	A PREHISTORIC INFERNO	39
VII.	A STROLL IN BUFFALO LAND	44
VIII.	CROCODILE LOVE	48
IX.	THE FAMILY STRUGGLE FOR SURVIVAL	53
X.	A DAY IN CRANE LAND	58
XI.	QUAINT FACTS ABOUT CROCS	62
XII.	THE "SLAVES" PUT IT ACROSS	68
XIII.	BATTLES OF GIANTS	74
XIV.	THE FRONTIERS OF ADVENTURE	81
XV.	IN BUFFALO LAND	87
XVI.	THE DUCK-HUNTERS	96
XVII.	THE OLD DAYS IN DARWIN	103
XVIII.	IN DANGEROUS WATERS	108
XIX.	NEW SHOOTING GROUNDS	115
XX.	WAGIS, QUEEN OF THE PUMPKIN	121
XXI.	EXCITING MOMENTS	126
XXII.	MEN OF THE WILDS	131
XXIII.	WILD WOMEN	136
XXIV.	WHERE ALL THINGS EAT TO LIVE	141
XXV.	LIFE OF THE WILD	146
XXVI.	DANGEROUS NIGHTS	151
XXVII.	THE CREW IN DISGRACE	158
XXVIII.	THE TRAPPER TRAPPED	163
XXIX.	THE FLYING PLAGUE	167
XXX.	FIGHT FOR LIFE	172
XXXI.	THE PATROLS RIDE OUT	180
XXXII.	NALGEE	187
XXXIII.	THE STONE AGE WILL PASS AWAY	192
XXXIV.	THE BLOOD HOLE	197

AUTHOR'S NOTE

THE incidents and observations recorded in this book were not all noted on one trip, but throughout years of wandering across the continent from the north-east coast to the north-west — little things that attracted a bushman's curiosity, or were pointed out to me by trappers or hunters, or by that incomparable student of the wild, the aboriginal. I must ask the reader's forbearance if there are errors in my account of the anatomy of the creatures described, for I am far from being a naturalist.

For photos other than my own I should like to thank *Walkabout*, Fred Don, Jack Mahoney, Ted Morey, Mr St John Robinson, the National Publicity Association, and the Department of Information.

I. L. I.

FOREWORD

THERE was no dustcover on the book that caught my attention while idly looking through the bookshelves of my Grandfather's country property. Just three words in faded teal writing – *In Crocodile Land.*

Little did I know then as a boy of around 14 what an influence this book of Idriess's would have on my life and the travels and adventure it would lead me on around Northern Australia after I left school.

So, what was it about the book that provided such inspiration for a city based private school boy. Basically it was the rawness, the frontier based stories and characters that Idriess captured so well along with the gritty black and white photos, thus nurturing a keen desire to seek adventure in the North just as he had done.

Luckily, I never had to encounter a character as bleak and callous as the Skipper that Idriess had to endure, described in the book by Idriess as "you were born to be one of the argumentative, obstinate cusses sent to plague the world". Moreover the racist language use by the Skipper is confronting and shockingly real.

Happily, the book displays Idriess's great story telling skills allowing the reader to immerse themselves in the steamy mangroves teeming with birdlife and menacing crocodiles. It was these depictions that meant most to me along with his admiration of the aboriginal bush skills and their knowledge and love of their beloved country.

His knowledge and admiration of our First Nations people can sometimes seem slightly strange by terms he uses but I greatly recommend reading *Nemarluk* and *The Red Chief* to understand his acknowledgment of these traditional owners and their pride of ownership of this great country.

Idriess has a unique way of introducing quirky and adventurous characters throughout his books and this is no exception and I often think to myself to how lucky I was to meet some of the same breed in my travels.

I'm sure that Cane Knife Jack who I met a number of times would have featured in one of his books as his reputation for wearing no clothes but just a cane knife on a belt as he traipsed through the rainforest between Cape Tribulation and Cairns was legendary. Likewise but with clothes on were the Watkins brothers of Cardwell who I became treasured friends with over many years. What amazing exploits Cocky,

Frisco and Micky got up to on along the Far North Coast and I feel forever grateful to Idriess who inspired me to head North to meet such seafaring legends.

Finally, thank goodness for Tom Thompson who keeps these stories alive especially in this case by publishing the 9th Edition after being out of print for 50 years.

Tony McKenna
Producer
Discovering Idriess

I

UPSAIL FOR CROCODILE LAND

How about coming crocodile shooting?" suggested the Skipper. "There's money in skins at present."

"That tempts me," I answered.

"Good—man was born to be tempted. Anyway there's adventure in it —and maybe profit. I've got the boat. We'll recruit a crew of sorts. You supply the petrol, and a share of the stores?"

"Righto!" I agreed. "That will do me."

And we strolled across to the pub.

It was a warm day in Darwin. The little port of "Happy-go-lucky" was dreaming away its midday siesta. I'd been wondering whether I'd take a trip west out to the wild Fitzmaurice River country looking for gold, or east across the Alligator Rivers buffalo shooting for hides. Or would I simply wait until the pearling luggers sailed, then cruise with them?

In that humid midday the pot of beer was cool.

"There's thousands of slimy reptiles lying along the coast just waiting to be shot," winked the Skipper.

I smiled. Crocodiles are not so easy. But the question of what to do next was settled. The dreamy North has a way of solving the problems of her lackadaisical sons.

From the hallway came the lazy voices of a few men taking things easy in cool whites. Business men, Government officials, a pearler or two, several cattlemen in from the back country.

The Skipper was an old acquaintance, a sea wanderer whose home and love was his little vessel. It brought him his living too, for there are out-of-the-way jobs to be picked up by such a craft in northern waters. It may be in running stores to an isolated lighthouse, or cable-repair work, or a salvage job on a wreck, or transporting a load of native lepers, or carrying a police patrol by sea, or a rescue party for lost airmen — unusual jobs come the way of such a craft apart from the job the owner may indulge in at his own whimsical fancy.

The Skipper sighed as he put down his empty pot. He was not a drinking man. We had pledged our word, so we strolled out into the empty street. My companion, though short in stature, was stoutly built as his singlet and shorts amply showed. Of a benign and apparently innocent countenance, this colourful roamer was liable to "turn up" anywhere.

"We'll stroll down to Jolly's and buy the petrol," I suggested.

"Right. Then we'll ship the stores, and sail with the dawn tide."

Surely neither man nor woman could have resisted such a night to start an adventure. Full moon silvering the water, a flying fish like a quivering jewel as it skipped down that silvered lane. A few stars only, for the heavens were a blue mist. The shoreline tiny cliffs velvet black below a tracery of treetops, an occasional bungalow light shining like a star. Farther south behind there Darwin lay dreaming. The *Lotus* like a lily in the night swinging to a full tide, the riding light on the jib stay brightly burning. In gentlest movement, the water was quietly lolloping her sides. Like a ghost vessel astern lay the white lugger *St Francis*, from Bathurst Island Mission. Just ahead the shadowy outline of a black-painted vessel from which came laughing voices from aboriginals aboard. The black figures stood out as they hoisted a hurricane lamp from the deck. She was the *Chantress* just in from Buffalo Land, loaded with hides. A buffalo shooter's vessel this—Bert Wills of Kapalgo station owns her. Dimly back on the harbour the hazy tip of a mast suggested a score of pearling craft at anchor.

It was the time of the spring tides; the vessels had been at sea, fishing through the neaps. They had come in to unload their shell, for outside in many places the spring tides run is dangerously strong and also dirty the water. At such periods the divers cannot see when under below.

"They've found a new pearlshell bed," nodded the Skipper. "Brought in some good pearls too."

"That will be good for the Port."

"Yes, liven up business."

We boarded the *Lotus*, breathing in air misty with adventure.

"You certainly lead a happy-go-lucky life, Skipper," I remarked as we tied the dinghy astern. "Your own craft which is your home, your own master, working where and as you like, liable at any moment to up anchor and sail on a cruise for new shores."

"Not bad," he replied. "Life is what a man makes of it and gets out of it, providing he's not pushed the wrong way. I'm always being pushed the wrong way."

You were born to be one of the argumentative, obstinate cusses sent to plague the world."

"I'm always 'agin th' Governmint'," he smiled. "Officialdom is a red rag to me. Come below and well stow away the swags."

Meet Herman our engineer, a quiet, cheery companion who laughs easily. His cheeks are wrinkled and he wears a thick necklace of split bamboo around his throat. Of wiry build, he is smart and active, his dark eyes flash in a smile, his legacy of Malay blood loves the sea and roaming and stringed music. Throughout the voyage on many a still night he will dreamily play the guitar. He writes a wonderful fist. His mother, a soft-voiced aboriginal, can read and write. His father, a Malay, son of a petty chief recruited in the early days, taught Herman Malay as a language which, with English, every seafaring man should know. Herman was educated at the Darwin State School, and later developed into a clever mechanic. A good seaman and rifle shot, his is an uncanny touch with an engine. In dangerous waters, through treacherous channels in a heavy sea, Herman will coax that engine to behave without a break-down throughout the cruise.

The Skipper soon has the kettle humming on the primus. We'll enjoy coffee and a snack before turning in. A surprise here below, for the vessel appears to be all cabin. Herman stands upright and his head just touches the chart rack under the roof. The vessel is a two-masted ketch, fifty-odd feet long, all open below like one huge cabin divided by bulkheads into three parts, the fo'c'sle, the cabin proper, and the cockpit. Climbing up the companionway one steps into the cockpit, thence up on deck. The little galley is at the stem, the water tap under the steps. The vessel seems very strongly built. In the main cabin are our bunks. We step over coils of rope and gear, over cases and bags of stores littered on the broad cabin floor. Two dozen kerosense tins full of fresh water, the water tank also full, the shelves loaded with tinned stuffs. There is a rack for the plates and pannikins, knives and forks. Another rack holding military rifles and boxes of ammunition, chains and hooks sufficient to kill one thousand crocodiles—if we can get them —which we won't. Crocodiles are not so easy as that. We dine hungrily, we will sleep well tonight ...

We had barely closed our eyes when a sudden drumming of the engine was drowned in a bellow of:

"Open up sails!"

Bare feet were pattering up on the cabin top. I tumbled up the companionway as the Skipper roared:

"Cast off gaskets!"

And we sprang to it to unfurl sails.

"Thought I'd wake you," the Skipper called cheerily; "hence my roar to the crew. There's only two of 'em so far but why shouldn't I roar! Here's where the captain takes the tiller. Heave up!"

We jumped to the windlass. The anchor chain came clanking in, grudgingly the hook came groaning up. Strenuous work for three men handling that heavy, wet ironware in the chilly dawn.

"Trice up the anchor!"

"Up jib!"

"Jib staysail!"

"Up mainsail!"

"Up foresail!"

As we made fast she gathered way.

"Coil halliards down."

When we'd made all cosy the Skipper smiled. "Ah! Smart crew. We're actually moving. And now, who is cook?"

We were rippling across the harbour with the sun a copper disc astern.

"We must recruit our crew," said the Skipper. "That is, if there are any benighted humans in this land of the brave and free who will deign to accept a job."

That was a cheery breakfast, steering towards a haze which developed into Talc Head standing up as a white and red banded cliff tipped with dark-green scrub. Wee beaches hedged with scrub gleamed white and gold to the risen sun. It was to Talc Head by swift canoe that the big chief Nemarluk sped when he made his sensational escape from Darwin jail. In this scrub his friends and Amazon wife were waiting, staring across the harbour. And it was to here that Constable Don and tracker Smiler tracked him. On a head-land here Smiler, surprising the big chief, closed on him with revolver against spear and, both weapons failing, they clinched and rolled down and down in a snarling fury of tooth and claw.

The Skipper and Herman scanned the beach, Herman pointing to a canoe and exclaiming, "See! Smoke. Just rising, and natives around it."

"Down jib!" called the Skipper.

"Down fores'l!"

"Down mains'l!"

"Down anchor!"

We rowed ashore and were greeted by a sophisticated old greybeard who immediately asked for tobacco. Gravely he enthused on the seaman-like qualities of his "boys" as we walked to the cool line of scrub back from the beach. By the scrub edge a group of the old folk were squatting; lubras were chatting as they chopped pandanus nuts for breakfast. Quite a number of piccanins were romping about. Men yawned and comfortably gossiped in the warming sand, shady trees beside them awaiting their pleasure when the sun grew hot. After a round of grave bargaining the Skipper signed on one lackadaisical man who admitted he would not mind a "holiday" at sea. He declared his name was "Freddy", under-stood all about boats, knew everything that was to be known about "alligators" and was not scared of the biggest of them.

"He'd run a mile if he saw one," declared the Skipper, "but he's been in a dinghy before and is the best on offer " He tried hard to enlist the services of several other huskies but they were too comfortable, hardly bothering to shake disdainful heads.

"The poor, downtrodden natives," exclaimed the Skipper with a wave of all-embracing sympathy, "enslaved by the whites! Oppressed! Forlorn groups of humanity! Consider their state. Who among us should have the heart to moan at income tax? Not to mention unemployment, and the butcher's and baker's bills!"

I grinned. The Skipper had a soft spot in his heart for the aborigines and in his own way had done them many a good turn.

"There's another side to the picture," I suggested, "here's old Paddy —one of the very last of the once numerous Darwin blacks. We're responsible. His tribesmen—like many others— have vanished. The handful of natives around here come from tribes farther east and west—they will vanish too."

II

THE CREW

HALF a dozen young lubras eagerly demanded to be "signed on".

The Skipper regretfully shook his head.

"You would certainly prove better men than these," he explained in pidgin, "but the authorities would never allow me to ship you aboard as seamen, the authorities being ignorant men."

"Sorry to disappoint you with visions of a floating harem, boys, he grinned to us. "They'd get our throats cut in the end. Come, let's go aboard and leave these poor downtrodden savages to their misery."

The lubras pouted, then demanded tobacco; while all claimed a present in return for the recruit they were losing. He meanwhile had gathered his spears, thrown a grunt to his wife and piccanins and was taking a touching farewell of his hunting dog.

"Up sail! Up anchor!" and we sailed away with our new recruit halloing answer to farewell calls from the shore. Those calls echoed long drawn out and tremulous with feeling as we drew away.

"You'd think he was taking a voyage to the end of the world," shrugged the Skipper. "Even his dog is howling."

Presently we neared West Point and a dozen black figures became visible on the beach. Others were wading the shallows spearing fish for breakfast. Among them a tall thin figure showed prominently.

"Something tells me," nodded the Skipper, "that that long black snake on legs is our man."

He was, the tall thin Jacky was to prove our best "'gator" boy. With a pained expression he signed on, which meant merely carrying his spears aboard then squatting down by the cookhouse.

As we walked along the beach the Skipper pointed to a powerful aboriginal walking ahead of us.

"See that ball of muscle? What would a Rothschild give for his physique! That prehistoric relic is richer than any millionaire. Perfect health, never worries over rent or depressions, lives free in God's own sunshine. In London he'd pay pounds to be bathed in 'actinic rays', which would mean the girl would switch on the electric light, take his money, bow him out, and giggle. Study this heathen savage, sublime in his independence. His only burden his fish spear, his only urge his stomach. He is not forced to toil even for the wherewithal to buy a hat. Nature gives him everything for nothing, and yet we try to force our civilization on the aboriginal. No wonder he scorns us as crazy."

"He's got his worries though, Skipper."

"What worries?"

"Well—maybe feminine ones."

"Why bring women into it," sighed the Skipper. "What a world it would be without women."

"We'd all be noble savages," I grinned.

"Yes," agreed the Skipper. "There'd be nothing left to quarrel over."

The native camp was tucked in behind a shallow arm of the sea, on warm sand and shells and loose sandstone crinkling underfoot as we trod the fallen leaves. Healthy clumps of tall bamboo, subtropical trees, vines and bushes sheltered this simple camp. Under two broad-leafed trees was their cooking place, their spears and dilly-bags of precious things, their piccaninnies and dogs speculatively eyeing us as our guides came shouting to camp. Here came a surprise, for with them sat a gaunt white man staring from below grey eyebrows. His grey moustache emphasized a lined face brown as the brownest berry. An exceptionally well-educated man, he had simply drifted back . He now lived the life that these people lead. The Skipper set the boys to cutting bamboo poles. They often come in handy on board such craft as ours. Work proceeded briskly, the bamboos ringing to the blows of the heavy knives. Then he signed on three more boys. The muscular Paddy was one. He could only grunt a few sentences of pidgin, but was to prove an excellent bush companion to me. They all of course wanted tobacco and scraps of ironware, the lubras smilingly insistent. We boarded the *Lotus* with our load of bamboos and crew and several "travellers" who cadged a lift down the coast to visit tribesmen. One of them was the "Old Man", a very tall, ludicrously thin specimen of wide-awake abo., cunning as a bush rat. Dawdling in movement, he measured us off from shrewd old eyes.

"That skinny streak of misery would make a good pull-through to clean the rifles with," declared the Skipper.

"Yes, he's near thin enough to crawl through the eye of a needle."

"His big hoofs would get stuck," said the Skipper, "but we could use him as a thread to patch the sails. What a wicked-looking old shrewdie he is, eyeing us off and planning just how he can use us to his own advantage."

And so it was to prove.

To the Skipper's command amateur feet stamped the deck in earnest now, except the Old Man's. He squatted on the cabin top smoking, his grizzled face a mask, calmly looking on. The anchor chain came rattling in with a will, pulley-blocks creaked and squeaked to real weight on the ropes, the *Lotus* shot ahead with the song of a live ship.

"Give me the old aboriginal" laughed the Skipper from the tiller. "He's thick in the head as you make 'em, but he's a jolly good sailorman."

"You're singing a different tune now."

"Oh well, I mean when he's not asleep. When he's not asleep he's hungry, and when his belly is full he's asleep." Fainter grew the farewell "yak-aing" from the shore. Jacky stepped quietly to the tiller and took it with the ease of a practised hand, Freddy proved familiar with shipboard routine. The other huskies were set to work at shifting the stores that littered the cabin top, and stacking them below.

Heading out between East and West Points the *Lotus* lifted to the swing of the open sea. A beautiful afternoon, the bluey-green water prettily sunlit, a light breeze. We were fairly on our way.

The crew soon settled down. Jacky, the thin one, proved a good boy at the tiller; an efficient dinghy man too. Strong as whipcord, the muscles of his legs and arms stood out like duck eggs.

"Just a piece of string with knobs on," said the Skipper.

But Jacky was much more than that. Behind his woebegone expression he was a deep thinker. We found this out as the voyage progressed.

"I wonder what plot that skein of misery is hatching out now?" the Skipper would remark when Jacky was quieter and more mournful than usual.

Surprisingly though, Jacky's face with its innumerable deep wrinkles would unexpectedly spread into a rippling grin of humour, often at our expense. But he knew his job. He dressed well—a rag around his forehead and one around his waist were clothes enough for him. Freddy's hair had been recently cut by pounding the tangled mass between two stones. The frayed ends looked pretty awful. His black moustache had undergone similar treatment, lending his furrowed face a comically rakish air. When he bent his head down the companionway to watch Herman working at the engine I could see daylight through the hole in his nose. It was large enough to have thrust a meat-hook through, let alone the bone he wore on gala occasions. His deliberate slowness of movement often annoyed the Skipper.

"I'd like to put a bundle of crackers under him," he growled.

"He'd move then!"

"No, he wouldn't. He'd sit on them and wonder what it was all about."

Billy was middle-aged with pipe-clayed hair and one of those good-humoured, Semitic faces sometimes seen in aborigines. A wink, any gesture, would urge him to smile and then the deep wrinkles down his cheeks would spread and deepen into canyons. A thick necklace of bamboo around his throat was clothes enough for Billy. This occasionally annoyed the Skipper.

To think that that untutored savage can wear his beauty unadorned," he would exclaim, "while I must buy expensive clothes to hide mine."

"The world is missing something," I'd agree, and Herman would grin at the Skipper's ample proportions in singlet and shorts.

Paddy, the shaggy-browed he-man, was the quiet, solemn boy. Besides the deep cicatrices across chest and back and shoulders that denoted warrior-hood, he sported four large scars from spear thrusts. Of these scars he was very proud, as was Jacky of his single scar. Although it ran right down one cheek of his backside, Jacky was no less proud of it for that. One day when Jacky was boasting of his prowess the Skipper remarked, though in pidgin:

"No doubt you're a brave warrior, Jacky, otherwise you would not have got that spear in your face."

And the roar of laughter showed that the Skipper, if not the spear, had hit the mark.

Paddy wore only a perpetual frown, trying to understand what we wanted of him. A willing if clumsy worker, most of his time when he was not sleeping he spent laboriously carving spearheads. It was a labour of love. And he could use his weapons too; he was an expert with the spear. He had fairly recently "come in" from an outside tribe and was well on the first stage to becoming "civilized".

"He'll soon be spoiled," said the Skipper glumly, "under the enervating influences of civilization."

I reckoned Paddy the most dependable of the bunch. All the crew were fairly efficient, fairly willing, fairly interested, generally caring little whether they happened to be here, there, or anywhere—until such time as they did get a definite urge to be somewhere else. A carefree life. But each possessed more mentality than the average white man would give them credit for. Mostly when we were sailing they sat gossiping and smoking up forard, happy with their brand-new pipes, their stick of tobacco and box of matches daily per man. And this peaceful scene, especially when they were sprawled on the broad of their backs puffing up at the sky, seldom failed to draw a speech from the Skipper.

"Take a look at these poor downtrodden slaves of the Far North, this wonderful land with its undeveloped potentialities, its immense, untouched resources. Are these poor heathens worrying about building railway lines, and developing harbours, and building new cities so that we and our children's children may slave all the more? Are they worrying about their income tax? Are their many wrinkles brought about by the high cost of living? Glance at their fires merrily blazing under the trees ashore there. Do they toil to produce coal and gas, then buy it by the sweat of their brow? Do they consider we are fools, lying awake of nights, flogging the cat as to how to pay the rent? No. These people and all their wild bush brethren have enjoyed their breakfast this morning, breakfast provided for them by nature, or by their taskmaster, the silly white man. They have dined so well, they who are supposed to be starving and in misery. Not one of these lads knows what a dole ticket is, doesn't know what it means to walk the streets on a winter's night!"

"Why should they? They've got plenty of firewood in the bush!"

"He doesn't know the meaning of a doctor's or a landlady's bill," went on the Skipper unheedingly. "He's advanced too much, has our prehistoric man. He's far beyond depressions and relief work and taxation and zip fasteners."

The suggestion of our naked crew dillydallying with zip fasteners seemed to tickle Herman.

"Go on! Laugh your sides out," brooded the Skipper. "All the same, it's true. Ages ago our prehistoric genius learned to live without all those things. He leads a sporting life, but you don't see him slaving at physical-culture schools nor sweating away his fat in a Turkish bath. No, he's a poor benighted heathen who knows nothing about our highly developed modern culture. All he's got is a healthy appetite, perfect sight, a sound sleep system, and a physical body that is a ball of muscle bound together with whipcord for endurance. The poor fellow knows nothing whatever about the triumphs of modern dentistry. He is blessed with a full set of teeth that are the envy of every white man who sees them—this downtrodden wretch who never yet sat in the dentist's chair can crack bones with his teeth. Neither does he know anything about our modern and expensive sewerage system. Yet he possesses an unimpaired alimentary canal." "You'll make us envious of the aboriginal directly."

"Envious! Who wouldn't be envious! He's got nothing that we've got, hut he's got everything we haven't got!"

"It's too comfortable to argue," I lazily replied. "I'm going to follow the aboriginal's example and go to sleep."

"You won't sleep as soundly as they do. You're sure to have some debt, or other trouble, on your mind."

"Oh well, lots of the poor old aboriginals are troubled by diseases we've given them—and they've rarely a doctor to treat them either."

And Herman smiled sadly.

Tom Cole, buffalo hunter and crocodile shooter in the
Northern Territory throughout the 1930s, whose exploits
were the the catalyst to write this book.

III

THE CREEK

WE were slipping dreamily by a low coastline where sunlit beaches peeped out between dark-green fringes of trees. Miles back inland loomed an indistinct dark silhouette of hilly country. Through Shoal Bay the water glinted yellow-green, betraying the bottom just under below. Gun Point stood up nearby, with a long bamboo flagpole standing up on the outer tip of Gun Point reef, a sure sign that the survey ship Moresby had been working hereabout. Herman lay snatching forty winks near his precious engine. We steered into the entrance of the South Passage through the Vernon Islands, the Sou'-west Vernon, Nor'-west and East Vernon. Low-lying islands, dense with mangroves.

"There's a clump of tiny islands across there." The Skipper nodded towards Apsley Strait. 'We call them the Buchanans. There's a monster 'gator lives on one, hangs around on the nor'-east side of Buchanan Island. He's taken three gins and a buck. One day he rose up and splashed his big paws on a canoe. The natives panicked, and he got away with a young girl. He's said to be three times the size of a dinghy. When he lies on the mud his barrel is as large as a dinghy turned upside down."

"I'd like to shoot him."

"So would I. I hate man-eaters."

The big Melville and Bathurst islands lie just north of here. These islanders are probably the best in physique and most cultured of any aboriginals in Australia. From Melville Island the aboriginals at times set off in canoes with the tide and make the Vernons. There they camp, fishing and generally enjoying themselves while waiting for the next tide, which carries them to Gun Point, on the mainland. The following tide takes them to Casuarina Beach. Here they beach the canoes and walk the ten miles farther into Darwin.

They stay as long as they like, they please themselves, the poor benighted slaves!" and the Skipper waved dramatically at the crew peacefully snoring on the cabin top. "When they've played up enough and the police want them they just put their fingers to their noses, take to the bush, jump in their canoes and go singing back with the tides. A fat lot they care for us and our civilization! What hope would a white man have if he broke the law as they do?"

I gazed at Escape Cliffs standing up like a bright red-and-white wall among the trees.

Now look here, Skipper. Perhaps on more than one occasion you may have sheltered an aboriginal who has seriously broken the law."

"Of course I'd shelter an outcast. I'm agin the Government anyway."

"You can't have it both ways."

"Yes I can—so long as I can get away with it."

A few men were at present making a crust on Melville Island by an unusual industry—snake hunting. To my knowledge Dave and Tom Woods were the pioneers. At that time there was a market in Sydney for better-quality snake skins, because the fashion was for snake-skin shoes, belts and lady's handbags. There are plenty of wrigglers on Melville Island, comparatively easy to capture during the wet season. For then the water overflows the swamps and low-lying areas, and creeping up over the grassy flats forces the reptiles up on to higher ground. In such havens their numbers continually increase and they fall easy prey to the aboriginal.

He's an adept at catching snakes with the bare hand. A lightning-like thrust at the back of the neck and his fingers have closed and pressed tightly on the base of the jaws. With open mouth the snake helplessly winds itself round and round his arm.

Another method is to grab the end of the reptile's tail, with the same movement snatching it off the ground and swinging it around and around; then "crack" it like a whip and off flies the snake's head. This is an expert's job.

With edible snakes I've often seen the aboriginal grasp the reptile's head behind the jaws, but with a finger grip this time that keeps the jaws closed. Lifting the wriggling thing off the ground he opens his capacious mouth and calmly thrusts the snake's head inside. Closing tightly on its neck with his magnificent teeth, he smartly jerks the snake's body, thus dislocating its neck. He does it calmly and easily in a matter of seconds, unless pausing to make some remark or joke with a friend before thrusting the reptile's head into his mouth.

But when it is a question of catching snakes in number a forked stick is generally used. It is about the length of a walking stick, the forked end narrow, each prong about two or three inches in length. Unerringly choosing a locality where bushcraft tells him snakes will abound, the hunter soon sees one and jabs the fork of the stick around its neck and presses down, thus pinning the wriggler to the ground. It can be killed then as the trapper has directed. The body must not be bruised as this could spoil the skin.

The most sought after by the trapper are the python and carpet snakes, often very prettily marked. They must be large, with a good breadth of skin, to satisfy the southern market. That market has since vanished, for the fickle fashion changed.

Near evening we rounded Cape Hotham and came gliding towards Mary Island, its waters now deeply shadowed by mangroves.

"Lower away fores'l!" yelled the Skipper, and as they sprang to it down came the sail.

"Lower jib!" and we came gliding in to anchorage.

"Down stays'll"

"Let go anchor!" and down she plonked while the chain rattled out quite musally on the now calm water. The main-sail was idly flopping from side to side.

"Down mains'l!"

"Make fast everything!" Two purposeful aboriginal horsemen came riding along to the store, well "Tucker time!"

Which order was greeted with a yell of delight from the "slaves". That's the only time they're human," growled the Skipper, "when tucker time comes—and when they're asleep."

Jacky, with a sly grin, passed some remark to the crew forward. Their black backs nearly convulsed with laughter.

"That fella talk that one?" called the Skipper.

"That one buffalo story," replied Jacky over his shoulder. "Him silly feller. Belly belonga him full up too much—he bog longa mud."

"What did that streak of misery say?" demanded the Skipper of Herman.

"I didn't quite catch it," smiled Herman. "It was something about a conceited old bull buffalo. Even when he admiringly gazed at his own reflection in the water he did not know how foolish he looked."

"Oh yeah!" snapped the Skipper. "And am I the buffalo?"

"Oh no, answered Herman. "It was only a simple native yam."

"Just because I don't know their lingo," growled the Skipper, "doesn't mean I don't see through their little tricks." And he grumbled his way aft.

I glanced at Herman and he smiled at me. We both knew the crew's nickname for the Skipper.

The boys often enjoyed a sly joke at our expense. Seldom a day passed but we did something that appeared childishly silly to them. They even grinned when we cleaned our teeth. They never cleaned their teeth, yet what perfect teeth they had. They thought us silly to work too when we had plenty of tucker and plenty of time to eat it. If that tucker had been theirs they would have sat down in some nice place and invited their friends and feasted and enjoyed it. They would have yarned and sung and slept, and awakened to eat again until it was all eaten. Only then, when they became hungry, would they lackadaisically have started out in search of more food. But no, we stupid white men insisted on working when there was no need to; always seemed to be in a hurry to go somewhere when haste was needless. In lots of ways white men are silly people to them, something to be quietly joked at. The aboriginal world is not our world.

While enjoying that appetizing meal a wonder moon peeped coyly from behind a wee cloud that was resting on the silhouetted treetops on the opposite side of the island, a moon of burnished copper and gold born from that wee cloud. As it emerged it grew into a swimming disc that sheened the treetops and sprayed a path of silver across the water to the white-painted *Lotus*. A fish sped through the silver in a comet's tail of brilliant bubbles.

Throughout the cruise our boys were like animals in their desire for sleep. At sundown after the evening meal, if they had not arranged for a murmurous corroboree song up for'ard, they came aft to the cockpit yawning, sleepy eyed, ready to lie down, pull the tarpaulin over them, and sleep. This despite the fact that throughout the day, unless it was a continuous hunting day, they would be snatching an hour or two's sleep now and then. With all this sleep it was difficult for them to awaken at dawn. And although the weather was beautiful they were often cold at night. Very strangely so, for a black's body, when he is asleep under even a slight covering, usually gives out a staggering amount of heat. Often in passing I've touched a tribesman sleeping thus and could feel the warmth coming from him.

Herman went below and set the gramophone going. It sounded rather well in the dreamy night. The Skipper undressed and accompanied the gramophone in a shuffling hula-hula. Having lost all youthful slimness, in his singlet the Skipper presented a paralysing spectacle. His exhibition of a South Sea dancing girl was priceless. If only he'd bumped his head on the cabin roof!

Suddenly, awake to the dramming of the engine, patter of feet above.

"Up anchor!"

I peeped up on deck, amazed that it was already dawn. Herman was at the engine, the crew hauling at winch and sails, the Skipper handling the tiller, not a breath of wind. A lovely dawn. Grudgingly I stayed below and lit the primus and cooked the bacon while the early morning sun winked down the companionway. The dawn sun, the moon, the breeze, the sea, and the bush are friendly companions—when in their gentler moods.

We ran in close to the shore, which was thickly treed with that densely growing, sinewy variety of subtropical growth often prolific on northern beaches. An hour later and Herman pointed towards some dark humpies, plain in the sunlight among the trees on the beach. This was the wet-season camp of Hutton the buffalo shooter—a lonely camp. We dropped anchor and landed. The camp was deserted, no tracks even, and yet we had seen the smoke rising amongst the trees. Natives probably, but they had vanished. Behind the huts gleamed a small, cold lagoon. Everywhere lay turtle carapaces, crocodile and buffalo bones. The bunks were of saplings overlaid with bark. Smaller huts were poked in among the shrubbery. A fairly large camp this, during the wet season when all hands would be here. A big old crocodile cautiously cruised out from the beach, but we saw no sign of human life.

"They must be inland on the plains, buffalo shooting," said the Skipper. "Dash it all. I'd hoped to pick up a boy here as a guide to Hunter's Creek farther down the coast. The natives say the 'gators are swarming in that creek. But the mouth of it is so narrow and difficult to locate. We'll have to poke along and find it ourselves." .

Just at sundown Jacky's keen eyes saw the tips of two long poles like black dots poking above the water near the shore a mile ahead.

"Guides to the channel," said the Skipper hopefully, "to guide Hunter's buffalo lugger. We'd run aground if we attempted the passage now. We'll anchor for the night."

The tide was out, the water yellow-brown, dangerously shoal. Plain in the rosy sunset a battalion of what appeared to be white men lined the shore edge—pelicans. Several crocodiles were cruising among them, and the black fin of an enormous shark. Paddy longingly fingered his heaviest fish spear, but a shot from Herman's rifle sent the shark racing in a lather of foam amongst the indignant pelicans.

At sunrise, breakfast.

"Up anchor!" and on a full tide we slowly ran towards shore, the Skipper in the bows anxiously swinging the leadline, Herman steering to orders as the leadline proved deepening or shallowing water. A few yards too far to port or starboard meant we would run aground. The navigation of the average sea-roamer may be rough but it gets places. The tips of the two long poles were now only just visible, a dense wall of mangroves behind them, no sign of an opening that might be the mouth of a creek. Slowly we skimmed past the sticks, then Jacky at the masthead saw the tip of another pole some quarter of a mile distant. We made for this, passed it, and were running bow on straight into the mangroves, all hands staring for sight of a creek, the Skipper continually heaving the leadline. When within a few yards of the man groves we turned and followed them along, a wall of trees on one side, a treacherously shallow sea on the other. Presently there appeared above the water the tips of young mangroves just out from the shoreline.

"Those mangroves are growing on a mudbank," said the Skipper, "mud that's been washed out of a creek. Must be getting near the creek mouth. If not, we're ditched."

We continued in a curve for half a mile, making the mangrove wall a guiding bank. Suddenly there appeared an opening in the trees. We turned outward to skirt the tree edges and the opening now showed a narrow street of water running straight into the mangroves. We turned sharply left and the creek opened out, a narrow, muddy creek walled by trees.

"Alligator! Alligator!" called Jacky and Billy. And pointed to two ugly snouts just on the surface swimming across the creek. They sank noiselessly as the white bows of the *Lotus* came knifing up the creek.

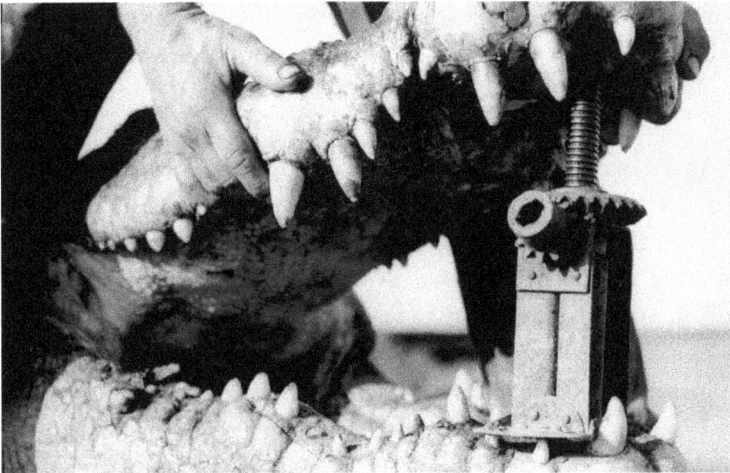

Crocodile shot by Hugo Schmidt at Port Alma in 1963.

IV

IN THE HOME OF THE CROCODILES

"'NOTHER one!" pointed Freddy casually, as a big fellow slid from the mangrove roots down into the water. Ugly brutes.

The creek was narrow as a walled-in street. Shadow caverns appeared among the trees and the maze of exposed roots looked like entanglements of snakes petrified as they had writhed up out of the mud. The trees were two walls of dull grey-green, the water muddy as the swift tide carried sticks and leaves upstream. A brilliant sky directly above deck, sunlight streaming down into this murmuring brown lane. Difficult to believe this was an Australian tidal creek. It was much more like an African jungle scene.

A harsh, metallic clanging rang out from deep within the mangroves.

"Pid!" exclaimed Paddy, and presently a steel-blue crane flashed out of the mangroves and winged low over the water upstream. The call of that bird coming suddenly from deep within the water-sodden trees sounded like the clang of metal.

"Look! 'Nother one!" pointed Billy.

And there appeared the snout and ridged tail of a crocodile crossing midstream. The boys for'ard were growing excited, anxious for the rifles to speak. As we steamed slowly along yet another saurian splashed down from the tree roots. Always there were crocodiles in sight, either swimming or silently sinking at our approach. I was to see them just as plentiful in other streams, but had not believed before that they occur so thickly in Australian waters. In northern Queensland waters and far west along the Kimberley coast in Western Australia the rivers only carry a few crocodiles each. But here they were everywhere. Seldom we saw them completely on the surface. Just the tip of the nose parting the faint ripples with, behind it, the knobby ridges of the eyes like two walnuts part submerged. And away behind, a few ser¬rations along the tail visible. A creepy spectacle, this gliding along just below the surface; no sign of the hideous bulk that in an instant could rise in a snapping fury of fang and claw.

Presently there appeared the tips of masts near the tree-tops, then the red-painted stem of an old lugger poking from the mangroves. We passed her and saw she was lying where her crew had cut a possy for her among the trees. A rough landing place for cargo was logged up, while farther on where sunlight showed in a cleared patch was a stack of bags of salt, and farther on dim stacks of buffalo hides.

We moored the *Lotus* fore and aft to the trees. It was a race to get the ropes out before the tide could smash us against the branches. With rifles handy we sat on deck to a jolly good feed.

"Big feller gator!" hissed Jacky and there were the ugly ridged eyes staring at us not twenty feet from the vessel.

"Bang!"

He plunged up convulsively, hard hit, and sank in a turmoil of water. He came up again all crumpled up and rolled half out of the water, his right forepaw held quaintly over his eye. He sank, but he was done. The boys jumped into the dinghy and prodded for him with the bamboos, but the tide had swept him downstream, rolling him along the muddy bottom. The tide was now racing back past the *Lotus* out to sea, hurrying brown water gurgling and hissing back from the mangrove roots. A continuous, heavy splashing too from shoals of mullet racing out to sea. Sometimes a shoal would be wheeled back by larger fish and, forced to beat the tide, they would leap against it and whack the onrushing water into clouds of spray.

When the tide had gone down somewhat we manned the dinghies and drifted quickly downstream. The thickly muddied water was still hurrying and hissing out to sea, the mullet shoals still racing with a continuous splashing. But in another hour or so the water would be steadier and clearer and shallow, except for an occasional deep hole. To shoot a crocodile at high tide means that he sinks, or slides down rom the bank and sinks, with the strong tide rolling him downstream towards the sea. Any that we shot now would disappear similarly, but would be stranded upon the mud-banks downstream as the tide receded. Those that slid down into deep holes might escape us, except those we located by prodding with spears, then lifted by means of long bamboos to which were attached steel hooks. This cruise was not for pleasure alone. We were shooting for crocodile hides, which, some little tune before the war, were a marketable commodity. but that market did not last long.

"Tch! Tch!" whispered Paddy as there arose the eyes, then the snout tip of a crocodile, and just past him two more walnuts breaking surface. They sank noiselessly as I aimed, the almost instantaneous, utterly silent movement of the brutes is uncanny. The splashing of the mullet was a continuous noisy sound, but these big brutes moved silently when they wished to.

We drifted on more slowly now, Jacky steering with the oars, the abos eyes intent on the water all around and higher up among the tangled roots along the banks. Below this maze the banks were becoming visible as sloping, slimy, blue-grey mud with a glistening, oily film to its surface. Every here and there up these mudbanks was a runway, like a slide that children might use in play. Each runway was the slide of some particular crocodile. Up this he crawled or rather slithered to get from the water up the bank to the mangroves and wait for prey, or sleep, or bask in gloom or shaft of sunlight Been shoot 'em!" pointed Paddy.

And there was the yellowish belly of a crocodile just visible upon an emerging sandbank. He was the one we'd shot from the *Lotus*. The bullet had smashed the back of his skull He was only nine feet long, a black and yellow skin.

We carried on downstream until Paddy's warning "Tch! Tch!" was a signal to Jacky to hold the dinghy motionless towards the bank. Blessed if I could distinguish a thing except muddy water with the slimy bank sloping high up to the terrace of roots. We pulled quietly across and there was the runway, cunningly camouflaged by now exposed roots.

But even from midstream the aboriginal's eyes had seen the crocodile's tracks up that runway, had seen that those tracks did not come down.

Gazing up into the roots I at last distinguished his head watching us from among the roots for all the world like a gigantic lizard, peering down, erect on forepaws. At the first shot he staggered, his paw rising in a helpless sort of way. He collapsed on snout and chest.

The aboriginals laughed and dawdled the dinghy towards the bank. But the crocodile wriggled convulsively forward and came slithering down the runway, his yellowish neck crimson. When almost at the water the second shot staggered him but he struggled once frantically and just managed to roll into the water and sink. I thought that if the boat had been a few feet nearer the bank and the crocodile not so badly hurt he might easily have slid straight down into the boat and then my aboriginal hearties would not have laughed so loudly.

We continued downstream until "Tch! Tch!" and Paddy pointed to the opposite bank. I stared at the slimy mud, but for quite a time could not distinguish the crocodile. In the gloom under those dull-foliaged trees his moveless, slate-grey bulk appeared like a muddy thing growing amongst the roots. The first shot lifted him and he made a desperate plunge up his runway, seeking shelter among the mangroves. He reached the steep summit of the mud when the second shot knocked him, causing him to twist round with snout to tail, clinging desperately with his claws. Too hurt to move he just seemed to shrink closer to himself. It was quite a time before he slowly slithered hack. He could not reach the water's edge. Even so, and although he was a small one, the abos had such respect for him that they hesitated to sling the noose over his snout and make certain he was dead.

"He dead feller finish?" I suggested to Jacky.

"Maybe!" answered Jacky and doubtfully eyed the crocodile.

As the boys stepped cautiously overboard they sank to their knees in mud, awful mud. Paddy reached over and smacked the crocodile's tail. It wriggled. Paddy snatched upward for a mangrove branch, which snapped, and down he flopped in the mud. But the crocodile was done.

We enjoyed a laugh at the bashful Paddy, clawing handfuls of mud from his bare tail, just like us whites, the aboriginal enjoys a hearty laugh should a comrade "come a flop".

An occasional shot from the Skipper's dinghy told us that Herman was having good shooting too. The Skipper was not keen on the rifle. His job was to captain the *Lotus*, an arrangement which suited us all. We continued downstream right into a lively nest of them, eyes and snout tips appearing ahead of us only to disappear as we advanced. Very difficult targets for a man standing in a rocking boat, aiming an inch below the farther two of four "walnuts" awash on the ripples.

They were always in sight, but vanished before a man could get confident aim. From away downstream came a hoarse, bullish bellow, a swirling and splashing of tails where two big fellows were fighting. As the Skipper's boat came paddling downstream he called out:

"I'm going to land and climb up into the mangroves and shoot from there. I couldn't hit a haystack on this rocking boat."

As his boys pulled him towards the bank my boys grinned and winked in delighted anticipation. I let Jacky dawdle at the oars so they could get their laugh, whatever it was to he. The Skipper stepped from the dinghy straight into that awful mud. As he struggled slower and slower ahead so his swear words grew hoarser and stronger. The Skipper is of short stature and amply built, and his temper under difficulties is none of the sweetest.

At last he struggled to the roots, pulled himself up and sat upon them to shake his fist at my grinning boys.

"Wait till I get you back on the *Lotus*, you swivel-eyed sons of jellyfish!" he roared.

"He got come back now!" howled Jacky gleefully.

The obvious fact had not struck me; when the Skipper awoke to the inevitable problem of getting back he'd say a lot about it. The crew would enjoy their laugh aboard tonight.

Our dinghy carried on downstream and I got a quick shot at a slithering grey shadow streaking down from the man groves. His tail whipped up and lashed the mud, but he gained the water and sank. We nosed farther downstream into another swarm of them, the water before us always thickly dotted with those four knobs of nostrils and eyes, ever sinking as we approached. An exceptionally difficult target to hit fatally. To the man standing in the bows with rifle raised almost to his shoulder, finger on trigger, ready instantly to sight and fire, it was exasperating that the plentiful targets, so close, would seldom raise themselves that one fatal inch.

We came to the bend where the creek mouth was emptying into the sea. Young ones were swarming here. The last of the tide was rushing out, leaving not only the banks hare but portions of the creek bottom as well. A six-footer suddenly oozed up from the mud on an exposed portion of the bottom and slithered along in rapid, twisting motion. At the shot his tail lashed up and his curiously helpless-looking paws churned the mud as he ploughed frantically towards the water. He just got there, and although we prodded the shallows with harpoon and spear we failed to locate him. But a flurry of water stirred the mud and showed we had disturbed others. One big fellow broke the shallows with a surge like a torpedo.

The Skipper's dinghy joined us, with the Skipper recovered and in great form at sight of the numerous crocodiles. Everything pointed to a profitable cruise. The only thing to do now was to get the crocodiles.

Not nearly so easy as it appeared.

"I'll go ashore," called Herman in his soft voice, and shoot from the top of the bank. I'll be able to see them better from up there."

Discarding his trousers, he plunged up the bank. In mud almost to his thighs he struggled up, and just managed to gain the top with the support of the umbrella-shaped roots. Even here he sank to his knees, pulling himself along over root after root. We saw a crocodile rise to the surface and waddle up a runway only fifty yards past Herman. We beckoned and slowly Herman plugged his way along the bank. At last he got right above the crocodile. He stopped, crouching among the trees. We saw him sinking even as he levelled the rifle. He fired and the crocodile flurried the mud and slithered back down into the stream. Herman had an awful struggle pulling himself out of the mud; he was nearly exhausted by the time he had pulled himself up on the tree roots. And yet heavy crocodiles, ever so much bigger, three times longer and incomparably heavier, can slither with quick ease over this slimy morass.

Apart from the incentive for hides it was great sport, ceaselessly alert for those ugly knobbed things that at any second might rise right beside the boat. A thrill to take the quick sight and see the death throes of this thing that otherwise might have lived to take to a horrible death a horse or bullock or buffalo, or even a human being. I've long since lost all lust for killing things except for food, other than crocodiles or sharks.

And then the falling tide grounded both dinghies on a mud- bank, leaving the stream but a chain of waterholes connected by shallow water or mud. It would be maddening, being forced to wait here for the return of the tide with all those crocodile targets ahead of us and in the shallows behind.

"Crack!" and a crocodile was thrashing the mud below Herman. Jacky and I managed to pole our dinghy across to where the blinded crocodile was wallowing in mud and shallows. We got a rope around him and killed him, and then the boys commenced skinning. Soon with their exertions they sank nearly to their waists in mud. So far as this particular creek was concerned, skinning the saurians was going to prove a tedious, beastly job.

Tired of inaction I began climbing the bank to seek a shooting possy. The attempt was a nightmare. My foot would sink down as if a clinging weight was dragging at it. To put the other foot down in a step forward meant sinking to the knee in mud. As I leaned to drag out each foot the mud followed it and clung, thick gluey blue mud. In the strain to lift one foot the other sank deeper and this necessitated a struggle to lurch forward when the foot came gulping up. When half-way up the bank I went down to well over the knees and realized that if I went down to my thighs there would be no chance of moving the feet at all. I would just stand there and slowly struggle from the belt up while I sank—sank. It put the wind up me and I turned and ploughed back down towards the dinghy.

"What would you do now if a crocodile chased you?"called the Skipper.

There was only one answer to that. Herman had shot another crocodile and it was giving trouble. He was trying to harpoon the writhing, snapping thing while Jacky was swaying in the mud with a long stick in one hand and a rope noose in the other, trying to rope it. He made more attempts to swing up the mangroves though than to swing the rope. Herman jabbed it vitally at last. They hauled it down to the shallow water edge, hoping the mud might be firmer. It was interesting to watch the big saurian sliding easily down the mud to the tug of the rope while the three boys sank almost to their thighs. When they reached the water's edge their chests were heaving. Now came the skinning. To make sure the crocodile was really dead Paddy reached out his knife and tapped where the eyes should have been. Eyes and skull were quite smashed by the military bullet.

"Him proper feller dead!" grunted Paddy with satisfaction.

He flourished a brand-new skinning knife and, being - ambitious to use it, knelt over the crocodile and plunged the knife at the back of its neck. The knife point turned up and looked at him while the crocodile's head snapped up with roaring jaws and Paddy was slung violently back into the mud.

"Hitch the rope to a tree, you fools," shouted the Skipper to the stampeding boys.

Much easier said than done. The crocodile was writhing over and over with liquid mud gurgling down its throat, its great tail lashing the mud in showers. Paddy scrambled up with bovine astonishment on his mud-spattered face, staring in turn at the bellowing crocodile and the twisted knife.

"Brand new knives! Two bob each at the Darwin Chinamen's, howled the Skipper from the dinghy. "Jump up! Keep clear, Paddy you fool! 'Gator catchem you proper feller."

Though its head was quite smashed, though the twisted harpoon had pierced it again and again, still it thrashed and clawed in a lather of mud. I kept well clear of those awful claws; they could have tom a man to pieces. It was fascinating to watch how its hideously writhing body could twist so lithely.

"What for you pightem (fightem)," admonished Jacky from a safe distance. "More better you die pinish (finish) altogether."

"Blurry fool you! shouted Billy. "Make we feller plenty feller trouble."

Billy suddenly leapt in and snatched the end of the rope. In a trice it was hitched to a tree. The running noose tightened around the saurian s throat, but he was churning round and round like a propeller. The boys now felt very brave. Billy leaned over and threw a handful of mud into the already blinded eyes of the crocodile.

"M-m," said Paddy as he straightened out the knife. "You die proper first time more better you. Now you die proper finish."

And he leaned over and struck quickly. The beast with a choked, hoarse gurgle whipped around its tail and splattered Paddy with mud. For the second time he sprawled back into the churned-up stuff, throwing himself backward with out-spread legs and arms.

"What for you play up?" they shouted. "You got die! What for you humbug?"

They admonished the crocodile as if it were an understanding being, which they really believe it to be. Before that crocodile was "proper fellow dead" it and the three boys were, except for their movement, quite indistinguishable from the mud. I wish I'd had a movie camera with me on that trip, as on other trips.

Taking onboard two crocs, the Daly River, 1934.

V

"LITTLE FELLER" CROCODILE

THUS one day's shoot, from notes written aboard the *Lotus* that evening. The fact that they were written at the time may lend the little incidents a shade more interest.

And now I must keep faith with quite an army of youthful readers spread over the continent, and in Tasmania and New Zealand. Constantly they write asking for more detailed description of animals and birds and "live things" to be mentioned in future books. Of localities too, and of the men and women and children of all colours living there, and of the manner of their lives. These young readers desire to learn more of their country and of wild things living in the lesser known areas. I deem it pleasure and honour to comply, only wishing I could do a much better job. So that if this simple record from a wanderer's notes deviates into a little detail now and then, it is to please and, I hope, in so far as space allows, teach a tiny bit more about our country to the citizens of the very near future.

Do not imagine that all Northern Territory rivers and tidal creeks are thus swarming with the estuarine crocodile. Although in occasional localities along the length of the Territory coast crocodiles are as numerous, in most waterways they are not nearly so plentiful. Away on the distant eastern and western coasts, even in unfrequented north Queensland rivers and along the Kimberley coast, you might not see more than three or four in a week.

Our crocodiles inhabit the rivers and lagoons, the creeks and swamps and island tidal ways of northern Australia. Generally they are called "alligators". However, there are no alligators in Australia. The alligator of Florida (U.S.A.) is slu88ish and tame compared to an Australian estuarine crocodile. The alligator would be "easy meat" to our big, swift, powerful, bad-tempered giants. Indeed, an instance has been reported of a small Australian crocodile being placed aboard train in the same cage as a large alligator, en route to an American zoo. In the morning it was discovered that the crocodile had tom the alligator to pieces.

The overseas alligator only averages about ten feet long, the big fellows among them up to fifteen feet. Whereas an Australian fifteen-footer estuarine crocodile is quite ordinary; many of them grow to twenty feet. More than one giant has been measured at thirty feet (one such was shot in the Gulf country and is now, I understand, in the British Museum). Years ago I remember one shot in the Pioneer River, Queensland, that measured thirty-two feet. Such a monster when partly submerged would appear like a "young submarine". Neither man, horse, bullock, nor buffalo would have any chance once such mighty jaws crushed upon him.

The estuarine crocodile's powerful jaws are armed with cruel, conical, interlocking teeth. I've a large tooth in my possession six inches long and four inches around, but have seen even more monstrous teeth than these. The fourth tooth on either side of the lower jaw is exceptionally large and fits into a notch in the upper jaw. The tooth can occasionally be seen when the jaws are closed, lending an ugly leer to the hideous snout. The alligator's teeth do not interlock. The upper teeth bite on the outer sides of the lower jaw, while the first and fourth tooth of either side of the lower jaw fit into pits in the upper. Then again, the overseas alligator's snout is shorter and rounded, while the crocodile's much more powerful snout is longer and more tapering.

The reason why bushmen have named the estuarine crocodile the alligator is to distinguish it from the Johnstone River crocodile. For we have two distinct species of crocodile in Australia, the Johnstone River crocodile, and the estuarine crocodile. The estuarine crocodile is the one we have been shooting at today. The Johnstone River crocodile is an agile little fellow seldom growing longer than six feet. He keeps to the fresh water of rivers and inland lagoons and swamps. A cautious reptile, he rarely tackles a man unless cornered, and then only snaps viciously in a frantic effort to escape. His long tapering jaws are armed with needle-sharp teeth, his forepaws grow hooked claws which can snatch out and grab a fish in a flash. I've seen aboriginals swimming in a water- hole thick with these small crocodiles. The crocs keep out of the way, hiding on the bottom and under submerged logs and in caves under the banks. Towards the end of the dry season, when the rivers dry up and form into waterholes, the crocodiles follow the water as the fish do. In such pools the fishes' lives are daily misery, constantly being chased by the crocodiles. No doubt the survivors long for the wet season which will fill the rivers again and scatter both crocodiles and fish. In such a waterhole, or in a shallow lagoon, the natives spear these crocodiles by first entering the waterhole at its deepest end as a living chain, extending from bank to bank. The elder children generally come along just behind the chain. They wade slowly on, stirring up mud with their feet while the women clap their hands underwater. The discoloured water not only camouflages the legs of the aboriginals but also clouds the vision of the crocodiles, who are further startled by the thunderclaps underwater. They speed ahead into clear water and thus they are gradually "mustered" as a mob of sheep are mustered together. Near the end of the hole the water shallows while the banks close in, thus enabling the line of aboriginals to draw closer together. And now with vigorous mud-stirring, shouting, and clapping of the water, they drive the crocodiles to the very bank. The water now is ripped and agitated by the crocodiles confined into an ever narrowing space. Again and again they attempt to break through, but are driven back by the shouts and spears and noise. But in the final spear-throwing their terror knows no bounds and they charge through their tormentors who leap high with wild yells as the slithering bodies surge between their legs. When the hunt is finished it is quite possible that some luckless tribesman will limp to the bank with a piece bitten clean out of his leg. And the only sympathy he gets is a joke.

"Bunderoo the Brave entered the water to feed on the crocodiles," they laugh, "but the crocodiles fed on him." The young girls especially laugh and jeer at the luckless one.

I was watching such a hunt one day when a terrified crocodile fastened on to the cheek of a warrior's sit-me-down. The yell as he leapt above the water startled the cockatoos, but the crocodile hung on as the frantic man tried to leap for the shore. He tore at his behind and yelled in anguish as he splashed and leaped, while all the hunters looked on, shrieking with laughter. It was only when the stricken one thumped straight down to the bottom and sat hard on the crocodile's snout that the thing let go. Simply crying with rage and pain, clinging with both hands to his buttocks, the badly bitten man staggered to the bank amidst the helpless laughter of the tribe.

The cunning, swift reptiles are difficult to kill outright, but are vulnerable should one prong of the spear pierce the inner body. For this allows the water in, and actually "drowns" the saurian. The crocodile when speared vanishes to the bottom of the waterhole and hides under log or rock. But next morning the aboriginal strolls along the bank seeking his breakfast and there is the white belly of the crocodile as it floats dead on the surface.

A few among the aboriginals of the swamps and lily lagoons of the Northern Territory and Kimberleys are expert at catching this fresh-water crocodile with their bare hands. The victim may he basking upon the water, his nose tip and eyes barely visible as he watches the tree-lined bank, waiting for some incautious bird come to drink. Silent as a shadow the aboriginal creeps around the bank behind the crocodile, and vanishes in the reeds. Amongst this cover he slowly wades out. The water grows deeper and deeper. Reeds and water-lilies break the faint ripples which otherwise might warn the crocodile. At the edge of the reeds the hunter takes a few deep breaths, then sinks and swims deep underwater. If the crocodile is far out the swimmer rises for breath under one of the broad waterlily leaves. Under this cover he can fill his lungs again, can see if he wishes to. He sinks again. Swimming deep, he now distinctly sees the crocodile ahead of him up on the surface. The white belly is plain, claws and tail and every underpart of the moveless reptile beautifully distinct under sky and sun above. A picture of primitive grace, the aboriginal suddenly shoots up under the crocodile and his hands have closed tight around its snout. His head in triumph bursts through the surface before the bewildered crocodile can struggle. Though it does struggle now to the limit of its frantic dismay all effort is hopeless. That grip is "scientific". Impossible for the long tapering jaws to open, while the claws on the forepaws are helpless because the snout has been gripped in such a way that the man's forearms have levered the forepaws apart and up. Just as you may grip a big crab in a certain way so that no matter how his claws struggle and champ he cannot reach around to the fingers that hold him. With triumphant laugh the aboriginal surges towards the bank and his grip is such that the wildly thrashing tail cannot touch him.

I've watched the natives catch them another way. Occasionally the crocodile must rise to the surface to breathe. The hunters, cleverly spaced all around the lagoon, have been waiting, their wonderful eyes searching the water. The only sound is a chattering of parrots, or the hoarse, melancholy call of a black cockatoo far away. A crocodile comes to the surface to breathe, only his snout visible like two nuts floating on the surface. Moveless, he stays there. Suddenly a hand grips the point of the snout as a black head breaks water and an arm is thrown around the crocodile's "shoulders". It is thus both "muzzled" and unable to claw. The hunter kicks out for the bank and jams the long, pointed snout deep into the mud. And thus the crocodile slowly chokes, struggle he ever so hard.

In the heart of the really wild bush at night a lonely lagoon can be very beautiful, sometimes eerie too. I got a great fright one night when camped alone in such a place. In deathly silence, faint moonlight made ghostly the white trunks of the paper-barks, made even more chilly the utterly still water. A shadow came and vanished. Again, towards the end of the lagoon, I could have sworn a shadow moved. A horrible croaking followed by loud cackling made my hair stand on end even as I realized it was only a Nankin bird.

Yes it was so—vanishing shadows were stealthily encircling the lagoon! It was fact—spearmen noiseless as ghosts were taking up vantage points all around the banks!

I reached for the rifle, and crept behind a tree. For a long time there was not a sound—only at times when a shadow moved again—the faint thumping of my heart. Then —

Two stones were sharply clapped together underwater. Quickly the lagoon resounded to an agitated but quiet barking as of young puppies. Spears whizzed into the water and I breathed again.

When stones are thus sharply clapped together underwater the vibration and sound effect are startling. But why it should agitate the crocodiles and cause them to rise and cough and "bark" I don't know.

Such is the Johnstone River crocodile, so named because it was first found in the Johnstone River, Queensland. To the best of my knowledge this species is not found elsewhere in the world.

The aboriginal of course cannot thus capture the monster of the river mouths and sea coast, the estuarine crocodile, the one that bushmen call the "alligator".

Young Aboriginal poised to strike (photograph by Francis Birtles 1922)

VI

A PREHISTORIC INFERNO

OCCASIONALLY though our aboriginal cobbers do claim a victim. They spy a suitable runway, one so enclosed by trees and roots as to offer them both cover and protection. Away up on the bank, at the very top of the runway, they tie some unlucky dog. One man crouches down within spear reach of the dog. The others hide within leaping distance of the runway on both sides, right down to the water. Another half a dozen crouch in among the roots enclosing both sides of the runway. Beside each of these are blobs of mud kneaded to a throwing consistency, just thick enough to be thrown. The job of these particular men is to hurl mud into the crocodile's eyes and thus, by blinding it, make it an easier and less dangerous target for the spearmen. Choosing a time when they know the crocodile is liable to respond to the decoy, they plaster their bodies with mud to deaden their primitive odour, then lay their ambush. The man away up top prods the dog with a sharp-pointed spear, the prods being tempered to the urgency of the dog's howls. Now, a dog is a tempting bait to a crocodile; he hears, slowly floats around in the direction of the sound, listens a while, comes cautiously swimming. He stops out towards midstream, just his snout tip and eye ridges visible as he listens and watches, his greenish, slanting eyes staring towards the bank. Suddenly a dog leaps among the trees up there, howls agonizedly. Its leg must be caught in the roots. With noiseless speed the crocodile glides to the bank. First the hideous snout, then the huge barrel emerges as it waddles on to the mud, comes creeping up the runway, a horrid thing.

They let him creep right up the runway. When just about to snatch the dog he is blinded by balls of mud. As he writhes around, spears pierce him from both sides. With a snarling bellow he slithers down the runway through a gauntlet of spears. In his blindness, in his frantic alarm at the agonizing spear thrusts, the hoarse grunts and maddening yells of the hunters, he may become momentarily entangled amongst the tree roots. Every second's delay brings more spears ripping into his hide.

He generally reaches the water only to die. The triumphant huntsmen recover his body from the shallows.

Another hunting method is as simple and effective, although in this case no decoy can be used. The prey must first be surprised at a great disadvantage. Crocodiles will sometimes waddle overland. They can smell water a considerable distance. It may be but a few hundred yards; it may be but a few hundred yards; it may be half a mile or more from a creek to a lagoon and back again. Or from the sea coast overland to a swamp. They fancy a change of diet, for in the swamp or lagoon there are juicy duck and geese, pelicans and swans and tortoises, as well as fish, while such choice morsels as kangaroo and wallaby and wild pig also come to the lagoons to drink. Thus, wandering crocodiles are found at times in a fresh-water lagoon quite a considerable distance from the nearest salt-water creek.

During the wet season, in those areas of country where rivers flood over and for miles turn plains and level country into shallow swamps, you might meet a wandering crocodile anywhere. For he can waddle across the water-soaked flats in the confidence that his natural element is all around him. Eagerly he explores miles inland, having the time of his life. He may come across a hogged bullock or horse or buffalo. He can lie like a log amongst the flooded grass, where emu or kangaroo may step upon him. No wonder he grows fat.

Can I pause a moment and tell a little personal story of the crocodile's love of wandering thus.

It was during one of the heaviest "wets" known in Cape York Peninsula. My mate and I, looking for gold, were travelling overland. He was a good mate in most ways, one of the best bushmen I have known, but a "queer" mate too.

His nickname was "Silent". Day after day we travelled slowly, often hour after hour with water nearly to the horses' knees. This exceptionally heavy wet had caught us between the ranges and the coast, where the numerous watercourses had all flooded over and submerged the flat country. Silent generally led the way, the laden string of packhorses following him, with me riding in the rear. Silent's job was not only to find the way through wild and trackless bush, but also to dodge the countless boggy patches along three hundred miles of country. A super-bushman's job to do it.

Day after day we rode on and often from sunrise to sunset we never spoke a word. Day after day, riding a hundred yards ahead, the long, thin, saturnine Silent slouched in his saddle as his horse plodded through the water among the trees, followed by the labouring packhorses who kept so faithfully to his tracks. A wonderful bushman was Silent. In many and many a place had a packhorse deviated but a yard from those tracks the poor horse would have quickly sunk, down, down, and in the worst places without hope of recovery.

In the gloomy chill of evening it would be Silent's job to find a camp. Always he did so. A tiny knoll, often but a few feet above water level. Sopping wet ground covered with ironstone pebbles but—it was above water. Here we would unload the packs, with difficulty make a fire, eat hungrily while the horses wandered off to find dry ground of their own or if not then to crop what grass they could snatch from under the water.

We talked a little then, but not much. Silent would answer. He seldom talked. Hunched up smoking on a log, he stared into the fire, thinking and brooding. The wild, trumpet-like call of wild geese swifty flying overhead, the whirr of wings as whistling ducks sped through the darkness at times was almost more company than he.

As day by day went by, night by night, week by week, I noticed that my mosquito net was always nearest any river, or watercourse that the phenomenal floods had made a river. Tired by the hard day, we would light the fire, greedily devour our salt beef and damper then I would rig the net against the ravening mosquitoes. Turning in, I would be dozing off to sleep, but Silent would be out there amongst the humming millions, still carefully piling wet logs on the fire. And I would notice that my net was nearest any river, while his blankets would be near mine, and the fire on the other side of him.

One evening I pulled up the side of my net and said: "Hey, Silent, I notice that when we camp my bunk is always nearest the deep water."

"Yes," he answered.

"Why?" I inquired.

"Because you build it there," he replied.

"Which means, I said, "that you let me lay my blankets down first, then you build your bunk between me and the fire."

"Yes."

"Which means that any prowling crocodile would come from the deep-water side, and take me first."

"Yes," he answered.

"Stone th' crows! You're a flaming nice kind of a mate, aren't you!"

"You have the brains to reason it out for yourself," he replied.

I grunted, and let the net fall and went on smoking. And did not sleep too well.

But it did not turn out exactly as Silent anticipated. He forgot that he always put the meat bags beside him and that their contents with the humidity and wetness had developed a quite decided smell. And when the big old-man crocodile did come he waddled around the islet nearest Silent, nearest that smell of meat.

Sleeping uneasily, as I slept all those nights, I awoke, and glanced towards the now dying fire. There it was. The Thing was coming, just there, at the water's edge, with the wet, horny serrations along its back dully visible in the glow of the coals. Not on my side, but on the side opposite

Silent's net, with Silent now sound asleep inside. As I stared there arose the hideous snout, a gleam of fangs played rosily on by the scarlet coals. Silently it emerged into the huge, awful head of an old-man crocodile. With a yell I snatched the rifle and leapt up through the net as the startled crocodile rushed straight up and through Silent's net, making for the deep water on my side. Silent was rolled over and over in his net and blankets as the huge bull crocodile tore across the camp and splashed back towards the deep water.

After that, each evening Silent and I discussed how to build a number of fires around us, and set our nets to mutual advantage and protection. Although all that remained of Silent's mosquito net was only just as much as would protect his head and face.

On land the crocodile can run straight ahead a short distance with surprising speed but cannot take too sharp a turn, and this the aboriginals know full well. When charged by a crocodile they leap aside only to double back at the critical moment.

The aboriginals are constantly on the watch out for these reptilian adventurers that prowl overland from river to lagoon. Should a lone huntsman or "boy scout" come upon such a one, or the tracks of one, then immediately the long-drawn hunting cry rings far and wide over the bush. Men instantly snatch their spears, the whole tribe comes running, giving distant answer to the cry. Then silence. For the crocodile must not be alarmed or he may hastily turn back for the nearest water. Also—this is very important—the hunters must keep to cover as they advance, for certain birds "tell" the crocodile of the hunters' approach. So the aboriginals over a vast area of country have earnestly assured me. It is one of the laws of the wild. Certain birds seem to go out of their way to raise the alarm at man's approach.

The huntsmen reach the scout. Silently they follow the tracks away behind the crocodile, allowing him to keep travelling until he gets midway between creek and lagoon.

Then, in a wide circle, they close around him and set the grass on fire. Quickly he is encompassed in a ring of smoke which, fanned by the breeze into flame, roars down upon him. Alarmed by the crackling, startled by the blind dash of a frightened wallaby, scared by the leaping flames he wheels around, but on every side flames are approaching while acrid smoke is now poisoning his nostrils, smarting his eyes. He shakes his head and coughs deeply. He makes a short rush for safety, but is met by flame and smoke. He wheels back and rushes in another direction, but again is turned back by smoke, and now the ring of fire is rapidly closing in. He becomes frantic; agitatedly paws the smoke from his eyes. He is driven back again

again and again until he is wheeling almost within his own length, a monstrous, terror-stricken thing enveloped by heat and smoke and leaping, half-seen demons that hurl weapons at him.

The heat now is suffocating him. He coughs despairingly and writhes away into fiercer heat that scorches his belly. He bellows, lashes out with his tail, scrambles away. He rears to the full height of his short legs, with parched snout gasping to catch a breath of fresh air that may suggest a way of escape. Coughing violently he shakes his jaws, strives to see through smarting eyes, when to a bedlam of howls a shower of spears hisses upon him. Blindly he charges. But his tormentors leap aside and he receives their spears as he rushes by. With a throaty bellow he swerves and crashes into a burning log with leaping, howling, jabbing men above and all around him. He charges away at frantic speed but crashes into a tree and swerves drunkenly aside while his tail tries to thrash the spears from his body. Again and again he is surrounded; again and again he charges through the gauntlet. He bellows and writhes, twists and turns, wheels around and around and rolls over and over in torment, with his great tail lashing out and sending smoking sticks flying yards away. At last, suffocating in heat and smoke, pierced by many spears, he slows down to a tortured writhing he dies.

I have seen some great battles thus, inferno scenes that have shown me a glimpse of the dead past brought into the living present, for these battles in the flame and smoke are battles between living prehistoric man and a living repre-sentative of the prehistoric reptile. If the grass is not long and dry, also if there is no light breeze blowing, the crocodile then has more time and opportunity in which to fight for life. The flames do not rush upon him, there is less smoke, he is but partly blinded, he can and does put up a better and longer fight.

But he is out of his element and unless he is close to the water he is doomed.

VII

A STROLL IN BUFFALO LAND

NEXT day Paddy and I took the dinghy and rowed across to Hunter's lugger, then walked to the camp. There was no one there, but tracks proved that the camp had been visited recently. There is a story in tracks. Tracks are the authentic news of the bush, if you can read them aright. These told us that some three days previously a white man, aboriginals and horses and aboriginal dogs had visited the camp. The horses had come heavy laden, the white man had supervised, the aboriginals had toiled. All hands had stayed the night. Then they had loaded the horses again and vanished back to the plains.

Apparently the absent shooters were doing well, judging by the stacks of salted hides, each greyish hide solid as a board. We followed a track out through the trees into an open, black- soil plain stretching far away. The track apparently led to Hunter's shooting camp, eight miles out. To that camp he brought the hides by horse. From there when dried they were transported to this coastal camp to be loaded on to the lugger *en route* to Darwin. The plain was brown under grass, slate-grey buffaloes grazing far and wide. The distance was haze and mirage of long, shallow water pools that melted as we trudged on. A warm quietness was over all. We could do with some buffalo meat, so we skirted out around the nearest little mob. Two old bulls suspiciously watched our approach, their long, unusual-shaped horns sticking straight out from each side of the head. As we drew nearer, cows and calves nervously edged back behind their guardians. Suddenly the bulls tossed their heads and wheeled at the run back across the plain, the cows and calves following.

But we were making towards a distant belt of trees around which were buffaloes scattered here and there. There would be others among those trees and, under cover, we might get a shot at some "meaty" beast. The plain was covered with coarse tuft grass; the buffaloes were in good condition, but this grass did not look good cattle grass. I've often wondered whether the type of black soil of these big plains would grow rich grasses if seed were planted there. Almost certainly, but the grass would have to become acclimatized to flourish under the local conditions, or be some rich imported seed which had proved itself in similar soil and climatic conditions elsewhere. These plains are at times water-logged during periods of the wet season. Probably they would make good ricefields, or grow crops suitable to the soil's particular environment. These big plains at present offer a living for a buffalo shooter only here and there over large areas. The time will come when they surely will support thousands of families, still leaving some land to be the preserves of the aboriginal and buffalo for posterity.

As we walked on and on, buffaloes were everywhere, as I have seen them on other trips distant from here. They were in mobs of fifties and hundreds. No matter how far we walked these mobs were always around us. And everywhere were the carcasses of beasts that had been shot. Just the carcasses, or skeletons, and always the great horns. Only the hides are taken. What a shame it is that year by year so many carcasses of excellent meat are left to waste upon the ground. Though unavoidable, it is a tragedy when so many millions of people are hungry for beef. But surely modern transport and treatment processes for meat could alter that.

Sometimes as we drew closer to suspicious little mobs we were not as confident as we looked. For trees are generally far apart on these plains and the buffalo is at times an uncertain animal. Should one decide to charge while we were in the open, well

They stared at us until we got to within a hundred yards of them and then each mob would lumber off, only to come to a standstill, turn around to stare back, snort hoarsely as we came on, then again lumber off at the trot. I did not fire. We were not desperately short of meat and I hated the thought of shooting a fine beast only to take what beef Paddy and I could carry. For tantalizing but interesting hours we walked on, seeking some small beast that yet would be in the pink of condition. As we walked the miles so the plain seemed to move with little mobs moving along. As we advanced farther so mob after mob moved before us, the nearby mobs, those a little farther away, those farther still, until many little mobs were slowly moving before us all across the plain. The farther we went, the more mobs started moving and the farther the horizon appeared, until mobs were all around us as far as the eye could see. I was thinking it must have been like this in the old Red Indian days of America. Those days have long since gone, but they exist today in Buffalo Land in our own Northern Territory. Few Australians know it.

It was while walking through a pandanus thicket that a roar like a bushfire sent Paddy and me leaping for the palms. The frightening noise subsided as the buffaloes galloped out on to the plain. Paddy was well and truly up a palm, the whites of his eyes glistening as he grinned from ear to ear at me only half-way up a scraggy palm. I swore at him all I knew to disguise my fright and outraged feelings. The buffaloes had been dozing under the palms and as we entered the thicket simply arose en masse and charged straight over the long, brittle leaves. Any man in a hurry trying to monkey up a prickly pandanus palm expecting the horn of a buffalo to prod the seat of his pants knows just what I expected to feel.

Not caring now whether we got a shot or not, for the distance to carry the meat was too far, we walked on in the pleasant sunshine. Then through a thicket of pandanus palms we emerged on to a sunlit clearing hedged far away with groups of other pandanus palms, a lagoon in the centre. Around its green edges were big red kangaroos cropping the grass while giant jabirus and smaller cranes fished the lagoon edge, buffaloes staring at us solemnly.

It was out on a sun-dried portion of the plain, the nearest tree half a mile away, that Paddy grunted and pointed. We walked over to the sun-dried carcasses of a horse and buffalo lying nearly side by side. They told their own story, simply read. The wounded buffalo had wheeled around and charged, and the horse had not swerved aside in time—the hole made by the buffalo's horn showed clearly through the sun-dried hide. I wondered what had happened to the rider. He could never have reached that distant tree. Paddy circled around and soon picked up two old, discoloured cartridge shells. Probably the rider's mate had fatally shot the buffalo from there. All tracks had long since gone; it was impossible to tell. I wondered if the rider had been stunned, or whether he had leapt up and run during those fateful seconds it had taken his mate to kill the buffalo. He must have been a swift and deadly shot, for the buffalo had dropped in its tracks only a few yards from the horse.

We entered another far-flung pandanus thicket with red 'roos hopping before us, a crackling thunder as startled buffaloes lumbered over the dry leaves. Those long, fallen, sun-dried leaves of the palms crackle like pistol shots under the hoofs of lumbering buffaloes. Even the footsteps of a man make a startling sound when breaking into that thick, brittle carpet.

The buffaloes are slate-grey, their dried wallows in last season's mud are slate-grey, the antbeds are slate-grey and nicely rounded where the buffaloes have been rubbing their itchy hides against them.

We were seven miles out on the plain when we stopped at the sound of a voice, a creak of wheels, such unexpected sounds away out there. Around a clump of pandanus palm appeared three horses harnessed abreast, then the creaking cart they were pulling. The driver was Fred, a big smiling aboriginal, Hunter's right-hand man, as surprised to see us as we were to meet him. Hunter wasn't at the camp, he explained, but had moved five miles farther out to Buffalo Camp. So we returned w'ith Fred, an awful ride, jolting over devil-devil country all ploughed up from last wet by countless buffalo hoofs. No wonder we'd heard the creak of the cart.

The thump of the wheels as they jerked down into and over those hard-baked hoof holes was audible a mile away. Fred was a cheery companion; life was a joke to him. He is one of those many aboriginals who have always been invaluable to pioneering whites throughout Australia. He could tackle efficiently almost any bush job, and knew no fatigue. I've always been keenly interested in the aboriginal, though in the wild ones particularly. It has seemed to me that study of this "Freddy" type of aboriginal would solve the problem of those unfortunates that we drive to the increasing townships as we take their country. From admirable men of the wilds they degenerate into pitiful travesties of what they once were. But always, scattered throughout the country, a few of them are like Freddy, quite good at an ordinary job, mentally all that is required. If only we could turn the derelicts around the outskirts of civilization into "Freddys" we would not have quite so much to reproach ourselves with.

Freddy's main job in the season is transport man to Hunter's large buffalo camp. He transports the hides from the shooting camps to the lugger, sails the lugger to Darwin when loaded with hides, sails it back loaded with stores and transports those stores out to the camps. He was now en route to the landing to prepare the lugger for sea. In between cheery encouragement to the toiling horses he enlivened that uncomfortable trip by stories of narrow escapes during buffalo shoots, of encounters with native "wild men", of "alligators" and snakes, flood and fire, native vendettas and vengeance bands, of adventure by sea, river and land. All true stories that were merely ordinary events to him but, if put into book form, would be classed as adventurous fiction. For we have come to believe that frontier adventure is dead.

VIII

CROCODILE LOVE

WE went back to our crocodile shooting, back to the gloom of jungle and swamp after the sunlight of the plain, back to the lurking stealth that seems the life of everything in those gloomy places. As the days dreamed by we proved this cunning crocodile, terror of the salt-water estuaries, to be most tenacious of life. Very close behind his eyes is the most vital spot. If a bullet smashes the skull there he may be left lying on the mud—dead. Should you happen to stand on the tail two hours after death the tail will probably swing around, perhaps violently. Maybe it is a "main nerve" that does not die, not until hours later. Even though shot dead, its body may wriggle down the bank in a last struggle to reach its mother, the water.

Strangely enough, though, should it be poisoned it will quite often struggle back up on to the bank to die. Probably it is forced from the water to escape drowning, for it struggles to get rid of the bait and to do this must open its throat. If the bait will not "come up" then water pours in the open throat. He then crawls ashore to escape drowning, and to get rid of the bait.

Should the bait have been in putrid meat, then the croc, is done. But if the meat was solid flesh he ejects it.

Many a wary old saurian too cunning to be shot or trapped has at last fallen victim to poison. Among them, I remember one well. He was a beast of a thing and his home was just below the falls on the lonely but beautiful Bloomfield River, in northern Queensland. Already he had badly mauled two young lubras, bright little things before he crippled them. He was a constant menace to the children of the few settlers, and had killed half a dozen horses. Sooner or later he would take the life of a child or woman or man.

He met his doom by strychnine in the bowels of a goat dead three days. By dinghy the goat was left at high tide to be stranded on one of the islets towards the mouth of the river. The bait proved irresistible.

Experience is needed in poisoning crocodiles just as know-ledge of the wilds is essential in poisoning dingoes. Like the dingo, many a crocodile becomes notoriously alert to the ways of man. The bait must be not only temptingly but artfully set. Unless a crocodile is hungry indeed he will not touch the bait unless it is "tasty", which means near putrid. This fact enables the hunter to turn one of the crocodile's keen senses against itself—the sense of smell. From away upstream or down, a waft of air brings odour to the nostrils of a cruising crocodile. With an imperceptible twist of the end of its tail it turns slowly around until it gets the scent fair in its nostrils. It pauses then, head on to the smell, awaiting the eddies of air to bring it yet more of that tainted odour. Its smelling organs then analyse that smell, whetting its appetite and assessing whether the distant meat is just to its liking. Slowly, cautiously, it cruises downstream to locate the bait. But does it come straight inshore? Oh, no. It awaits outstream, just its nostril tips and horny rims of the eyes visible. For its personal safety it is using four keen senses that we know of, the senses of sight, hearing, smell, and instinct.

It is staring towards the gloom of mangrove or jungle, seeking the faintest unusual movement. It is smelling not only the tainted meat but is smelling too to detect the possible odour of white man or black, to distinguish odours unusual to that of decayed mangroves and mud, and to the incoming and fall and outgoing of the tide. It is hearing the usual sounds of the waterways—the gurgle of the tide reluctantly receding from the tree roots, the "plop" of a mangrove seed, the splash of a fish, the gasping of funny things that make bubbles in the mud, the hiss of spreading waters, the familiar call of water birds, the queer sighings and suckings of mud and tide receding from a maze of tree trunks and roots. Now and again the mewing call of a kite, perhaps the cackle of a wild goose, the screech of a cockatoo. Maybe all he hears is the dull knocking of the bill of a water bird upon some water-soaked log. The crocodile may sink, to rise later barely visible, just four seed pods upon the hurrying waters.

And thus, if he isn't ravenous, he may float for hours. And beside him may rise other seed pods. Finally one crocodile sinks, vanishes. Then on the shoreline an ugly snout appears, rises silently, and the hideous bulk emerges creeping slowly up the bank. Takes the bait.

Unless the crocodile is ravenous that bait must be putrid, for the saurian has no digestive organs as we know them. Neither has it a tongue; but it has a palate. When it slowly, cautiously, slithers up the bank and finally takes the bait it turns its head to one side as it does so, probably reaching out a paw and clawing the bait to its snout. It waddles back to the water and disappears with barely a ripple.

However, unless he is a big fellow he will not get away with the delicacy so easily. There is a flurry in the water, a splashing and lashing of tails as his fellow crocodiles pounce upon him and struggle to snatch away the tit-bit.

I've watched them do this a number of times. They wait about if very suspicious; they may hang around for even two or three days, not too sure of that tempting morsel ashore. Finally they send a small fellow in and as he comes back to the water they pounce upon him.

When shooting crocodiles we used the military rifle, because the shock of the high-powered bullet is very great. And shock counts a lot. Gives you just a moment or two in which to rope a paralysed beast. For a brute may appear quite dead, but in another moment he is a whirling fury and is hack to the water and gone. He is finished, but you probably lose the skin and with it goes the time, effort and expense. A sixteen- foot crocodile is a huge target. However his brain is very small, and unless the bullet completely smashes it there is little hope of killing him so "dead" that he will not move again. The bullet must strike about half an inch below centre between the eyes, or if side on must strike the eye, or if fired from behind it must strike the skull just behind the level of the eyes. It is waste of a costly bullet otherwise, unless you are shooting for pleasure and don't mind whether the skin gets away or not. Every shot is at a different angle of course; almost all are under different circumstances. You may be up on a high bank, or a low bank, or on a sea beach, or crouching among the roots, or shooting from a lugger's deck, or standing up in a dinghy or flimsy native canoe. The crocodile may be motionless in the water facing you, or slowly swimming up and down stream, only his eye ridges and nostril tips visible. Or he may be lying like a log on the sea beach, or high up on a muddy creek bank. Every target is at a different angle but you always aim at, or a fraction below or behind, the eyes, to place that bullet right into the little "skull-box".

A military-303 bullet striking most angles of the skull generally makes a mess of the crocodile. If not instantly killed he rolls and writhes like a blinded snake and surges up to the surface, giving the boys a chance to rope him swiftly. The shock of the bullet acts somewhat like an anaesthetic, paralysing the nerves. But allow him to get over the shock and he writhes into a snapping, clawing, tail-thrashing fury, raging from the surface to the bottom and up again ana down again as he fights death. Should he be vitally hit thus on a mudbank and have time to get over the shock, he may lie there apparently stone dead. But he awakes to a fury when touched. Snakes, smaller members of the reptile family, are also very tenacious of life. The crocodile clings to life long after he "should" be dead.

There is a knack in aiming at a crocodile in the water, apart from the angle of the shot. You have only an inch to "come and go on" and water is very deceptive. Probably all you see are four "walnuts", just above the water, and for all the world like four nuts that have dropped from a tree and gone floating downstream. Maybe five, or six, or seven feet behind these "nuts" appear a few serrations of the tail. Maybe not. If the water is clear your practised eyes will see the partial shape of the big brute below the "nuts", but you must be anticipating that shape for the thing often lies motionless and all that the casual eye might note would be four walnuts upon the water. Often the water of these tidal creeks is discoloured, if not actually muddy. It is very difficult then to distinguish anything but the snout tip and eye ridges, unless of course the thing is surging across the surface. Again, these creeks are often gloomy and shadowed, walled by trees and jungle growth. Sometimes the water is dark and discoloured by vegetation, particularly so in swamps. A quick and ever alert eye is needed, with instant control to halt still as a shadow. Then you aim to send the bullet just between the two eyes, but a trifle lower, according to the height above the target that you may be. And now comes deceptiveness of the water. For instance, if you can see a fish in the water, he is not exactly where he appears to be but a little ahead of that position. To overcome this my aim was suited by aiming an inch lower (that is, ahead) than I would have done had the object been completely upon the surface.

To aim otherwise means the bullet strikes behind the skull and almost certainly the shot is wasted.

If the crocodile is swimming towards you, then you must follow his movement with a corresponding movement of the rifle. If he is side on, then still fire a little low, and a fraction ahead of where the target actually appears to be. If he is moving side on, the rifle muzzle must follow that movement.

There is quite a little knack in it, which only experience teaches. A walloping big target at close quarters certainly, but there is only one spot where a bullet will effectively stop him.

Should he be sunning himself on a mudbank, the whole big target lies exposed like a moveless log. But still you must hit him in that part of the skull that carries the brain, otherwise he plunges up and in a flash is back to the water.

Strange it seems that these huge, lumbering monsters lay eggs. Yet the females do, at the beginning of the wet season, and are very serious about it. Particularly savage too, if disturbed.

Perhaps more surprising still, that the male and female actually "make love". But such is a fact. The hideous, cold-blooded brutes actually make love. Become "all worked up".

On the still, breathless nights you hear them. The smooging, unhappy, love-lorn bellow of the male. After a while a splash, then two splashes. Playfully he is chasing her. He nips her tail. She swings her tail around and lands him a dinnyhaser on the snout. Rebuffed he hauls off, coughs bashfully. Then he cruises after her again. Playfully she eludes him. She is not much interested —perhaps. Becoming a little anxious, he chases her and nips her a little harder this time. She grunts and swipes him with a savage forepaw, at the same time swinging her tail at him with a "bang!" that wallops the water. If he happens to stop that tail-bashing he knows all about it. Makes him "sulky feller", as the aboriginals say. But soon he is chasing her again. For there are plenty of pebbles on the beach, as the lady knows full well.

So does he.

After a while she relents. Her tail-banging loses its sting. They become quite matey. He sidles up beside her with a plaintive "moo", rubs shoulders; she does nothing. They come to an understanding.

Woe betide any jealous fellow who should seek to interfere. The accepted suitor will tear him to pieces—if he can.

IX

THE FAMILY STRUGGLE FOR SURVIVAL

BEFORE the great event, the egg-laying, something seems to worry her. She becomes secretive and crafty, avoids her bad- tempered husband, eventually slinks away on her own to the loneliest place she can find in river, creek, swamp, or along the sea coast. Hugging the bank, she hides underwater until assured no lurking old-man crocodile is following. When cer-tain no danger awaits her on land, she climbs ashore. Swiftly, stealthily she vanishes. Into the mangroves, or jungle, or tall grasses, or creeper-entangled shrubs, depending on what part of river bank or coastal shore she has chosen. With extreme caution she creeps through the underbrush, often pausing to listen, moveless as if carved in stone. She is seeking a home, a safe home. It takes a lot to satisfy her. Again and again she comes to a likely place, gazes all around spying out its advantages. She has almost decided when some little thing displeases her. She pushes determinedly on, or waddles hack to the water and cruises slowly farther along the bank.

Nothing will do her but the best, the safest.

At last she finds it—the best home in the world.

It may be quite close to the water, or some distance in among the mangroves.

Perhaps it may be a coastal home, a tiny cleared patch surrounded by dense vine scrub. The centre is sand upon which grows coarse, tufted grass with creepers stretching out from the scrub around. Down on to this little sand patch beats the warm sun from the blue sky above. A death-like quietness is all around. Distantly comes a low murmur—the lazy sea.

She becomes busy. Her paws make the sand fly as she scrapes out a hole, but not a deep one. When this is to her satisfaction she hurries out from the hole and her paws root up the grass tufts, scratch together the leaves. She scrapes these into the hole and thus roughly lines it with vegetation.

Then comes the serious business. She lays her eggs. She takes her time over it, not displaying the energy she did in preparing the nest. Eventually the important job is done. She has laid from forty to sixty eggs, even more. I have known as many as eighty eggs to be in the one nest. The egg is about three times the size of a hen egg, but the shell is soft and leathery, not brittle.

When the last egg is laid, with a grunt of satisfaction she slowly moves out from the nest, then begins tearing up the grass left in the tiny clearing, and scraping from deep around the edges of the scrub all the leaves available. She works hard now, and it is really marvellous how lithe her great bulk can be, how she can twist and turn as she scrapes the leaves together in a heap then, with a sweep of her tail, pushes them back towards the nest. Thus she works until she has made clean as a new pin the scrub edge and sand of the little clearing. Next she pushes all the grass and leaves into the nest and over the eggs. She pauses then, head a trifle side-ways, carefully surveying her handiwork. Perhaps she may paw a few more leaves to this side, a few more to that. When finally satisfied she creeps aside a little, then with her tail sweeps the sand back over the leaves, circling the nest as she does so. The finished nest is a large, sand-covered mound, perhaps three feet high.

When all is finished she lies there quietly, eyeing the completed job. She listens quite a while. There is not a sound, there has been no sound but her own all this time. The precious eggs are safe.

Realizing she now is very hungry, she creeps into the scrub and stealthily waddles to the water.

The days go by. The warm sun beats down upon that speck of sand on the earth far below. The decaying leaves and grass within the nest slowly grow warm, then develop surprising heat. Generally, within fifteen to seventeen days the eggs are hatched.

The baby crocodile is a few inches long when he breaks through the shell. In silence, he is buried within a suffocating darkness. He immediately begins to burrow upward. With many a pause to gain strength, he fairly pokes and wriggles and claws his way up through the rotted grass and sand. At last he emerges—panting. Blinking in the sunlight, he lies there drinking his first breaths of pure air as his eyes develop sight, his lungs gain power, his ears begin to hear. Then he crawls from the sand, rises on his forepaws exactly as a lizard would, and gazes around.

From noisome silence and suffocating darkness he has broken through into a fascinating new world of light and beauty.

Just so do we, I believe, after death.

Already he is what he is going to be while he lives, a vicious, active, cunning, fightable atom of life.

With surprising speed he runs down the nest mound and into the scrub, with unerring instinct making for the nearest water. He will meet his mother there, for if able she "hangs around" to guard her offspring as they take the water. Enemies await them and not the least of these is "old man" crocodile. He has no compunction about scoffing a baby crocodile, all of them should he get the chance. But he dare not try if the enraged mother is near. Big fish also seek to make a mouthful of the baby before he grows large enough to make a mouthful of them.

As the baby crocodile scurries to the water's edge he sees mother silently waiting there, camouflaged by the shadows of the trees. He pauses, surveys her, glances calmly around. All is well now. He may see beauty in the hideous jowls of his mother, in her greenish, slanting, coldly watchful eyes. I doubt it though. I think the vicious little pest merely feels instinctively that all is well. He slips into a shallow pool beside the stream, and feels water for the first time. Somehow he knows that he must wait—for his brothers and sisters.

He slips into an inch depth of water, his sharp little head on the surface as he breathes, stronger and stronger now.

It must be fascinating to feel tbe organs inside awakening to their wonderful duties.

In this pool there comes over him yet another transformation, this brutal little thing that already has experienced such marvellous transformations, this speck of life that was conceived under water, came on earth within a shell planted underground, formed within that shell and broke up from darkness to light, grew lungs and sight and hearing, found cunning and instinct and the power to run. Now he slides into the water and lies there in the shallow, his bright, wicked little eyes staring at his huge, motionless mother.

A faint movement beside him—a little brother has come. And now a sister nestles at his other side. Soon there will be a score and more of them. A hoarse, raucous cry breaks out from the trees above. He hears, cocks his eye—but does not move. His mother has not moved.

And so time dreams on, until the whole family is there— except the old man. He is not wanted. In fact, about the last thing on earth they wish to see is their father.

And now it is drawing towards sundown. For the first time, mother slowly moves. She stares at them, then very slowly turns outstream and lies motionless, waiting for them.

A sudden fierce new feeling seizes the baby crocodile. He is hungry, ravenously hungry. He creeps into deeper water, begins to swim. One by one his brothers and sisters follow him. They are all going to be taught how to swim.

She takes them only a little way, through shallow water where her huge bulk will scare away large fish, to a secluded sandbank just out in the stream.

Here, surrounded by water, they will find protection from land enemies, while that little portion of the sandbank above water will protect them from the far more numerous enemies of the submarine world. The mother, for ten days or so, will protect them from any prowling crocodile.

She crawls up on the sandbank. The string of them scurry up just behind her tail tip. She claws at the sand and instantly the ravenous little devils are fighting around her snout as the fearsome smell of much-decayed meat enlivens their nostrils. They tear into the soft stuff—they have learned to eat.

Thus, for long but interesting hours at a time I have spied on mother crocodile building her nest, laying her eggs, and finally meeting her babies.

The aboriginals have told me something interesting about the baby crocodile's first feed, though I have never seen this happen myself. The aboriginals say that, if by any chance the mother has failed to kill game and bury it until it becomes softly putrid enough for the babies to eat, she disgorges food for them from her own stomach.

This appears to me to be quite possible.

Very soon baby crocodile experiences another wonderful sensation. He crawls into the water, keeps going until he has crawled underwater, in the shallows. He finds he can now live, for a little while, underwater. He comes to the surface, with all his might fills his developing lungs with air, then crawls underwater again. He is learning fast—he has to.

His mother keeps him at the swimming lessons. She wastes no time. He must learn very quickly indeed if he is to survive; already a number of his brothers and sisters have gone down the bellies of big, swift fish.
The mother is very particular that he loses no time before he learns to float properly; and it is a wonderful float, that rippleless, almost invisible, lurking, effortless float of the crocodile.

One bright morning while sunbaking on the sandbank another experience comes to the fast-growing baby. A sudden terrifying rush of wind and a squirming brother is snatched aloft in the talons of a sea eagle.

And so the baby crocodile learns that nowhere is there safety for him, that death lurks for him in the water, on the land, even from the air. And every moment of the day and night it will be so until such time as he grows large and powerful enough to fight large and powerful things. So he grows with surprising speed.

In about ten days or so mother has become tired of her much diminished family. She believes they are agile enough to look after themselves. Feeling very hungry she glides away to seek relaxation in her distant haunts.

The youngsters know she has gone. They show no regret, but they know. They are on the sandbank. They all glance warily around . Instinct tells them the time has come when they must look after themselves. They seem to be taking a breathing space, letting it fully sink in before they take the final plunge.

Already they have learned a very great deal, especially about the things that count. Two have been scoffed by sharks, eight fallen victim to large fish, three have incautiously crawled ashore and been knocked on the head by black men, one has been taken by the sea eagle, and one caught in the roots underwater and drowned. But now the survivors' wits are sharp, their bodies agile little mechanisms in tune with their environment. Our first baby though only a few inches long, is a vicious, snapping, swift little terror. He now takes the plunge, scuttles down the sandbank and into the water—dives swiftly straight down and hides under a log. It is a plunge against death to reach the bottom and hide but he does it—not so some of his luckless brothers, for big fish are awaiting them. He tackles small fish himself now and soon will be chasing large fish. But for quite a time yet he will need all his cunning and swiftness and growing strength to survive in the fierce battle for existence.

Fortunately very many would-be crocodiles never reach the water. For the aboriginals love crocodile eggs and feast upon them whenever they find a nest. So do the aboriginals' hunting dogs. These prowlers find many a nest and immediately scratch their way down to the eggs. I saw one hungry mongrel get the shock of his life one day. He was busily digging down as a baby crocodile was digging up. The needle-sharp teeth of the little crocodile fastened on the nose of the dog which leaped with an agonized howl into the scrub violently shaking his head.

Wild pigs also root up the nests and gobble the eggs. But perhaps the greatest indignity of all is the goanna. To think that this cunning lizard can undo all the labour of the mighty saurian that built the nest is humiliation indeed. The goanna burrows into the nest, locates the eggs and eats them, making the nest his home while there remains an egg to be eaten.

If it were not for this great destruction amongst the eggs our northern rivers soon would be alive with crocodiles.

X

A DAY IN CRANE LAND

EARLY dawn and quietly beautiful. From deep sleep we were rudely awakened by the "slaves" washing down the deck, making as much row as the crew of a liner. It was extraordinary for the boys to awaken, let alone actually work till ordered.

"What's their little game?" yawned the Skipper. "They're up to something, believe me."

"Perhaps they feel like earning their pay."

"Bah! The slaves have sense—they only work when they've got to. And now they're working a point. I'll bet that skinny-shanked old heathen is at the bottom of it."

The "old heathen" was the Old Man, the shrewd old passenger who did nothing, said nothing (to us), saw everything, held unquestioned influence over the crew. All this time he had sat tight. Did not attempt to go ashore though this was his alleged destination.

"Why should he go ashore," growled the Skipper. "He'd have to find his tucker—instead of having it found for him— cooked for him—presented to him on a plate."

"You're a father to him," I remarked kindly. "Next thing you'll be putting his nightie on for him and tucking him into bed."

Herman sniggered to the Skipper's disgust. He was itching to order the Old Man ashore, but this would have made the crew turn "sulky feller", even if they did not .desert and go bush with the Old Man. The obvious fact bothered neither Herman nor me; life was too pleasant to worry over little things.

Yawningly we climbed up on the deck. A flight of red herons, their necks quaintly bent, skimmed just over the masthead as they seemed to glide through the air upriver. It was full tide, the bush very still and quiet. In the creek now clear green water welled up to the lower branches of the trees, the white ketch throwing an entrancing reflection prettily hedged among that dense greenery. The Skipper yawned, with a suspicious glance at the boys. The Old Man as usual was curled up for'ard watching the boys at work. He hadn't done a hand s turn since coming aboard. His skinny legs had been saved from walking many a long mile. He'd travelled in a luxury that was the millionaire class to the abo., but he wouldn't soil his bony old hands to help pay his passage. The most voracious eater amongst them all, he still was too lazy to spear a fish for the pot. It was interesting though to note how silently he bossed our boys, and any others who happened to come aboard. He wised them up to many a trick, and got his own way in everything he imagined concerned him. It's the law of the tribe, the Old Men have the say.

That old rascal is up to something," growled the Skipper.
I can feel it in the air. He has put some devilry into their fairy-like minds. He toileth not, neither doth he spin, but he collecteth all in. Poor ignorant heathen. The white man is feeding him, sheltering him, providing his smokes, transporting him at the cost of good benzine. When that same white man reaches his age there will be only the workhouse for him. I'd like to know just who are the slaves!" Grumbling to all and sundry he strolled aft to see about breakfast.

Paddy and I took the dinghy and rowed up a miniature creek. But it soon petered out amongst the mangroves. We stepped ashore and wormed our way through the mangroves out into bright sunlight. Here was a plain stretching in brown grass far as the eye could see. Here and there an isolated clump of trees with, upon the plain itself, the grey-black dots of feeding buffaloes. Away on the horizon a mob of them, one behind the other, walking out to feed, looking much like a string of camels in the distance.

Where the creek emptied out on to the plain the edge was all mud, but firm. We followed this creeklet. It was an ideal place for any crocodile waddling inland seeking a meaty breakfast. There were numerous arms of the sea and tiny creeks creeping in through the mangroves to end in claypans along the edge of the plain. But not one crocodile where we could have expected a score. We stepped back into the mangroves and presently were worming our way along the banks of an inlet. We were conscious of a deepening sound—the hoarse croakings of apparently numberless birds. Paddy the aboriginal in his bare pelt walked easily and noiselessly ahead, stepping over the mangrove roots and edging his body among the thick-set trunks in an effortless movement. His black skin tinged dully with copper merged perfectly with the gloom and dull grey of the mangroves and mud. Instinctively he appeared to know which mud was firm, and which was treacherous. He turned his head and his perfect teeth flashed in the gloom, his eyes shone as he pointed upward. Overhead above the foliage a riot of sound, the still air heavy, tainted with odour of birds. Soon the noise was of a huge fowlyard at feeding time, only the croakings and duckings and coughings and flappings and belligerent cawings were immeasurably harsher and wilder than any ever heard among domesticated fowls. Now and then only, away up through the foliage, we caught a peep of treetops russet coloured from masses of herons and cranes with long beaks and quaint, stumpy tails. The mud absorbed all sound from our bare feet; it.was not that sucking, gurgly sort of mud. It was littered with feathers. They were floating upon the stream and thick on the bank opposite, from which also came a riot of cawings and squawkings. A tattoo of alarmed gruntings signified that wide-awake birds had spotted us even through the dense leaves intervening. With a noise like wind swaying many branches, a flock flew to a bedlam of cawings. Others followed and the noise of their wing-beats in myriads rising up from thousands of trees sounded like hoofs of cattle vibrating into the rush of a stampede. Paddy gazed eagerly around and pounced on two sticks.

"Good feller tucker!" he hissed, and crouched away seeking some clear spot up amongst the branches. We came to a place and he instantly doubled down and back, and threw. The stick missed all those branches and leaves and whizzed up to strike the outspread wings of a bird. Russet feathers flew and the bird somersaulted down with a startled squawk. I admired this son of nature. Food in sight and he grasps the first weapon of man, a stick lying upon the ground. And uses it efficiently despite a maze of natural obstacles.

The rising tide was creeping up over the tree butts thus blocking us from going nearer the creek. Paddy's eyes were up at the birds, but mine were down amongst the water-covered roots lest I step on a log that was not a log. In distant northern Queensland I'd done that years before and the shock as the thing grunted and lurched away was still a creepy memory. The next one I stepped on might not be asleep. Paddy pointed time and again towards deep water where little bubbles occasionally rising may have been from a big fish or a crocodile. But no ugly snout arose. Apparently they were fishing in deep water. We might see only an occasional one until the tide went out. So we wormed our way back among the trees, the branches above violently swaying to rattling of leaves as again and again flocks of cranes took noisy flight. From the open plain we gazed back at the treetops lining the creek. They were a mass of russet and pink amongst which the black dots of the cranes' heads stood out vividly. Even at that distance their hoarse croakings made a wave of sound. Then as Paddy stepped down I heard that sighing, sucking gurgle. He leapt back instantly. And I realized yet again that even an aboriginal does not always know which is safe mud and which is treacherous.

When back on the launch the Skipper's wrathful face told that trouble was brewing.

"What's doing?" I inquired.

"These downtrodden slaves," he growled wrathfully. "They want to move on—they say we've scared the crocodiles and they won't come back."

"I saw very few this morning."

"It s high tide—there'll be plenty of crocs when the tide goes down. All that these charcoal Romeos want is for us to sail along the coast so they can meet their giggling Juliets."

Herman had just stepped aboard.

"What do you think?" I asked.

I only saw five crocs the whole morning," he replied quietly.

"Call yourselves crocodile shooters," said the Skipper disgustedly. 'Why you couldn't shoot pussy if she was tied up by the tail!" And he glared at the Old Man squatting stolidly forard.

Unblinkingly the shrewd old warrior returned him glare for glare, then thinking better of it gazed down and meditatively scratched his toe.

"I'd dump that swivel-eyed bag of bones overboard," declared the Skipper, "only he'd poison the alligators."

Herman grinned. Paddy suddenly threw his spear and a yell of delight followed the haft as it sped through the water, the leaning weight causing the frantic fish to swim side on as the buoyant spear came to the surface.

We'd finished a hearty meal when Jacky came aft and put the case before us, his eyes bulging with earnestness.

"More better we go," he declared. "That feller 'gator he cunning feller too much. Chute (shoot) him—he clear out. This place pinish! Before *orright*. Now no *good*—too much man he come. More better you-me try Mary River orright! Catch him plenty feller 'gator that place—*full up!*" and he used his hands expressively.

Thus the aboriginal, anxious to move on after a few days in any one place.

"We're staying right here," declared the Skipper definitely. But I knew he felt uncertain. Rightly so. Several days later and the crocodiles appeared to have vanished. It was always so. A few days' shooting in the one locality and the saurians disappeared, apparently cruising up the coast and into nearby creeks. It was rather uncanny that in such a lonely, extremely isolated creek where very rarely a white man trod, they should realize within sixty hours, and even less, that the place was now decidedly unhealthy for them. The crocodile possesses a very small brain, but there certainly is capacity for a sort of reasoning in it.

We lifted the mudhook and took to sea, sailing east along the coast, then into another creek. And the crocodiles here also were plentiful, the shooting lively—for a few days.

XI

QUAINT FACTS ABOUT CROCS

THROUGHOUT the years I've often camped in lonely places, and occasionally thought it fortunate there are no man-eating animals in Australia. But it would not do to fall overboard here.

While anchored in any tidal creek the crocodiles were all around us. We'd hear them at times in some vicious splash, or a hoarse, muffled cough. Otherwise there would be utter silence in the inky-black night. But flash a torch on the water and near at hand it was certain to reflect on two cold, green emeralds that turned fiery under the torch then vanished. Occasionally one would hear a crocodile calling to its mate. The sound was like the distant, dull "moo" of a plaintive bull. Sometimes there would come a hoarse, throaty bellow as two "old men" challenged or fought.

Why is it, I wondered, that fierce land animals that once roamed our continent are now extinct, whereas these slimy brutes remain?

Survival of the fittest maybe, though probably the correct reason is geographical upheavals and subsidences, and climatic changes throughout the ages. Australia has been under an Ice Age. Such drastic climatic and physical changes might easily cause many animals to become extinct, whereas salt-water reptilian life could retire to the coasts and sea. The estuarine crocodile is a survival, a living relic of prehistoric times, as the aboriginal is a Stone Age man. Australia in prehistoric times had an inland sea fed by large rivers in whose waters lived and fought sharks and crocodiles and lizards. If man lived in those ancient days he must have felt small at times. When our inland rivers dried up and the forests vanished like the animals and birds that roamed amongst them, the crocodiles retreated to the river mouths and the sea. It is their descendants we had been shooting at today.

They are repulsive brutes, but there is a grim interest in them when you come to know them, as shooters and trappers know them. There are hardly more than a score of these men. The very few trappers mosdy seek live crocodiles on order from zoos. The shooters shoot for skins during the rare occasions when skins are in demand, after which most return to other occupations, probably roaming the coast seeking crumbs of wealth from the sea.

A quaint thing about the crocodile is that he has no tongue, only a palate; his "innards" contain a filthy, slurry liquid. His digestive organs are made to treat only soft, decayed, or partly- decayed food. This is one reason why, if he takes a bait that is in fresh meat, he can disgorge the solid meat.

The crocodile, as a rule, seizes its prey then sinks, quickly drowning it. But he can also drown it on the surface, while breathing himself. To succeed, he must grab the animal's head in his own jaws, then pull the victim's nostrils under-water. Although its own mouth is partly open the water cannot rush down the crocodile's throat, for this closes as a valve would. The crocodile breathes through the nostrils, which are on the tip of the snout. From there .the long air passages do not enter the mouth, but travel away up the snout and along the head and discharge the air at the back of the closed throat. So that the crocodile can still breathe so long as the tip of its snout is above water. When the crocodile submerges, the small air opening in each nostril closes tight.

Thus the crocodile not only takes its prey by surprise, but also enjoys a tremendous advantage in the struggle. Even large animals, bullocks, buffaloes, horses, fall victims to its attack. If the first shock of the attack drags the victim into the water, the crocodile closes its throat valve and fills its lungs with air. Then the nostril valves close as the monster sinks and drags its prey underwater.

Whether in daylight or at night, in water or on land, the crocodile possesses keen sight—especially underwater. Human vision underwater is limited to a few yards, to a few feet only when the water is discoloured. Under such conditions, the pearlshell diver has to grope for the shell. It takes but little tidal discoloration of the water to force him to cease work until with the gentler tides the water clears again. For underwater service the crocodile's eye is incomparably more efficient than ours. We can outsee him easily on land, but all the same he can see a considerable distance when in the open air. Try to sneak on him through open forest country and if you do not take every advantage of cover he will detect you from hundreds of yards away. In northern Queensland rivers the crocodiles, being few in number and liable to be shot at now and again, make good use of eyesight. At times I've watched a horseman winding his way along the low hills fringing such rivers as the Bloomfield and Normanby. A crocodile floating out in midstream has been watching the horseman too. Should he dismount in view of the crocodile the saurian quietly sinks. Experience has taught it that the man has probably dismounted to aim a rifle. So it is not only the crow that has learned the meaning of a pointed rifle.

The cold, baleful eye of the crocodile is one of the countless wonders of nature. So that it can see in bright sunlight, and in the gloom of jungle creeks, in black night, below clear water, in muddy water, and in water which grows denser with changing depths, the eye is fitted with a number of filaments. To my rough examination there appear to be three. Just as the reptile rises to the surface there is a "flick" over the eye instantaneous as a camera shutter and a filament thus protects the eye against the sudden change of light, and makes vision effective for that light. When the crocodile sinks and goes deeper another film automatically operates as the light dims with changing depth, while still another film comes into service as the saurian glides down to greater depth with correspondingly less light. No matter whether it be fresh water or salt water, no matter whether the crocodile glides quietly down to the depths or whether he chases prey at great speed, these filaments react automatically and enable him to see distinctly his elusive prey, or the snag, or log or reef, or enemy in the shape of lurking brute who may be more powerful than he.

Perhaps these filaments possess a property of magnifying the dull light that penetrates the depths. Or maybe they act as a kind of filter sensitized to something other than light. We must leave that problem to the naturalists.

As the crocodile can also see quite well at night then he must have "cat's eyes" also. Or miraculous nature has added to his already marvellous eyes the property that enables the owl and other night birds to see at night. Occasionally, when a crocodile is submerging in clear water immediately below you, you might notice "pin head" bubbles rising. These are not the larger air bubbles which he occasionally sends up. In clear, sparkling water these small bubbles shoot up like a puff of tiny diamonds. Hunters believe these come from the eyes, or from some gland in the eye socket.

The crocodile possesses extraordinarily keen hearing. I have watched him become instantly alert at a cautious footstep, even upon mud, a bare foot gently placed upon mud that is not "gurgly". Perhaps his ear registers more than hearing, may register vibrations which do not react on the human ear. And yet, with all its cunning and alertness, with its senses of smell and hearing and eyesight, there are times when you can creep up to within a few yards of one. Not often, but I have done it, and seen other men do it. I've even stepped on one brute, but I'll admit he was sound asleep. We were both wide awake the next instant, flying in different directions.

All wild things, just occasionally, whether asleep or resting or even at times fully awake, allow their "instinctive sense" to fall sound asleep. At such times you may creep up almost to touching distance of wild animal, bird, reptile or fish.

The ear of the crocodile is not like the ear of an animal. It is an almost indistinguishable slit in the dull-grey, horny hide. But the cavity inside contains a very efficient instrument.

The hearing part of the ear, set behind the eyes, is a horny bar working on gristle. Alas, I am not a naturalist or scientist so cannot tell you how the thing "works". With it the crocodile can hear perfectly when upon land, on the surface of the water and down in the depths. The "slit" of the ear appears to open just a trifle when the crocodile breaks surface. This allows the entry of air, through which sound must now come. The slit, which closes when he submerges, is a neat protection for the cavity inside, whether the saurian be in the open air or deep below. Occasionally when on the surface a drop of water gets into the open cavity and proves a nuisance. On a choppy sea and on a river where tide and wind have freshened the water into sharp little splashes, I have sometimes seen a cruising crocodile lift his head from the water and shake it just as a dog does when water gets into his ear.

At first thought we might wonder why the crocodile, spending so much time in and under the water, should need such good sight and hearing both on land and underwater. But without it he may not have survived from possible enemies of the past, and certain enemies of the present. On land or on the surface of the water his hearing tells him many things that he may not see, distant yap of a dog that warns of the presence of aboriginal huntsmen, the thump, thump of a likely meal as kangaroo or wallaby approach the lagoon to drink, or the snort of a wary buffalo on the same errand. The ring of an axe betrays human beings nearby, or the click of rowlocks tells of a dinghy coming downstream. These and many other sounds tell him things, often warn him, or help him in his quest for prey. He knows the call of the birds and these too can reassure or warn him. So does the screeching agitation of a colony of alarmed flying foxes. When deep underwater you might think it would not matter whether he could hear or not—there might not be anything to hear! Not so. Down in the depths is a world where gloomy quietness reigns most of the time, but sometimes there is sound. And sound carries a long way underwater. It comes in the form of vibration. The human ear can also hear underwater but not nearly so many sounds, nor so distinctly, nor so far away. The crocodile lurks at the bottom of the water seeing and listening for hours in comfort. A man underwater struggles to hold his breath, his vision is very limited, he can listen only a couple of minutes at a time. Underwater there are sounds that both may hear, though the man can listen only momentarily.

At the bottom of a river the crocodile can hear a swimmer crossing the stream above, can hear the paddle of a canoe and by the sound follow its course, can hear too the splashing of a horse as it is forced to cross a stream. If the crocodile has travelled overland into a fresh-water lagoon, he knows when natives have entered the lagoon seeking tortoise or mussels, for he hears them, hears them distinctly through the water. He listens, judges their approximate number and remains warily hidden if there are too many. Otherwise, cautiously he crawls along the bottom, then glides underwater towards the sound to spy what is doing and whether there be a chance to grab some unlucky swimmer or wader. A terrifying menace when working thus, the hideous bulk camouflaged deep among the water grasses, the grisly head horribly alert and magnified like some nightmare thing, the baleful eyes cold dull-green emeralds.

When in the big swamps he hears the splash as a flock of wild duck or geese alight on the water. Hears the splash of a startled tortoise, or water rat as it dives to safety.

In river or sea he hears other sounds, the smack of another saurian's tail, the thump of an anchor coming to rest, the "clapping" of a crayfish. For the salt-water crayfish who lives in colonies in the reefs and coral gardens betrays his presence very distinctly when under below. To swim, or rather surge backward, he smacks his tail and this clap sounds a long distance underwater. It brings the shark with a rush. Brings the crocodile too, for he also is fond of succulent crayfish. A few other fish also betray their presence by noise.

Vibration also reacts on the crocodile's ear, enabling it to hear and analyse noises which are beyond our range. Vibrations of the water, the sea with its underwater vibrations of tides and currents, storms and varying depths, the passage of large fish racing to the surface or diving down into some great black hole in the cavernous floor of the sea. The river waters too have their sounds, their vibrations, and so too have the still lagoons, and the great swamps. Vibrations which mean things to the crocodile's ear but not to ours.

So not only the crocodile's eyes but his ears also are of great value to him on land and in the water.

Another quaint thing about this hideously efficient brute is that he grows two sets of ribs, longways and crossways. These are not solidly fixed ribs like those of an animal. They are much more pliable and can move and expand. Doubtless this arrangement is to help him in his two lives under such different "atmospheres" and pressures, his life on land and his life under the water. I cannot say to what depth he can descend but as I have seen him swimming fifteen miles and more out to sea, he can probably descend to considerable depths where these sets of ribs would protect and regulate his body against the water pressure.

He is a voyager, this fellow; an explorer when the fit takes him. He will cruise away out to islands a considerable distance to sea. I've seen him away out towards the Great Barrier Reef, preying on turtle twenty miles from the mainland. And out there the sharks quite often cruise in shoals, not in ones or twos. But the big sea-going crocodile is not afraid of sharks, nor anything else in the world that I know of—except man. And I don't think he is really afraid of him. He treats man with extreme caution while always on the alert to take him unawares.

Alas, mankind is very proud of the modern submarine, terrible weapon of destruction. Fortunate it is for humankind that we cannot invent a machine with the efficiency of nature's submarine, the estuarine crocodile. A submarine that can operate on land as well as on or under water; that can dive to the depths without the possibility that mechanical failure may prevent it surfacing again. A submarine that is not "blind" but can see and also hear as it submerges and cruises underwater; that can operate at night equally as well as in the day; that can charge its batteries and fuel up from the natural materials around it. A submarine independent of home port or dock; that can transport itself overland and operate at will in shallow swamp, snag-filled river, or deep sea. We could get quite a laugh at thinking out more advantages of nature's "submarine" as against man's. For the crocodile can carry on and still successfully fight the battle of life even if he has a paw or half his tail chewed off. But a submarine with its rudder blown off would be a helpless wreck. The submarine underwater makes a noise often fatal to it when picked up by instruments a long way away. The crocodile's efficient method of propulsion is noiseless in comparison. However, we'll let it go at that, being thankful that man has not been able to add to his underwater death machine the decided advantages possessed by the crocodile.

XII

THE "SLAVES" PUT IT ACROSS

FROM the ketch one afternoon we noticed a large crocodile away downstream. He swam to the bank and leisurely waddled up to sun himself on the mud.

"Cunning as a warehouse rat," declared the Skipper. "Keeps just out of range, but holds an eye on us all the same. If we make a move he'll waddle back to the water and be damned to us!"

"Crocodiles know things," said Herman in his soft voice.

Generations of Malay blood were behind that belief, jungle superstitions that attribute to certain crocodiles powers part human, animal, and supernatural. Since the dawn of time men in savage lands have held such beliefs.

"They know too much for you blokes," growled the Skipper.

And the crew chuckled, though no shade of expression crossed the gnarled face of the Old Man, squatting on his haunches for'ard. We were not getting nearly enough croco-diles for the Skipper's satisfaction. We were shooting plenty, but shooting to kill instantly was another matter.

"These crocodiles possess the 'debil-debil' eye," I protested. "They see the bullet coming."

"Don't give the crew ideas," snapped the Skipper. "They're full of crazy ideas already. The reason why my shooters cannot kill crocodiles is because they can't shoot straight!" And he glared in disdain.

Paddy glowered from deep-set eyes, sullenly fingering his spears. I'm sure he liked me. I was glad to see him finally choose a fish spear. He stepped to the rail, scowling down into the water. I lit a cigarette, picked up the rifle and stepped into the dinghy astern. Then rowed carelessly upstream away from the crocodile, gradually pulling towards shore. When the trees hid me from that distant eye I stepped ashore and walked in through the mangroves and came out on the edge of the great plain. I'd pit the wits of man against the cunning of the crocodile. My plan was to walk down the plain with the mangroves between me and the creek until past where the saurian was sunbathing. I'd then enter the mangroves and edge in to the creek bank, then come up along it from the seaward side. The crocodile would have his "one eye" up-stream. He would not expect danger to approach from the downstream side. I carried out this deep-laid scheme and through the mangroves reached the creek bank well below the crocodile. Then came the stalking, cautiously edging up-stream with a sharp watch on the water lest some other tempting target appear, while scanning the tree butts immediately ahead lest I step on a crocodile not supposed to be there. They've got a disconcerting habit at times of being where least expected. The mangroves were so thickly placed that I had to squeeze through among them. All was eerie gloom and smell of mud and still water and deep silence, the one sound a sucking gurgle as the mud reluctantly released each foot. Not deep mud. The feet only sank three inches at each step so long as a man quickly pulled each foot away. Here and there I crossed a greasy runway, not before peering along it to be fairly sure no crocodile was up among the tree butts. Should a brute detect me between him and the water he would almost certainly charge down the runway. And everything would happen in a hurry. There is quite a little thrill, hunting a dangerous thing that is capable of fighting ferociously if cornered out of its own element. A very different proposition this to stalking a 'roo or turkey. A harsh, metallic shriek urged me to leap for a tree though it was only a crane trumpeting close by. But the old heart was thumping, so I knew that if a crocodile made a rush for the water I'd beat it to a tree. A man alone in such a place is not nearly the hero he is when accompanied by a mate.

Presently, peering out from the bank, I got a peep of the ketch, a picture in reflections upstream. The crocodile must be very close. Yes, there he was, basking on the mudbank, a beauty all of eighteen feet, lying in such a position that one eye had the ketch in full view. To detect me he'd need to look almost back along his tail. Presently, in the gloom I saw I must cross one of those little ravines that the tide occasionally washes out amongst the mangroves. As I crept forward an express train slithered down the ravine splashing me with mud. A glimpse of horny bulk of the biggest crocodile ever, then the splash as he took the water. A further splash as the other took the water.

And a tattoo of drum beats that was the old heart racing its hardest.

I hadn't had time even to jump for a tree. That wasn't a ravine at all; it was the runway of a huge crocodile. Hedged by tree roots, it was not visible as a runway until one peered down into it. It was now churned with a metallic blue mud like dull-blue, polished grease. A dinghy could have been launched down the thing, but that old man crocodile was assuredly larger than a dinghy.

Having had enough of the mangroves, I crept back out on to the plain and with a sigh of relief in that glorious open sunlight turned towards the seashore. There might be a crocodile or two on the beach, safer prey than seeking them in the mangroves.

But there were only two of them, cruising out from shore. We'd apparently "shot out" this creek too. The crocodiles had moved and we'd have to move also. Idly I wondered what tale the slaves" would put across the Skipper now. We had not sailed for the location they had recommended, much to their disgust. Half a dozen of their aboriginal acquaintances had passed by on a walkabout down the coast to some corroboree, first disgustedly impressing on the boys that they were not of much account, considering they were the crew and could not make the Skipper sail where they wanted to. I've often got a quiet grin out of the old abo.—he's such a human fellow.

The tide was well out, leaving exposed mud away out to the sea edge and as far right and left as the eye could see. The mudbanks were alive with the queerest little fishes Wee frog-headed fellows playing everywhere in countless thousands, enjoying a myriad "at home" under the late afternoon sun. They were hopping and jumping, and some actually "flying", most energetically. As they hopped they momentarily raised a tiny reddish fin just like a sail. The wind would catch these sails with quaint effect. Lots among them would keep their "sails" erect and aided by a puff of breeze jerk themselves over the mud a considerable distance, giving an energetic twist to their movements by the flip of an eel-like tail. Among them were many quaint little things constantly flipping a white flag the size of a threepenny bit. These were little signal crabs and everywhere among the jumping fish, like tiny dots and dashes, their little white "flags" were flapping.

It was sundown when I boarded the *Lotus*. An appetizing smell from the galley told that the evening meal was well under way. The crew up for'ard were busy over their fish and rice, the Old Man scoffing the lion's share as usual, his long, skinny fingers lapping the rice into a cavernous mouth. Several tough-looking strangers daubed with ochre and feathers squatted among them, big fellows, heavily bearded, with knowing eyes that glanced swiftly from under shaggy brows as I stepped aboard. I noticed that the Skipper had made them leave their spears ashore.

"Any luck?" he asked.

"No. That big fellow got away. But I nearly stepped on to one bigger than he."

"I saw the splashes. They're cunning as a basketful of monkeys. And a darned sight quicker. Any fool who thinks he's going to make a living out of crocodile shooting has another think coming. Better hop into some tucker."

"Righto. You're a good cook when there's none better. Who are the strangers?"

"Myalls from down the coast. I bet they'll put mischief into the slaves' heads—as if they're not cute enough already with their natural instincts—let alone the Old Man."

"The slaves will be the death of you yet," I grinned.

"Quite apart from joking, that could be if I'd let 'em," he declared, but this mouse is falling into no trap while he can smell the cheese. I'll bet you before two hours have passed they'll come aft and tell us about a river that's so full of crocodiles the banks are crawling away. Thousands and thousands of lovely crocodiles just waiting to be shot. And if that doesn't catch us they'll make the bait young lubras who will dive for us and bring up plenty feller trepang! Altogether too much! And it will be in a land flowing with milk and honey. I know the symptoms. I've been watching those latest cut-throats—the stage is set."

Still, it might be quite all right. We'll have to move else-where anyway—this creek is shot out."

"I know. But we don't necessarily move to the slaves' playground."

Sure enough, soon as our pipes were nicely going, Jacky stepped aft, a half-kindly, half-ingratiating smile on his deep-lined, innocent countenance. With glowing eyes and effusive hand talk he proceeded to tell us all about a river swarming with crocodiles, with the added attraction that the sea coast thereabouts held wealth untold in the form of pearlshell, trochus, and *beche-de-mer*.

"Plenty fellow crocodile there," he earnestly explained, "plenty feller pearlshell, plenty feller eberyting! Long time before me been go along that place, longa schooner. Catchem pish, tchell, we feller been fill up that schooner *all* about. Fill 'im up till no got room down below. All feller sleep up top!"

And thus Jacky whetted our appetite with a description of the wealth obtained so plentifully that every inch of space down below in the alleged schooner was filled right up. As he got well into his tale Paddy and Freddy and Billy came and squatted beside him, urged to give moral support by some unseen signal from the Old Man.

The Skipper heard them out, then nodded towards the strangers and innocently asked, "Those feller belong that country too?"

"Ou ai!" they nodded.

"I thought so," grunted the Skipper, "and you want me to give those ruffians a lift down there so they can introduce you to their lady friends while I'll be called upon to feed the whole camp with my good tucker and tobacco! Oh yeah!"

"Him feller good man!" protested Jacky with a jerk of his chin towards the warriors for'ard. "Plenty feller work! That place good one, plenty got him lubra savvy this work. Him gib it hand. Him savvy cook, wash 'em does, clean 'im shell, skin 'im 'gator, cut 'im trepang."

As on similar occasions they watched our eyes to see how we were taking it. Then, if we appeared at all interested they would add softly, "Plenty young fellow lubra too. Young lubra work hard feller."

"Alligator shooting!" snarled the Skipper. "I should have stuck to two-up in Sydney. Then I might have made a living! Tell you morning-feller time," he added to Tacky. "Clear out of this!"

As the black diplomats stepped softly for'ard I knew why the Skipper had added that last sentence. The boys would believe they'd won their point. We could sleep fairly soundly and they'd be aboard in the morning.

"Are you going?" I asked.

They want me to sail east," he replied. "I'm sailing west."

And I knew again what was in his mind. A number of men on trips somewhat similar to ours had been killed farther east. I should have liked to sail east, for it is an interesting coast, apart from the fact that Jacky, in his own cunningly primitive way, had painted an attractive picture of this river of wealth and mystery. With ordinary precautions there would have been no risk at all. But the Skipper throughout the years had known things happen that made him very cautious, bloody incidents along this very coast. Attack and ambush, death by the broad-bladed spear, tomahawk and nulla-nulla. The blood-stained decks of small craft with their crews chopped to pieces. Looted luggers blazing in the night with only dead men aboard.

Every sea wanderer becomes very strongly attached to his vessel, it is in his thoughts day and night. Some skippers think more of their little vessel's welfare than they do of their own. To them it would be tragedy indeed to lose their vessels. They seldom run a risk that can be avoided.

We smoked on deck for a while. Far above, brilliant stars kissed the quiet water between the black walls of trees. Now and again a sigh as a fish broke water, swift, vanishing shades of flying foxes speeding upstream, then far above wild geese speeding overhead with harsh, mournful trumpeting.

Early next morning fate intervened, on our side. We stepped up on deck to see the boys sprawled out very sick indeed. The Old Man lay groaning as if in mortal straits. Billy was near foaming at the mouth. Jacky lay caressing his stomach moaning, "Me feller plenty sick too much!" Paddy crouched with yellowing face, his eyes upon us with a pathetic expression of bewilderment. The strangers had vanished, sick and frightened men.

"Something is quite wrong," exclaimed the Skipper. "Now how in flaming blazes could these benighted slaves have poisoned themselves?"

He glanced around and his eyes lighted upon an empty tin of engine grease.

"My good grease!" he howled. "Four shillings a tin, all gone to feed a crowd of lazy blackfellows! Beautiful grease filling their gluttonous stomachs and now I'll have to get rid of it for them!"

And he did, with some awful mixture which he dosed liberally with Epsom salt. The boys were sick before, but it was sheer rude health to what happened soon after they swallowed the Skipper's "cleaner out".

"And now I'll have to fry them johnny-cakes to fill them up again," he stormed. "Of all the heathenish things invented it is the Australian aboriginal!"

The unfortunate crew stretched across the deck were writhing and moaning pitifully, but to me it was a funny little episode. There was plenty of dripping for cooking aboard, two kerosene tins full in fact, but the engine-room grease happened to be up on deck that morning and it was easier for the boys to reach for it than go below for the dripping.

Next morning we sailed, the launch a picture in the sun-light as we ran down that narrow lane between walls of greenery. From the bows we got a parting shot at a crocodile. He vanished in a flurry of spray. There was a fathom of water over the creek mouth and mudbanks. No doubt the quaint little frog-headed fish with the sails, and the little white signal crabs were all snug and deep in their burrows waiting for the tide to recede again. With a lift of the bows we took to the open sea, heading west. A bright day and beautiful, the sea like a rippled yellow-green river. The engine gently purring, the water slipping past astern, the Skipper at the galley, Herman sawing a plank, Jacky steering, the Old Man sleeping in the bows, Billy too, with Freddy and Paddy lying naked on the cabin top snoring peacefully.

"Poor slaves!" called the Skipper from the galley. "Not a care in the world, while the master cooks their tucker."

But the fresh breeze laughed his words away. It was good to be alive.

XIII

BATTLES OF GIANTS

HORRID things, crocodiles. But when you are hunting them for months, when you seek them out in the hushed gloom of jungle creeks, in the shadowed beauty of the lily lagoons, in the festooned tangle of the tea-tree swamps, then they possess, in their own repulsive way, a creepy fascination. Their repugnant existence is not the open life of wild animals, the beauty of flowers, the joy of birds; it is a thing of the gloomy places, and of the depths. You seek to creep upon them and kill them to take the one thing they possess, their life. Quickly they come to know you, to pit their instinctive craft against you. Day following day, week following week, the world grows smaller and smaller until it centres on you, the stealthy hunter, and the suspicious, vanishing crocodile.

He knows *you*.

Experience brings you realization of this, and you wonder why. Maybe it is because of some vague link of life between us, between the hunter and the hunted. Primordial life came from the crawling depths, so we are taught. I cannot believe the same of human life. To me, despite our deep-grained faults, human life has come from the stars—no — from far, far farther away.

Perhaps there is something psychic, some cosmic link between us. For all life is—Life. Anyway, the crocodiles soon come to know—when we seek their life.

These hideous brutes in their still-primal fastnesses held a strong curiosity for me, whether they were on land or water, by night or day. It seemed repulsively strange and yet hazily understandable that they were, in their hideous way, almost human. They will manoeuvre to protect and, if necessary, fight for life with a sometimes human cunning frantically mixed with the animal courage of despair. Yet again they were so crafty, so alert. And yet they could be so sleepy and stupidly careless. Also, they are so inquisitive and, as we say, "curiosity killed the cat". Anything strange, anything they do not understand, any unusual movement, unfamiliar sight or sound, attracts them with a curiosity which may prove fatal to them. Curiosity sometimes gets human beings into trouble, but without it and the mental powers to investigate we would not have advanced beyond prehistoric man. If the human race had been born with the urge of curiosity developed twenty times stronger than it is, I wonder how much farther ahead we would have advanced by now.

The crocodile, in his own way, is keenly inquisitive too, keen to find out what some strange thing is, curious to know what the other fellow is doing. Should he notice a fellow crocodile on some mysterious business bent, he will lie low and spy on him, and as like as not spoil his little game if he gets a chance. He is a bushranger also. If he notices a weaker fellow snapping up a morsel, he will surprise him and take it if he can.

He will pirate the other fellow's lady love, will surge in with a fighting grunt and take her if he can.

They are interested too should something disturb a colony of flying foxes that often mass like a gigantic swarm of bees on trees overhanging the bank. Should lurking saurians be within hearing of the deafening screeching then "seed pods" suddenly appear on the water. They surge in, and any foxes knocked down by stick or gun that fall into the water—fall into open mouths. Crocodiles are very curious about anything unusual upon the bank, or some strange object floating down-stream. They will stay about for hours, seeking to find out what some unusual happening or thing may be. They want to know what it is all about. Only the tip of the snout, the top of the eyes above water staring at a familiar spot upon the bank upon which some queer change has taken place, or where there is movement of animal, bird or mankind.

They vanish, to rise silently again. This near-human curiosity is taken advantage of by shooters, trappers and poisoners.

In another way too, like humans, the roving spirit comes into their cycle of life. The younger ones travel, eager to be moving about and seeing things. They may travel hundreds of miles. Gradually they think about settling down. Many return to the waters in which they were born. Afterwards, as age comes slowly on, they do not move very far afield. Later on the individuals claim some particular possy and here or hereabouts he is always to be found. As the Englishman says, "My home is my castle, and here I stay".

Then, again, comradeship is a feature of their lives, as it is with all things of the wild, and with humans too. A crocodile's mate is seldom far away. Should you trap one, his mate will soon be near by. Very often she will come next sundown and lie just near where he was caught. She is waiting for him.

Again, should you set a 'gator trap with the flesh of a crocodile, others will not return to the place. Not until six weeks afterwards, certainly not until the tides have washed away all taint of crocodile flesh from the mud. We, too, hate to return to scenes of tragedy. Crocodile instinct tells him one of his friends met violent death there and—he may be the next. Like many living things, he has an instinctive dread of death. Scent and instinct tell him to avoid the place.

Though very inquisitive the crocodile is also extremely cunning. By his inquisitiveness he learns things, and his cunning teaches him how to profit by what he learns—according to the limits of his environment.

So far as my limited natural knowledge allowed me learn by observation of the saurian in the waters and on the land, and from his carcass, his bulky body is surprisingly lithe, while from below the shoulders to tail tip, most "sections" seem almost able to act "independently", as it were. Though he waddles on land "straight ahead", and cannot turn swiftly, he can act with incredible swiftness under water. Can dive and turn in the water while twisting on back or side and use his claws and fangs and tail as he speeds by or wheels around. The skin, or rather hide, in sections appears to bewooded cliffs, roofs that are landmarks peeping above the little jungle composed almost of horny plates. Even where those "plates" are absent the skin is made up of large, tough, pliable scales. These are joined together by a sort of gristle, even to the smallest "scale". Thus all is watertight while at the same time wonderfully elastic, especially the latter half of the body. To see the massive bulk of a big old crocodile quiescent on water or land you would not imagine with what speed it can travel and turn in the water. In a fight particularly. At the same time it can be motionless, for hours if necessary. Should prey fall into the water it surges ahead like a comet, open-jawed.

The legs have a bony framework, but these squat, stubby things are more of a very tough gristle. As he swims, or rather "float-swims", up on to the mud he "carries" these paws. They slither in under him. The forepaws are armed with terrible hooked claws. Most crocodiles are webbed between the claws, but a few are not. One crocodile may be partly webbed, and yet again another may be webbed on one forepaw and not on the other.

These creatures are the monster "lizards" of the world. Yet the female lays eggs, while all have feet like a duck. But anyone who might think the crocodile a sissy would be very much mistaken.

Many a time I've watched the ugly bmtes crawling up on to the mud. I was curious to learn just how they do it. Though they are crawling, their bulk appears to slide along over soft mud where a man would become bogged. They put pressure cn the mud and seem almost to slither along; not the same pressure as a man's foot or an animal's hoof, but the long, "creepy" pressure of a wonderfully elastic, pliable, almost torpedo-shaped body. Their tracks on soft mud are long, shiny slithers.

Unless in the water and perfectly sure of themselves, the crocodiles will seldom snap at prey, unless it be fish; even then I've seen them snatch out with a lightning clutch of the claw. Just submerged near the bank they wait for prey at some spot favoured by animals as a drinking place. As the beast leans over to drink the fore-bulk of the crocodile rears up from the water and his terrible claws snatch out and paw the prey to its jaw. One sideways twisting writhe of the crocodile and the prey is jerked into the water and is being dragged under.

This is the method when the victim is a kangaroo, a wallaby, a wild pig. Though he will sometimes knock them into the water with one sweeping blow from his tail. It is the usual method also when he fancies a diet of poultry, for he occasionally snatches a tit-bit in the shape of a wild turkey. Turkeys quite often have their favourite drinking place and quench their thirst at the same hour each day. The scrub turkey, continually approaching the drinking possy, may wear quite a little track to that one particular spot. Wallabies quite often do the same. Should a lurking crocodile thus spy a turkey's regular drinking place, he will be waiting there next day.

I've seen a crane on the wing get the last shock of his life from a crocodile's tail. On urgent business bent, he flies too low over the water. The tail whips up and the crane is knocked into the open jaws. As a mouse might play with a lion, so does the willy-wagtail with a crocodile. I've seen them quite often, the great brute floating downstream with the tide, the wagtail dancing back and forward along the ugly head, singing and whistling right merrily.

Large, weighty animals put up a terrible struggle for life. To overthrow these the crocodile plans beforehand. Motionless in the shadows, with only his nostril tips and eyes above water, he notices some animal coming to drink. He estimates its size, its caution, the 'lay" of the bank down which it is timidly stepping. The animal drinks, hurries away. With a flick of the tail the crocodile is at the spot. Its cold eyes are taking in the tactical advantages and disadvantages of the ambush to be. According to the nature of the bank, the surroundings of grass or shrubs or trees, the depth, clearness or discoloration of the water, it plans to hide to the best advantage to take its wary prey by surprise. It will return day after day until it gets its prey. Or until it attacks and the prey escapes.

Towards sundown one day I noticed a young buffalo bull coming cautiously to a creek bank to drink. He was only a youngster, but he was a buffalo for all that, versed in the ways of the wild. He had come to the waterhole often before. This evening he snorted as he advanced, hesitated some twenty feet hack from where he usually drank. He pawed the earth, and sniffed towards the water. But all was still and quiet. The pandanus fronds were drooping, the long shadows stretched across the waterhole—all was as usual. He approached the water's edge, his eyes staring into the shadowed depths. He planted his fore hoofs firmly, and sniffed towards the water. His neck leaned over. As his muzzle touched the water, the outspread paws and ravening snout of a crocodile lunged up. Claws gripped the back of the buffalo's neck and pulled the muzzle down into a clashing snout while the entire forequarters of the crocodile arose above a surge of water. Its hindquarters writhed over as it dashed the young bull with terrific force to the ground. One agonized groan, the helch of wind sounded like the exhaust from a steam pipe. The crocodile gave a powerful twist to its tail and a lurch backward with all the weight of its body and the young bull splashed into the water, its legs helplessly thrashing the air. It vanished in a surge of water and the frantic hoofs were the last of it that I saw. The pool was a turmoil of subsiding wavelets. Bubbling up through the discoloured water came the last air the young bull would ever breathe.

The buffalo seldom drinks from a steep creek bank. He prefers to drink in the shallows, and then wallow in the mud. But in a severe dry, as the waters fast dry up, at times he has no choice. Should a crocodile sight him coming, it sinks to the bottom, gliding towards the bank. The water may be too deep or discoloured for the buffalo (or horse or bullock) to see the lurking menace. But the crocodile can hear the vibrations of the buffalo's hoofs approaching on the bank above. The awful green eyes are glaring up. At the first ripples the reptile surges straight up and his jaws fasten upon the nose of the drinking beast.

Thus the crocodile uses cunning, swiftness, strength and weight against heavy prey. Secures its grip by surprise reinforced by the shock of great weight, allied to leverage of the powerful tail to drag its victim straight into the water. If thwarted, then weight, leverage and strength are used to dash the victim to the ground. The crocodile twists and writhes upon the struggling beast, crushing the wind from its body, then drags it into the water.

Crocodiles use similar tactics when fighting among themselves. That awful rear-up from the shoulders, with clawed paws outstretched as they lunge forward with the head thrust sideways for the jaw grip. Once they secure that grip nothing can break the purchase. They can uproot a surprisingly large mangrove tree by this leverage. When two ravening beasts become fatally locked in one another's jaws it truly is a scene from primal depths.

One such battle of titans I witnessed fought upon the mud-bank of a jungle creek. The bank was wide and flat at the water's edge, then rose some twenty-odd feet in a gentle slope. Up that slope was the glistening runway of a crocodile and he was lying at the top of it, his tail to the water. This was unusual, for when basking thus they generally have the head turned, or partly turned, towards the water, ready at alarm to slither straight down to safety. This one was basking in the sunlight that flooded down into the creek. I was on the opposite bank, creeping among the trees for a shot at him. Down behind him at the bank's edge an ugly snout arose and a saurian emerged and began slithering up the runway. The silent, definite quickness of the huge bulk, its swift crouching wriggle across and up the mudbank showed he meant to surprise the other. Instead, he was taken at a disadvantage, for the other spun around and charged straight down the runway in a shower of liquid mud. They met with a throaty bellow. With clawing paws they rolled over and over locked in one another's jaws. Tails showering the mud, they rolled down on to the flat, the one with the advantage strove to break the jaw of the other, surging above him with straining neck, battling to wrench that jaw apart. Their forepaws with the cruel hooked claws gripped and ripped and tore. Their snarling gurglings and drum-like thumps of the tail started a bedlam amongst the cranes overhead. Mud and sticks flew out to daub the mangroves and splash into the creek. Over and over they rolled with a great splash into the water and under. The creek broke into agitated waves as the battle was waged below, suddenly to break surface in a writhing flurry of interlocked bodies that sent the water splashing to the tree roots. With a final lashing of tails the fighting monsters vanished. A few minutes later a violent surface disturbance higher up the creek told that the battle was still being waged. Gradually the waters subsided. The cranes settled back on the treetops with protesting squawkings.

I hadn't fired a shot. It had been all too swift for one thing; but I wouldn't have missed that fight for anything. I did not see them again. Whether the victor had wedged the other under some submerged log and drowned him—who knows? Perhaps their very fury took them both to death, entangled amongst the snags in some deep hole.

Two old-men crocodiles will fight with a beastly, bellowing noise, thrashing about in the water or mud as antediluvian monsters fought in primal ages. Their bodies writhe around one another. Their steel-like claws stretch to the uttermost as they strive to tear each other to pieces. If they cannot grip the adversary's jaw, a favourite grip is the "dog grip", the front paw. Hell breaks loose then. The bitten thing raves frenziedly as it struggles to break the grip before its paw is chewed through. The biter "shoulders" his enemy, heaving to keep his body pressed against the adversary, and pushes sideways and backward while levering with part-arched neck. The claws of one paw press down upon its enemy's snout. It thus holds every advantage, for the enemy can only follow it around and is unable to bring its own jaws into action. If the grip cannot be broken, then the paw will be chewed off. The maimed saurian may then possibly escape, proof being provided by the fact that a crocodile whose paw has thus been chewed off is occasionally shot or trapped. Occasionally, also, one is shot that has had two or three feet of its tail chewed off. One enormous monster that "Anzac" Bennett shot on the Endeavour River, Cooktown, had lost at least five feet of his tail in some submarine battle. It was enormous, that thing—the largest ever known to be shot in the Cape York Peninsula.

The tail is another "king grip" if the antagonist can hold it, for he thus can keep out of reach of the other. No matter how the victim fights and struggles, often desperately striving to "catch" the other's tail, if it cannot jam its antagonist against the bank, or a tree, or underwater log then the grip is held until the tail is chewed through.

But it takes a swift, cunning fighter to secure either of these grips. The crocodile can move his very important tail with lightning swiftness, while his forepaws have their own claws and strength and the great jaws to protect them. And both contestants fight like the furies they are.

Shot crocodile, Johnstone River, Queensland 1907.

XIV

THE FRONTIERS OF ADVENTURE

FOR a moment shall we look around us? For thus we learn that "things are not what they seem", neither in a drop of water nor in thousands of square miles of apparently empty land and sea. When we feel the ketch and its crew are but an utterly insignificant speck in a vast loneliness we are both right and wrong. Vast though the sea is, somewhere out there are other vessels. Despite our isolation we really are voyaging on the frontier lands of adventure. We used to speak of these things sometimes in the tiny cabin at nights, two thousand miles and more from the great cities that were so busy they could visualize nothing but what was going on in their own little suburbs.

Though adventure may not befall us, still we may as well see and learn what we can while we are here. To one side of us stretches the apparently empty Arafura Sea. It is not empty, for somewhere out there cruise the pearling fleets, seeking treasure of the sea. During this very season they are finding new and rich beds of pearlshell. They are Australian vessels that, in spite of shipwreck and cyclone and frequent tragedy, long since pioneered those valuable ocean beds. At one time big, modern-equipped Japanese fleets came year by year with fast-growing strength, seeking to make these prized seas their own. Yes, there are both adventure and riches out there, and tragedy sometimes for the diver as he gropes through the dull green twilight on the sea floor. He may slip down into a deep hole, his life-line may become entangled around some rocky ledge that hides a gloomy cavern, or some giant fish of the depths may attack him.

And now at this very moment appears a ship with a queer, nearly square-rigged mat sail above the high stern. That long bamboo stern, towering over the sea, has rough windows cut in it, like a terrace of huge black eyes. It is a terrace really, for here the crew sleep. This clumsy-looking craft can brave storms and sail with surprising speed. Surely a craft like this could appear from nowhere but out of the mysterious East — maybe it comes from the "Spice Islands" of the Indies. It is a venturesome Malay proa, trespassing in forbidden waters. Clad only in sarongs, her crew are brown, stockily built men, alert of movement and eye. She holds off while wary eyes watch our craft, suspicious lest police or Customs men be aboard. She seeks trepang: ugly crawling slugs of the sea-bed that the mandarin and other folk enjoy so much when cooked as soup.

We do not realize how blessed is Australia in the richness of her northern seas. Hundreds of thousands of square miles of rich fishing waters, vast beds of valuable shell, unknown expanses of marine growths that knowledge and progress will turn to the use of man.

For centuries past, the Macassar men have raided our northern shores for trepang, pearls and the lovely tortoise-shell of commerce. To the Malays the continent was a vast, inhospitable, mysterious land. They believed that fierce, war-like races of giants inhabited its unknown interior, and that among them were tribes of semi-humans that were half man and half animal, half man and half bird, or part man and part reptile. However, the shores of this mysterious land mothered pearlshell and trepang and uncountable fish, and they were not afraid to sail its strange seas and take what they could. These venturesome Malays were mostly Macassar men. Better seamen and bolder pirates seldom sailed the seas. Two hundred large proas and more would leave Macassar in the now Dutch East Indies in January during the westerly monsoons, in charge of an admiral, probably a native prince with lesser admirals under him. As the cumbersome but seaworthy fleet approached the great coast the vessels would split up into fleets of about fifteen proas each and, scattering, sail on to widely separated points along the coast, each commander favouring some special locality. While still a long way from land, signal smokes upon the coast rose like ghost wisps into the air. The wild aboriginals thus warned the tribes of the approach of the foreign brown men.

Thus, too, the watchers on England's white cliffs must have warned Boadicea's woad-painted warriors of the approach of the Romans, warned the tribes of the raiding Vikings.

The Macassar men, in order to "cook" their fish, that is to clean and smoke-dry and thus preserve the trepang slugs, must land and form a base ashore. They had to do this by force of arms, for very often they were opposed by the aboriginals, who fought as savage guerrillas fight. The invader had the advantage of disciplined training, fought with bows and arrows and the steel-bladed kris against the stone-headed spears of the painted savages. When the landing was consolidated, the smoke-sheds were built. Day by day the lazy smoke rose ashore, while out in the bay the fifteen proas and their numerous small boats were busy fishing, the loaded boats pulling to the shore. From each vessel a guard was placed ashore to protect the men working at the "cooking" houses. These men rarely ventured inland except in strongly armed parties to some nearby lagoon in search of water and meat as a change in food from fish. A man on land never left his arms for a moment, nor relaxed his caution. Should he stray but a few hundred yards away he probably would fall a victim to spear or club—or to the strangling cord.

A quiet death that. A touch as of a leaf as a man steps past a shrub, instantly followed by the jerk and bum as tbe cord is pulled tight. The victim on the ground jerking out his life as men kneel upon him and hold taut his limbs. Many a Malay went to death that way, within sight of his own camp, even within sound of the voices of his comrades.

It is not every aboriginal tribe that uses the strangling vine, but those that do are experts.

However, the Malays triumphed. Though their flotillas were scattered along the coast, though their men were greatly outnumbered and often in peril, they proved the stronger.

Not only by virtue of discipline and superior weapons, but also because the aboriginal tribes seldom combined in a mass attack against them. Though two or three tribes might occasionally combine, usually the tribe on whose country the Malays landed carried out the yearly guerrilla fight until the invaders sailed away.

As happens in civilized warfare as well as savage, there was a certain amount of intermixing among the Malays and aboriginals. This is the reason why, as time has gone by, in some areas along the coast the aboriginals show traces of Malay blood. And in such cases it has considerably improved their appearance.

Some among the aboriginals were not above trading with the enemy, just as "civilized" nations do. The aboriginals would collect pearlshell and pearls, and tortoise-shell. Raucous would be the laughter when some warrior held up a lovely pearl between his dirty fingers and joked at the foolishness of the Malay who would give such good food for it. None will ever know the wealth of pearls that have found their way to the Old World through the Malay sea roamers fishing the great South Land coast.

Despite the fact that the aboriginal never learned that the unity of tribes means strength, he is no fool. He occasionally used the plan practised throughout history by an apparently subdued people, to surprise and overwhelm the over-confident invader. Wrinkled old Malays with a curse and a glint in their eyes have told me such stories. A tribe even for three seasons would sham friendship to their conqueror. With each season, the tribe would not resist them; would come and help, quite unarmed. Help in gathering wood for the smoke-houses, help the boatmen in diving for trepang, while their hunters would bring in wild geese and duck and meat to the camp. Numbers of the young girls and piccaninnies frequented the camp ashore in friendly laugh and joke, and doing little odd jobs. Finally the Malays in that particular locality would become quite used to these friendly aboriginals amongst them. Then one morning weapons would be snatched as if from the very air and a howling massacre was upon them. From the grass, from the trees, from their very feet other warriors leaped up and hurtled into the fray while the lubras were screaming and stabbing with the bone dagger and often with a Malay kris. From out on the bay aboriginals had seized weapons and were massacring the boat crews, the one concerted movement so perfectly timed that nearly all the crews were helpless in the water. It was work only of moments and then a raging black crowd was tumbling into canoes and racing for the nearest proa. Heaven help her if she proved to be ill-manned.

Other stories too the old Malay sea dogs told of a combined tribal attack in the cold hour that comes with the dawn. Of canoes loaded with warriors drifting down upon a proa. Of ghost men swarming up and then the long-drawn, beast war-cry as the clubs crashed down. And pandemonium from the shore where the camp was being simultaneously rushed.

Yes, there was perpetual warfare between the aboriginals and Malays here and there along those thousands of miles of coastline. Those Malays who temporarily relaxed caution often paid for it with their lives.

The Malay fleet, with their proas loaded, would return each season across the Arafura and Timor seas to Macassar with the changing of the seasonal wind.

For many years after the white men came to Darwin the proas returned. As time went on they began to be harried by Customs officers, but the coast is so long that such policing did not make a great deal of difference. What eventually finished their seasonal cruise on a large scale though was the development of the pearling fleets—those of Thursday Island is particular, of Broome to a much lesser extent, and finally of Darwin.

The Thursday Island fleets as they grew soon took to fishing the Great Barrier Reef for trepang and the great quantities quickly obtained went far towards supplying the Eastern market. So that now we see only an occasional venturesome proa in these waters, such as that quaint vessel away across there. Yes, adventure sails beside the *Lotus* in the deceptively empty Arafura.

On our landward side is Buffalo Land, stretching from east of Darwin almost to the Gulf of Carpentaria. We will stroll ashore and dally a while in this land of the large beasts. Their country adjoins the waterways of the large "lizards".

Behind the dense fringe of mangroves and vine jungle that hedges the coast are great plains stretching away back to distant low hills. Intersected by shallow rivers and innumerable creeks, tea-tree and pandanus swamp and lily lagoons teeming with wildfowl, it is the home of the aboriginal and buffalo, marsupials and birds and snakes. Undisturbed except for a score or so of buffalo shooters, a wandering prospector, or a Mounted Police patrol.

During the wet season considerable areas of the plains are morass, too boggy to "work". The scattered buffalo shooters then retire to their own wet-season camps to "lay up" and repair saddlery and equipment and get stores ready for the next season's shoot from April to November. The end of the dry season leaves the sunburned land parched and grey. The wet season floods it with water. At the end of the wet the waters begin to drain off, the warm suns come and the land is transformed into riotous life. Vegetation seems fairly bursting to spring up and spread and grow and grow and grow. Animals and reptiles and birds gorge on the abundance nature is so swiftly providing. The buffalo herds emerge from their retreats and stream out on to the green plains. The shooters get busy. Life—and death—has come again to the land.

It is a wonderful experience, on a bright, warm dawn, to watch from a vantage spot buffaloes emerging to start out for their daily meal. The great plain gradually takes form amid the scattered clumps of pandanus palm. Litde jungle "islands" still are shadows. The sun rises brighter; the horizon slips farther away. An old bull has emerged from a jungle patch. He stands there sniffing the air. His horns have an enormous spread. He moves forward a few yards, stops. As if by magic another buffalo appears behind him. Yet another behind him is emerging from the jungle.

From a dozen different clumps of palm or jungle or valley a buffalo has appeared, followed by another and another. Then the first old bull walks straight out on to the plain and behind him walk a line of buffaloes, bulls, cows, calves. Line after line appear, walking out on to the plain until everywhere it is dotted with moving lines of buffaloes. As the morning wears on they will he dotted all over the big plain in litde mobs of forties, eighties, a hundred, occasionally much larger mobs. And on other plains not visible they will be there just the same, lazily feeding the day away.

The hunter lets them get well out from cover, miles out on the plain. Then he rides out amongst them, quietly selecting his mob, seeking the mob with most bulls. For it is the bulls' hides he wants. He turns his horse towards the mob, but does not rush them; if he did, they would bunch together and spoil his chance of a shot. They stare at his approach, uneasily shuffle as he comes nearer, then the outsiders wheel and rush towards the centre of the mob. Those farthest away turn and start out. He eases his horse then, while the mob slowly string out, one falling in behind the other. When they are strung out in a nice long line he leans forward and instantly the horse is at the gallop. Swiftly he is up alongside the cows and calves, galloping past up along the line as it breaks into a lumbering trot. He looks down on and ahead along that line of lumbering grey backs. Some appear to be pipeclayed, for they are covered with grey-white mud from wallowing. He notes the broader shoulders and long horns of the bulls, their heads held low as they gallop. With eye alert he is up beside the first bull and his rifle whips up, then down as he shoots into the small of the back. His horse races on and the rifle is whipped up before him ready for the next shot. So he races right up along the line, with left hand on the reins, right grasping the rifle. He fires into its backbone where the hide is thin. He must shoot at just the right time and hit the right spot or else.

His horse is as expert as he, and must be so. One stumble and rider and horse would be down, with the buffaloes gal-loping over them. Once the shooting starts, the horse must gallop not only straight up alongside and faster than the bulls, but must keep them going, for if a maddened bull breaks line a slip would mean trouble—the bull simply charges anything he sees. And so the shooter gallops on and rarely misses, though at full gallop he must place each bullet in one vital spot. Bull after bull crashes down until the shooter gallops right to the end of the line.

If the line was long enough, and there were enough bulls in it, providing he is an expert at the game he may even have got enough hides for the day.

For the skinning and transport, and the packing and treating of the hides takes time, limited by the horses and native labour available.

Just occasionally all may not work out to schedule. I remember one time when three pairs of shooters from different points of a big plain were converging, and as they did so the many mobs of buffaloes were also converging, until suddenly they broke into a lumbering gallop and soon were milling together in one mighty mob. The hunters just before then had started their shooting at the gallop and there came the thunder of several thousand hoofs, the clashing and tossing of mighty horns as the ground shuddered in a mad, uncontrollable stampede. Foam-flecked horses galloping for their lives, with a hundred aboriginal skinners, men, women and children, racing for trees—trees so very scarce when away out over the plain.

XV

IN BUFFALO LAND

OCCASIONALLY an accident happens. A bull horns a horse and it screams as it rears and crashes to the dust. If the thrown rider leaps to his feet, he shoots instantly. Otherwise it is a race between him and the buffalo to the nearest tree should his mate not be near. Some men are stunned by the fall. Some never reach the tree.

There are occasional areas of the plains which are honey-combed with little holes, somewhat like rabbit warrens. Horse and rider going after a string of buffaloes occasionally gallop over such country and the horse goes down with his fetlock snapped. The rider is thrown straight out and down into the midst of the lumbering buffaloes. More than one shooter in such a breathless moment has been saved by his aboriginal helper galloping his horse straight against the nearest oncoming buffalo and thus throwing it aside.

Perhaps of all Australian bushmen the buffalo shooter has the most adventurous life. He lives amongst natives and sometimes unavoidably becomes mixed up in their tribal feuds and vendettas, their killings and their jealousies. He has thrills in plenty in his buffalo shooting. At times he may be compelled to water from swamps infested by crocodiles, or wade across. Even though this country is a morass in the wet season, he may perish of thirst in the summer and leave a last message scratched on a billycan as Bert Combes did, as others have. He may face a lonely death from fever, probably with a faithful aboriginal squatting there not knowing what to do. Or the buffalo shooter may be called upon to face storm or shipwreck when sailing his hides back to Darwin. Especially did the early hunters face adventure when, not so many years ago, they pioneered this unknown country with its numerous wild tribes.

The buffalo shooter, like his horse, is an expert with unflinching eye and nerves tensed to take any strain. Necessarily a wonderful horseman, to succeed he must have full knowledge of the game, have his share of determination and endurance, be capable of handling and understanding the often complex nature of half-castes, and the primitive shrewdness in aboriginals. And he must possess the initiative to carry on his work successfully in roadless country distant from a civilized port, and, with the management of a fair-sized camp on his mind, have the organizing ability to keep his stores arriving from port, and his hides going back to that point. He probably sends fifteen hundred hides per season into port.

The knowledge, organization and skill necessary to secure the smooth running of the big camp, and deal with the problems of supply, treatment of hides, transportation, marketing, makes it a man-sized job quite apart from the spectacular shooting.

At the end of the wet season, with the break-up of the rains, natives come in to the shooter's camp eager to gorge on the plentiful meat that will be in abundance immediately shooting commences. Eager too for the tobacco, flour, tea, sugar, iron scraps —anything. They love the game. The shooter must engage the best twenty among these as skinners and keep an eye on them all, their relations and alleged relations and friends, for all hang around the camp, and all expect some share in the spoil. He must keep a very sharp tally on the skinners' knives, because these in particular may disappear miraculously. If he cannot handle natives, he will not stand much chance of making a success of the game.

Two expert skinners will skin a buffalo in ten minutes, but it is only trained men who can. And the shooter must pick these men and keep them satisfied. This means satisfying their numerous hangers-on also. When the men ride out to shoot, the whole crowd of natives follow on behind, the skinners, packhorse boys, and hangers-on with the women and children.

These latter will load themselves up with meat for the daily gorge by the campfire.

Even so, with daily shooting all over the great plains the natives can eat but little indeed of the thousands of carcasses left yearly to rot. It is a great shame, that waste of good beef. But under present conditions there is nothing that can be done about it. A time must come though when that yearly waste will cease. The beef will be saved and canned.

At present it is only the hides of the bulls that count. These tan into excellent leather of exceptional thickness and quality. The value varies according to demand from £1 per hide to 30s. or 35s.

The hides are so thick and heavy that two hefty bucks strain and grunt as they lift one hide on to a horse. Two extra-large hides are often a load for a horse, though as a general rule fourteen packhorses will transport about thirty-five skins.

When the buffaloes are skinned the loaded horses are led back to camp, followed by a chattering string of blood-stained natives carrying choice cuts of beef. There will be a busy time for the cooking fires tonight, even though these folk have already gorged themselves on raw meat, of which the aboriginal is very fond. Back at the camp towards sundown and the hides are spread flat upon the ground, raw side up.

The lubras squat on the raw hide and begin scraping the fat off it. The skins are dried and salted, and at the right stage folded. Experience is required here for, if the skins have been allowed to dry too much, they won't fold. If folded when too moist, they go "bad" before arrival at Darwin. Eventually the folded skins are stacked, and these stacks steadily grow as the season progresses. An average camp may deal with a hundred and fifty skins per week. Ultimately the stacked skins are loaded on to the truck or lugger for transport to Darwin, and from there to distant markets.

The packhorses are the ordinary sturdy bush breed, but the shooting horses are priceless. Only one in a hundred, if that, is suitable for a shooting horse, and when found he is an envied prize. Possessed of phenomenal endurance and exceptionally swift, sure-footed and agile as an eel, still they must first be trained like polo ponies. Above all, they must have "horse-sense", which is more common in animals than many of us suppose.

With training they quickly realize their job and its dangers, and how to avoid those dangers. Both horse and man again and again when racing and working at utmost speed will in sudden emergency be called upon to act in a split second. Many a man has blessed his shooting horse for saving his life, some of them again and again.

The horse not only does his job by racing after the string at the right moment, catching up to the hindmost on the right side and racing past him at exactly the right pace and distance, but he is watching those galloping ahead, alert for the least sign of an angry bull about to wheel and charge, watching the low-held heads with the great horns lest the neck twists a bit to look behind, following every individual movement of the beasts galloping ahead as he races with them while passing one after the other.

Those outstanding among the really good horses become famous. It was said of a horse of Paddy Cahill's that it could do everything in buffalo hunting except skin the beast. It could even kill a beast, by causing it to make a false step by pressure against its shoulder and in the resultant fall "breaking its neck". However, there are many true stories of the grit and sagacity of the buffalo shooters' pet horses. More than one horse was exceptionally well known to the aboriginals. Such a horse was trained to chase stray niggers from the camp. With ears laid back, fiendish eyes, lips bared to show awful teeth, it would charge a strange aboriginal on sight. I don't blame the aboriginal for running—I'd run myself!

Horses have been known to protect a loved rider after a fall, to charge the buffalo and break its rush against the fallen man. And more than one buffalo shooter, hard-living men though they may be, has near broken his heart when his favourite horse has been killed.

A few of the buffalo hunters breed their own horses, have taken up stations for cattle and to breed suitable horses. The station then is their wet season's "camp"; they go shooting in the dry. Perhaps one of the best known is Cecil Freer, whose Stuart station in the Wildman River country a hundred and twenty miles east of Darwin has bred hundreds of "shooter" horses. Freer, an excellent horseman in the bush or in sport, has won races with his own horses year after year in the Darwin races. The breeding of good horses for buffalo shooting requires similar care and skill and patience to that necessary in breeding racehorses down South.

There is a lot of hard work in buffalo shooting, a little danger at times, but a little fun too. Cecil Freer was the prime joker one day. The incident is still the theme for a campfire corroboree song. The day's shoot was over, but one wounded old bull was hiding somewhere in the long grass on the edge of the plain and the natives desired it for meat. Freer at this time was dismounted, so he carefully noted the only tree on the edge of the plain, just one little tree. Then on foot he cautiously entered the long grass. The old bull charged with a roaring snort. Freer just reached the tree ahead of the bull, only to find its branches black with struggling aboriginals who had climbed it to see the fun. Freer snatched at the tree and swung around it as the bull brushed his pants. He swung around and around the tree with the bull following wide out, hampered by its long horns. Freer brought the bull down with a one-handed snap shot to the forehead, then leapt back, gazed up the tree, and on occasion I've raced for a tree like that, an awful experience, battling to get every ounce of power out of the lungs with the great beast thundering behind and the tree seeming to edge farther away.

A different little thrill enlivened Freer one day, one of those warm, dreamy, slumbrous days. He dismounted, hitched his horse to a bush, and yawning stretched out on an invitingly green patch of young grass on the edge of a creek. Tilting his hat over his eyes, he fell sound asleep, blissfully unaware that the bank edge was deeply undermined. Gradually it gave way under him. In a flurry of broken loam and grass and startled insects he fell—on to something smelly that grunted and squirmed. Instantly he held tight, realizing it was a huge crocodile. It bulged up and lashed out and went for its life to the creek, while Freer leaped for his life up the bank.

"For the life of me I don't know who was the more scared,"

grins Freer, "the crocodile or me."

Of the "buffalo kings", old-time and present, familiar names to Territorians would be Paddy Cahill, Joe Cooper, E. O. Robinson ("Buffalo Bill" of the Territory), Fred Smith, Barney Flynn, Tony Madden, Fred and Harry Hardy, Cecil Freer. There are quite a number of other well-known shooters, "Mick" Feeney, James Stott, Hunter; quite a number more.

Old timers tell me the pioneer shooters used to stalk the buffalo, shooting from the ground. It was Paddy Cahill who was the first to shoot from a horse, shooting beast after beast as he galloped by: quick work, requiring skill, judgment, an iron nerve and an unerring eye. Perhaps Cahill got his idea from the most famous buffalo shooter in the world— Buffalo Bill, America's own Colonel Bill Cody.

And this offers me a chance to put in a plea for our own buffalo. Do not let the future exterminate him; give him a chance. There would be little possibility of exterminating our buffalo under the conditions which have existed in the north up to the present. But now that the war is over it is possible that an influx of new shooters, equipped with modem transport (not to mention the aeroplane), might come to Buffalo Land, with tragic results to the Australian herds that are so much smaller than were the American.

A tragic fate annihilated the vast herds that once roamed great areas of the United States of America. There were once more than thirty million head of wild buffalo in the buffalo lands of America; yet within a very few years they were shot down to less than a thousand head! Of this sad fact no American is proud.

A result of this slaughter was that it robbed hundreds of thousands of Red Indians of the food upon which they so greatly depended; it pushed them farther and farther hack until they had "nowhere else to go"; it resulted in numbers of the Indian wars wherein so many Indians went the way of their own buffalo.

We in Australia, when we look back over the past, have by no means a clean slate when we realize what our coming to this continent has meant to the aboriginal. He has not been hurt much by the few buffalo men of the north; the aboriginals there keenly look forward to the buffalo season. But we as a people, from the south-east, have driven the aboriginal back and back (into Shadowland) until now the remnant of him stands at the Last Frontier. One goodly stretch of this frontier is the coast of Buffalo Land.

With the exception of a few desert tribes, the aboriginal's back is now to the sea. So, while there is yet time, let us give the few tribes left a fairer go. And—remember what happened to the American buffalo.

My only knowledge of the American buffalo comes from the well-known book, *The Hunting of the Buffalo*, by E. Douglas Branch. I have not been able to get in touch with the author, but I feel sure he would not mind me using a very few extracts as a plea for the future safeguarding of our own small buffalo herds.

The American buffalo is really the bison, while the Australian is the Timor water-buffalo. The bison was noted for its massive head, shoulders, and hump. It grew six feet tall at the hump, and was up to ten feet in length, with long mane, shaggy frontlet of hair, and "beard". It weighed two thousand pounds, a lumbering, wild and woolly relic from the days of the Animals of Long Ago. Its horns though, were very small compared to the huge spread of horns on an Aussie bull buffalo. Its hide often was covered with a thick brown fur. The hide of ours is mostly slatey grey.

The bison grazed in small herds that at times congregated into large herds as ours do, only that the bison was in incomparably greater numbers. Frontiersmen rode for weeks amongst them, never out of sight of the herds. In the seasonal migrations they were dense, moving masses, covering the prairies farther than the eye could see.

The bison moved in a great yearly migration for hundreds of miles, south with the winter, north at the thaw. Some among the Indian tribes followed the migrations of the bison, living their lives with the wanderings of the great beast that gave them food to eat, and clothes for shelter. Our buffalo, although some among them wander great distances, migrate only when their numbers increase. Their seeking more sheltered country during the wet season, to spread out again across the water-logged, but drying plains when the wet is over, could hardly be called migration.

The bulls among the bison were the fighters and protectors of the herds, as are ours. To the Red Indian the apparently inexhaustible herds of the bison were part of his very life. From the hides came the warm robes that sheltered his wife and children against the snows and bitter winds of the long winter. The hides, sewn together, made the roomy, comfortable, rain-proof tepees of the tribe. Numerous tribes could muster six hundred large tepees. That hide made his comfortable bed, his blankets, curtains, moccasins, robes, belts, sheaths, shields, string. The bison, to the Indian, made life worth living.

The Indian's proudest possession was his highly trained buffalo pony, just as eventually was the American buffalo shooter's horse, as is the "shooting" horse of the present-day buffalo hunter in Australia.

An Indian tribe would shadow the buffaloes for some days, taking great care not to alarm the herd. At a propitious time and place they would attack. The buffaloes would look up to see horsemen galloping towards them from the skyline. They would turn and lumber away, only to find other yelling horsemen racing towards them. They would set off in another direction, soon to be met by other horsemen. No matter which way they turned the buffaloes would see horsemen galloping towards them.

The Indians had surrounded them in a thin, far-spread circle. But as the buffaloes again and again changed course, that circle was drawing rapidly nearer and closer together, until finally it was in plain view, but now galloping around and around the herd. By now the leaders of the buffalo herd, thoroughly bewildered at no sign of a desperately sought opening to safety, had begun to circle until the whole herd was a lumbering mass of buffalo galloping round and round.

They were "ringing"—as Australian stockmen at times ring a mob of cattle to prevent them scattering or breaking away.

The circle of galloping Indians rapidly drew to within arrow shot, and now began to shoot, marvellous horsemen, without saddle or bridle, sending arrows almost unerringly into the galloping herd. They had to shoot those arrows at a certain spot and angle below the shoulder-blade to inflict a mortal wound. The arrows must have been excellent weapons to penetrate the thick hide, and must have driven deep into the huge beast to touch a mortal spot.

This habit of "ringing" was fatal to the buffaloes. The Indians would keep shooting until every arrow in their quivers was exhausted. It was not until the inexorable advance of the white man was fast pushing them back that the Indians took to firearms.

The first advance-guard of the white men was soon shooting out the buffaloes, the hunters occasionally losing their scalps to the angry Indians—which brought overwhelming retaliation. But the swarms of men coming on behind the buffalo shooters wanted the lands of the Indian—and of the buffalo.

It was during the building of the Kansas Pacific Railway that Will Cody made his name. Like our own shooters, Cody rode a noted and favourite horse—Brixham.

For one of the construction gangs of 12,000 men he contracted to supply buffalo meat. Within eighteen months he shot 4280 buffaloes, and became the famous Buffalo Bill, his exploits in later years being celebrated in many a book and picture. Buffalo Bill was also a famous guide and Indian fighter, an extraordinarily picturesque frontier character.

I've no idea of Buffalo Bill's complete tally, using a breech-loading Needle rifle, I only know the construction gang record of 4280 head for eighteen months. Still, it is interesting to compare his tally with that of our own few "Buffalo Bills". The "kings" among these men shoot up to

2000 buffalo per season at the present day. I could not tell you the complete tally of such buffalo kings as Paddy Cahill, E. O. Robinson, Joe Cooper, Fred Smith, the Hardy Brothers, and others; but Robinson alone exported 23,000 hides in seven years. Of present-day shooters, Cecil Freer's tally, before these notes were written, was 30,000 buffaloes in twenty years.

When the Australian shooter kills as many beasts as his aboriginal skinners and bush transport can handle, he ceases shooting for the day. Our comparatively small herds would not last long if there were a big influx of new shooters, with modem transport to shift the hides much faster.

As the American railways pushed out into the undeveloped country, buffalo shooters set to work in swarms. At one time, it is estimated that there were five thousand hunters at work. No wonder that for hundreds of miles the country became a mass of rotting carcasses, and that the buffaloes were exterminated (and many of the Indians) within a very few years.

Under present conditions such, very fortunately, would not happen in our own north, for there are, all told, only a few score shooters. But there were thirty million buffaloes in America, and probably there are not much more than thirty thousand or so in our north.

One thing that has helped save our much smaller herds is that only the bulls are shot. In America cows and bulls were shot—they all had hides. Despite the big tallies our own men make, the herds are given a chance of breeding up.

Still, it would be a shame if, with the probably rapid development of our north, we did not guard against wiping out the buffalo, and the consequent injustice to aboriginal life. These things can happen so easily with uncontrolled development. Within a very few years the thirty million American bison had been slaughtered to such an extent that the nation had the greatest difficulty in collecting a few hundred together so as to breed and preserve a thousand head for future generations to see and wonder at. I'd hate to think that the same fate might befall the old aboriginal —and the buffalo.

After more than a century of acclimatization in the Australian bush, this buffalo is game to the very last. He is a fighter by nature, will battle while he has strength to lift his head. The first three were imported into Australia by Maurice Barlow, then Commandant at Melville Island, in 1825, as a source of meat for the garrison. A few more were later imported, then the settlement was abandoned. The buffaloes rapidly increased and expanded into great herds that later helped to make the name and living of the buffalo king of Melville Island, and the "kings" of Coburg Peninsula and the mainland.

On the mainland, at Port Essington on the Coburg Peninsula just north-east of the present Port Darwin, a settlement was garrisoned in 1838, and again buffaloes were imported from Timor. But this settlement was abandoned in 1849 and the Territory coast left to itself for a time. The buffaloes increased to herd after herd in the untrammelled freedom of a vast land empty except for the aboriginal tribes. Although the wild men regularly hunted buffalo, they made little difference to the herds. The animals were too big and strong, and their hides too thick to fall easy victims to bone- and wood-tipped spears. The buffaloes commenced a grand migration, working down the Coburg Peninsula and into the Alligator valley. Here were the Alligator Rivers, big swamps and plains, the start of the plain country that stretches far away.

In this natural environment the herds rapidly increased and many were forced to keep on migrating, spreading farther east on to plain after plain until tens of thousands stretched for hundreds of miles in wild, untrammelled freedom. It was in 1885 that Tom Cahill and his mates penetrated into the Alligator valley and discovered the buffaloes. What an experience that must have been, those few white men breaking into this new valley, these new rivers, these plains and wild lands stretching far away. A handful of horsemen pushing forward, all around them the long-drawn calls of Wild aboriginals, suddenly coming upon a plain covered with herds of buffaloes. How the buffaloes must have stared at sight of their first white men. And the white men stared too.

Paddy Cahill with Quilp on horseback, and Aboriginal team on foot.

XVI

THE DUCK-HUNTERS

AND SO the warm weeks went by while we dawdled along the coast, cruising into river or creek or salt arm of the sea for such time as we took to "shoot it out". And now through the little ship another smell arose to combine with shipboard smells, the tang of salted crocodile hides.

"What with the hum of stale lizards," growled the Skipper, "and salted fish and cockroaches and oil and petrol and bilge and tar we smell like nothing on earth. It only needs the sweet effluvia of the slaves down here and we'd have to cut our way out of the cabin with an axe."

The aboriginalss certainly did "hum". At times when they plastered themselves with stale grease their odour was awful. The more it smelled the better they liked it. When I asked Jacky why they indulged in this odourous pastime he sniffed and replied: "White feller he smell too much. We feller no more can smell 'im now!"

"Now isn't that nice!" exclaimed the Skipper with smiling sarcasm. "The delicate blackfellow smothers himself with stinking goanna fat to drown the odour of smellful white brother. Such a perfumed compliment."

"The Chinese and Malays also insist that we hum a bit," I pointed out.

"To hell they do," replied the Skipper indignantly. 'Why you can smell 'em a mile away. What do you say, Herman?" 'We've all got our own smells," replied Herman diplomatically.

"Strike a light!" exclaimed the Skipper. "What's come over you two? You'll have me bathing in odour of violets next." However, the crew (excepting Herman, of course) were under strict orders to keep to their cockpit, and for'ard. Other-wise the temptation to fool about with those rifles below might have proved too great. Except when it was cold, they slept up on deck.

Once, in the dead of night, a rousing corroboree war song startled the ship, a thumping on the deck to rhythmic time beats.

"What the devil!" exclaimed the Skipper and jumped for the companionway to flash a torch for'ard. It bathed the living corpses under the tarpaulin; they definitely were all sound asleep. The Old Man had started the song and the others joined in urged by primal instinct. To the Skipper's roar the song ceased abruptly. Indulging in a violent harangue, the Skipper climbed down and into his bunk again, his temper not improved by a chilly breeze up top.

"These wretched slaves will be the death of me," he grumbled and grunted himself again to sleep.

But when the corroboree broke out again he grabbed a tomahawk and howling bloodthirsty curses leapt up on deck. There he staged a corroboree of his own, threatening to chop off the first head that opened a mouth. The "slaves" lay quiet as mice. But they were thoroughly awakened now, the dream song driven from their consciousness. They must have been planning some big corroboree on their return to the tribe, or else the Old Man had been talking of past triumphs before they fell asleep.

"Explain it how you will," snarled the Skipper, "but they'll never talk again if I hear one more howl out of them."

I grinned, puffing at the pipe. The little differences of opinion between the Skipper and the slaves were amusing.

They got even a few days later. For some time past they had been hinting at the multitude of crocodiles that basked upon a certain island's shores, and at the "plenty feller too much" trepang only waiting to be picked up in shallow water just off those same shores. As to labour, it was there in abundance, just longing for something to do.

"D'you know," mused the Skipper one evening, "I've half a mind to see this isle of dreams. It's off our course a bit, and no doubt the slaves are putting something across, but still— there might he something in it."

"You're thinking of the trepang," I ventured.

"Yes and no. There might be a patch of trepang there. Probably there isn't. It's the natives that may be there I'm thinking of. If there really is a big crowd more or less permanently camped there then they'll be salt-water boys. They would come in very handy if a man sailed down there seeking trepang next season."

"Please yourself," I yawned. "The seas are wide, there's plenty of tucker aboard, time doesn't count."

"Right," declared the Skipper. "We sail in the morning." When still quite a few miles off the island the Skipper said disgustedly:

"Ditched again."

And it appeared so.

"Why that feller no more sendem up smoke signal?" he demanded of Jacky.

"Maybe he inside lookout tucker," answered Jacky dubiously. "Plenty feller boy he stay there."

I doubted it. Otherwise before now a lazy smoke signal would have warned any of the local hunting parties or fishing canoes that a vessel was approaching. Jacky's explanation was that all hands ashore probably were deep inside the scrub seeking food.

There was no one on the island. We were hardly ashore when we saw that. No fresh tracks on the little beach, no trace of fresh fires, no recent gunyahs or windbreaks. There were plenty of heaps of old shells and fish bones where natives had eaten their fill. This was only one of the islets fairly common along portions of the northern coast to which the nomads came according to the fish and plant-food seasons. When, for the time being, they "eat out" such an islet, they pile into their canoes again and sail away. Thus these children of nature give nature her chance to replenish the land.

"Where all this feller man?" raved the Skipper. "You lie longa me."

"That feller been go walkabout," frowned Jacky, while his fellow conspirators gazed about in apparent perplexity. "What's matter him been go way? Before, plenty boy, plenty old feller woman, plenty young feller lubra, plenty feller piccanin sit down here alla time."

"Well you flaming well go and find them," shouted the Skipper, "and don't come crawling back to the boat without them for you'll find no more tucker here."

And the abashed boys walked doubtfully towards the dark patch of scrub which clothed the centre of the islet.

"If it wasn't that I knew we'd be wasting our own time," growled the Skipper, "I'd make them dive for that trepang that isn't there until they looked like jellyfishes. Now what is their little game, I wonder?"

We knew at sundown, when they emerged from the scrub loaded with tapering, beautifully balanced bamboos.

"Spear hafts!" yelled the Skipper. "You miserable heathen! Inveigled me eighty miles out of my course just to cut spear hafts!

And so they had. A creek on this island grew clumps of slender bamboos noted as spear hafts far along the coast.

When later we would land these boys back to their distant tribe they would be welcomed not only for their pay and what they could scrounge from us, but also for spear hafts which carried a reputation far and wide. And, when the stars shone, around the campfires, Jacky and Paddy and Billy and Freddy would tell in pantomime how they had pulled the wool over the eyes of the white men and obtained the spear hafts. The Old Man would stage the corroboree and doubtless make a hilarious success of it.

"Do you realize," growled the Skipper in the cabin that night, "that we should form Mutual Protection Societies to help protect the poor deluded whites? Out here in God's great loneliness, at the mercy of the heathen. I'm sure the faraway cities would rally to the cause if they only knew of the peril of their fellow whites. Here we are, two poor wretches who've toiled hard for years and earned a comfortable boat; by the sweat of our brows we've filled it with tucker and the bare necessaries of our trade; here we are, pioneering a wild and uncharted coast at the mercy of wretched slaves who neither toil nor spin. We can't get rid of them, and they know it. They actually own the boat without having ever done a hand's turn to own it, nor do they carry the faintest responsibility. They just own the boat for it sails more to their whim than to mine. And when they get tired of it, or run it on a reef, they will simply jump overboard and swim ashore. And leave me to drown!" And he growled himself to sleep.

I lit a final pipe. It was such a very quiet night. Just the tide gurgling past the bows, Herman's steady breathing near by, snores of the aboriginals from the deck above, the rustling of a cockroach. Just a few men in a tiny boat under the vast heavens. Difficult to remember that far away there were great cities teeming with life. The slumbering quietness, the rock-a-bye of the boat, was sending me to the vale of dreams where aboriginals and half-castes and white men and all of us must go.

Back to the mainland, anchored in a snug creek, plenty of crocodiles for a few days. Then we had to walk farther afield. One day the boys led me to a lagoon inland. It was an oasis of white paper-bark trees, pretty under dense green foliage, clumps of palms, reeds and waterlilies in luxurious blue flower, singing birds. A beautiful spot. As soon as the boys turned to me with a warning hiss I knew their aboriginal friends were about. The boys were intent on a "sit-down" and gossip. There would he no crocodile hunting today. I grinned to think of how mad the Skipper would have been had he known.

We located the old folk taking it easy on a vividly green patch of tender grasses, then a group of fierce-eyed men heavily armed, women and piccaninies. Their eyes lit up, giggles and smiles at our approach from the women, stony glares from the men. They scented tobacco. They were squatting down on the lagoon edge, camouflaged under palm leaves and drooping vines. At a signal from Jacky we crouched as we went towards them so as not to disturb the ducks away out on the lagoon. As we squatted down, grunts of conversation broke out. A young girl with laughing eyes held out a grubby hand. Of course I had to give her half a stick of Nigger Twist tobacco. Then the warriors cadged a fill of tobacco from the boys and breaking it up with their huge stubbed thumbnails lost no time in stuffing the lumps into their pipes.

Ingenious were these pipes. Numbers of them were crab claws, or long, twisted shells. To fashion the crab claw into a pipe they burn the hard, bony end in a slow fire until it is breakable. As it cools, they snap off those parts not wanted. The "stem" is already bored, for running right through it is a tiny hole which once held oil or marrow, or a nerve. The shell pipes were about six or seven inches long, tapering to one end. The natives break off the small end of the shell and thus expose the hole running through. The hole of course grows larger up along the shell. It was in this hollow that the shellfish once lived. The mouth of the shell serves as the bowl of the pipe. Wandering aboriginals we thus occasionally met puffed away in delight when for some small service we paid them in the precious tobacco which stoked up their crab-claw and shell pipes.

The lagoon was a blaze of purple convolvulus trailing from the trees, with waterlilies in blue and pink flower emphasized by the snow white of egret birds. The still water was half covered by the gigantic flat lily leaves, two and three feet wide. Here and there across these was busily running the quaint lotus bird with his combed crest and funny long toes. Away across the lagoon where a splash of sunlight fell through the trees, solemnly stood two giants of the bird world, black and white jabirus. The bill of the old-man bird was large enough to have carried quintuplets, let alone one little babe. If that old fellow was not as tall as a man, he certainly appeared to be. But the aboriginals' attention was concentrated towards the middle of the lagoon, whence came the quacking of ducks. Scattered flocks of them lazing among broad lily leaves and floating masses of grasses.

Three expert hunters were hunting those ducks, though there was no sign of the hunters, not a sound but the whistling of tree birds and the cackle of a waterhen. And no sign of uneasiness amongst the ducks themselves. But every now and then one simply went under below, diving for some succulent morsel. But—that duck did not return to the surface. And still not the faintest sign of alarm from his fellows. Anyone who did not understand would not have known what was going on. Even had a duck disappeared before his eyes he would not have guessed.

It was so simple, but only an expert among hunters can do it. Drag the duck under water so naturally that even its mates around it fail to notice. Each of the three expert hunters out there amongst the scattered ducks was underwater, each breathing with his nose under a lily leaf. Moveless, quiet as a shadow he waited, clearly seeing every movement of the nearest ducks as they preened their feathers, gossiped in clucks and whistles, paddled around here and there. Now and again one would dive its neck deep into the water in chase of some tasty bit. A black hand would snatch out and the duck would continue its dive. A sharp tug, its neck was broken. It was thrust into the vine belt of the submarine hunter. Thus, every now and then, a duck vanished.

Such hunting is fascinating to watch, almost eerily so. There is neither sign nor sound of the hunter, not even a ripple. The victims still carry on in peace and innocence while one by one their mates vanish.

Of course, Jacky had to spoil it. There came a whirr of wings and a flock of ducks noisily splashed upon the water directly ahead of us. The long, skinny Jacky rolled his eyes at us, grinned, and snaked his way to the reeds at the water's edge. Very slowly he vanished underwater. He did it quite well. The young lubras giggled. The show of course was put on all for them.

Jacky got his duck all right, only one. That duck suddenly flapped up with an alarmed squawking that was agitatedly drowned as it was pulled underwater. Jacky had grasped a leg and made a mess of the job even then. Those ducks flew and their alarm was transmitted to other ducks all over the lagoon.

An alarmed quacking and whistling broke out, a whirring of wings as flock after flock flew up, and away. From away out in the lagoon three black bodies rose up, glaring disgustedly towards us. The lubras in hilarious glee shouted news to them of the now bashful Jacky's triumph. The hunters came swim¬ming towards us. Each man had half a dozen ducks hitched to his vine belt. Jacky came ashore with his lone duck, the target of disgusted grunts from the tribesmen, laughing jokes from the girls. Half a dozen of those young lubras were belles, with all their share of the usual feminine kittenish knowledge. All done up to kill too.

The women of most of the coastal tribes are very vain about their adornments to beauty. These are in the form of heavily raised weals, ten inches long, that go right across their bodies, just under the breasts. There may be two, or three, or four lines of these weals. They stand out from the skin in parallel lines like protruding whipcord, wonderfully well done. Some girls proudly show small weals, others larger and longer ones, depending on age and womanhood, and the skill of the operator.

He generally is the witch doctor of the tribe, the old medicine man, grizzled old bundle of sin. His surgical instruments are pieces of flint flaked to razor edge, or shell dressed similarly. If he has been able to secure a piece of bottle, then this is his lancet par excellence. The girl lies before him; not a sound—breathing tremulously perhaps with dilating eyes— but not one gasp, not a whimper. Squatting down beside her, he bends over her, then slowly draws the cruel blade right across her body. You can see her skin and opening flesh crying with pain but—not a sound. He fills the wound, taking his time; he slowly packs the long, raw wound with a specially prepared clay. So in the coming days, as the wound fills in, it grows up over the clay ridge. At the right time the "doctor" probes out the hardened clay and the ridge of flesh heals over perfectly. Some of the "lovely" girls had their designs done in fantastic patterns. These were very proud girls indeed. But what they had gone through to obtain these beauty patterns must have been rather awful.

Reuben Cooper, with his Aboriginal shooters and skinners, buffalo hunting in the Territory about 1934.

Bill Dean, croc shooter in Darwin in the 1960s.

XVII

THE OLD DAYS IN DARWIN

ON a glorious morning under the lightest of breezes we were sailing west. We must call in at Darwin for more petrol then sail west again. The *Lotus* was a goodly-sized ketch and used up a lot of petrol on account of the river and creek work she was called upon to do. On the open sea we used sail.

Herman was busy at the magneto. I was at the tiller. The Skipper cast one glance at the sky then went below to clean up, with his inevitable grumble at the lazy "boongs". The same boongs, just as inevitably, were yarning and stretching on the cabin top. The Old Man crawled under the slight shade cast by the dinghy lashed there. The sun now shone warmly, so the Old Man developed a brainwave. He grunted to the others to rig up the awning. Obediently they obeyed. With a sly grin at me they all coiled up in the shade and fell asleep.

I smiled at what the Skipper would say should he poke his head up above the deck. There really was no particular job for the crew at present, but sleep just now did seem waste of a glorious morning.

It seemed a bit humorous to me. Here was I, peacefully smoking, with eyes ahead as well as on the compass, one wary hand on the tiller guiding the tiny ship, responsible for all. Herman sweating down there at the engine, doing a good job as he always did. The Skipper down below poring over a chart, at the same time with an eye to the midday meal for all hands cooking over the primus. And the black bodies of the crew, bare backsides turned to me, snoring peacefully on the cabin top.

In due course we rounded the reef jutting out from Pussycat Island, then sailed between island and mainland and through the passage between Gun Point and Sou'-west Vernon, keeping straight on to dodge Gun Point reef which like a black line runs out to sea. We rounded the reef and turned her bows for Lee Point.

It was then that Jacky came aft and innocently asked the Skipper would he put the Old Man ashore at West Point and pick him up on the outgoing trip. The Old Man apparently had urgent tribal business ashore. But he'd be all ready to step aboard again when we returned from Darwin. The Skipper agreed with alacrity and Jacky stepped for'ard again.

"Of course I'll put him ashore," chuckled the Skipper. "The one thing that would give me greater pleasure would be to heave him overboard."

"I gather you won't pick him up again," I grinned.

"Don't make me laugh," chuckled the Skipper.

In the afternoon we were bowling along under a gentle breeze, the little whitish cliffs of Darwin in sight. East Point stood out in white cliffs hedged under dark green scrub. Then West Point appeared, a long strip of sandy beach, grey-green under scrub. This was where the Old Man had come aboard.

"Gottem swag belonga you ready?" called out the Skipper cheerfully.

"No more," called back Jacky. "Old Man no more go longa shore this feller time—he go longa Darwin."

"Oh!" snarled the Skipper. "Changed his mind, has he? Woke up, has he? Now prefers a taste of the delights of Darwin town, does he? Thinks he'll dally a while among the fleshpots of Egypt! He'd like to display his noble form in the Chinatown of the Great Metropolis, would he? Well now, I'll skin him alive if he hasn't his swag ready to jump into that dinghy within five minutes. He's going ashore—or overboard!"

But I knew the Skipper wouldn't. We needed the crew boys; should we insist on the Old Man going ashore they would merely desert at Darwin.

The crew sulked, indifferent to the Skipper's persuasive vocabulary.

"They know I know if he goes overboard they all go," he snarled, "and I can't do without them. Meanwhile I'm missing the tide. But oh! when we come back this way in the morning just won't that old schemer go ashore—with a sting in his tail!"

I knew what was in the Skipper's mind. Once reloaded with petrol and we would be sailing west, farther and farther from the men's tribal country. Once he could get them outside they would not dare desert. By the same token the Skipper could swing his authority, for the last thing they would then wish would be to be put ashore in country where hostile tribesmen might hunt them down.

On the mainland Vestey's huge meatworks stood out plainly, as did the white landmark of Point Emery light. Very pretty coming up the harbour, blue water rimmed by low cliffs heavily wooded. The town at the harbour end perched high up but away behind the little cliffs, a twisty, dusty road leading up to it, roofs peeping among the trees.

When we anchored there was a steamer at the wharf, but the harbour was almost empty. The pearling fleet was at sea fishing through the neap tides. Near us was a low, rakish-looking lugger with her coloured crew stolidly gazing towards our own boys. Several other similar vessels belonging to sea wanderers on quests more or less like our own were anchored nearby.

The Skipper and Herman and I were enjoying a wash preparatory to going ashore.

"Just note our gay Lotharios," chuckled the Skipper. "Actually washed their one and only Sunday best pants and singlet. Washed off the goanna grease and war paint—they're all set to cut a dash amongst the dusky maids ashore. They'll beat me, will they? Then you just watch!" And he stepped for'ard and sternly told them they must stay aboard, for the town law was that no native be allowed out of the compound after dark.

"No permit for sailor boy go ashore either," he added. " 'Spose you feller go ashore—policeman run you in."

"That will spike their little game," he chuckled as he came aft. "They won't be doing the grand ashore tonight."

And we stepped down below to don our own glad rags.

A little later, as we stepped up on deck, the Skipper received a great shock—mutiny! The crew advanced to meet us headed by the Old Man, his eyes fairly leaping with rage.

"What mean you say we feller no go shore?" he demanded. "You go shore, boss. We feller go shore too. More better you buy me one feller 'tinglet, 'tchirt, 'at, belt. Gib it tchilin! By and by me feller all about go pictures." The Old Man paused for breath as the startled

Skipper got his.

"Ho yes," he roared. "I'll buy you a swag of clothes and take you to the pictures, will I? Perhaps you'd like to borrow my evening togs and I'll escort you to dinner at Government House? You flea-bitten streak of nothing on earth—to hell with you! And all your uncles and brothers! You wall-eyed wash-out of a crab-faced alligator! Now look here, you downtrodden black slaves, you have been work my boat two-three-few feller day, plenty feller day. You get plenty money, tucker—does. You no more do work. Old feller gin do more work than you. She'd do it in her sleep. Now listen here, my hearties. You no more go shore now, you stop longa this boat. 'Spose you go shore you finish. You no more come back longa boat. You go longa calaboose quick feller. You stay there too—no more go hack longa home—you stay jail long feller time! Me, I sail about herly morning time. You-me heave up anchor—go 'nother place—lookem round crocodile."

Dismayed eyes greeted the Skipper's ultimatum. They cut out the rough stuff and subsided into gloomy silence.

The Skipper, still calling threats to the glowering boys, was heaving with righteous indignation as we rowed ashore.

"Do you think they'll come ashore?" I asked.

"I've got 'em if they do," he snapped. "The police will pick them up. Natives without permits aren't allowed to roam the streets at nights. They'll hang themselves doubly if they do go ashore, for they've got no right there and they haven't enough clothes to go around. So if they steal ours they'll be in a double pickle."

I felt a bit sorry for the crew. Jacky was a sophisticated hoy and knew his way about the place; Billy too. But for the others to have been treated to the white man's famous pictures would have been something to corroboree about indeed.

"Pictures!" snapped the Skipper as we climbed ashore. "They'll want violets in their noseholes next!"

Darwin will grow into a modem port. It will never be the same again. Just as well perhaps, for everything must progress. But many of us roamers will hold a lingering regret for the happy-go-lucky little far-northern ports of other days.

Up the road we climbed and the town began to spread out before us, with the bush as background. A wide street opened out, densely packed with Chinese shops. Quaint it was: Chinese women sitting shrilly gossiping on the doorsteps, Chinamen slouching about in Chinese pants and coat, others in khaki and singlet. Numerous Chinese youngsters with jet-black hair and large black eyes. Aboriginal town boys on errands, some on bikes, clad in shorts and singlet. Dim-lit shops, musty shops, and shops that did not seem to be shops at all. And the faint smell of the East over all. We strolled along, the Skipper throwing a greeting now and then to some coloured friend.

On a matter of business we visited a cheery little dark-skinned man. Born in Australia of Singalese parents, he had fallen in love with a dusky Broome beauty. His father, though, had other visions and packed the boy off to Ceylon to make an alliance that had been arranged long ago. The rebellious lover on arrival found that his bride-to-be was the eldest of eleven daughters. She was fat and cross-eyed. So he turned her down flat and hurried back to his Broome sweetheart. He defied his outraged relations, married the girl, brought her here and succeeded in doing very well for himself.

Among other accomplishments he was now an expert cleaner of pearls. We found him greatly disappointed. Almost with tears in his eyes he showed us something that had recently been brought in by the pearling fleet. It was a huge "blister" containing a forty-grain round drop. Within the pearlshell the blister had formed, and within it the big pearl. But the back of the shell was worm-pitted. Little fiends of the sea had bored down with their drills seeking to suck out the "heart" of the oyster. The big, round, nacreous blister had saved the fish within the shell, but through the tiny drill holes water had squeezed through into the blister and turned the lustrous pearl chalky. Our friend, with infinite skill and' patience, had carefully, tenderly, taken skin after skin off the pearl. Alas, to no avail. The very heart of the pearl was chalky.

And thus can a "microbe" of the sea turn to dust a treasure which otherwise might be worth a king's ransom.

We stepped out into sunset and into another street with a bungalow here and there. Then the European street. The shops not so thickly placed here, but you could buy anything from the proverbial needle to the anchor. Healthy-looking white men moving about in shirt and pants, or in cool whites. All cheery chaps; a quiet air of business about this quarter. And so the town spreads surprisingly away in broad streets with neat bungalows here and there, bright gardens, plenty of trees. The harbour hills used to be a blaze of red when the poinciana season was on. I remember the lovely flame tree in the back garden of the old Victoria Hotel; the dear old hostess, Mrs Gordon, and the poinciana trees and windmill.

We said cheerio to two tall men, Dr Cook and Judge Wells, known throughout the Territory. And enjoyed a spot with business men and pearlers, with cattlemen and Government officials, and wanderers from land and sea. In the old days of Darwin you could meet a lot of men and learn what was going on in the back country, along the coast, and out to sea, in a surprisingly short and pleasant time. And get through quite an amount of business too.

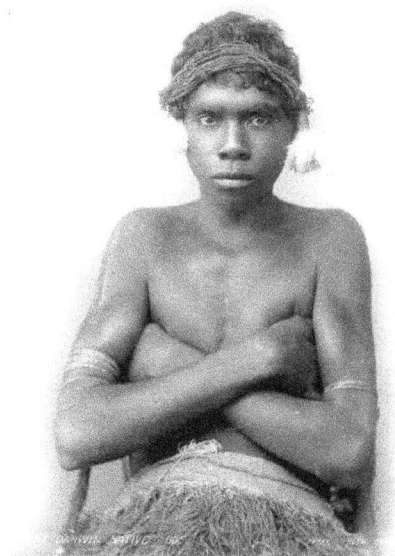

XVIII

IN DANGEROUS WATERS

NEXT morning we sailed from Darwin; a beautiful day. At West Point we hove to. The Skipper turned to the crew with a glint in his eye.

"Arright," he ordered the Old Man, "you catchem gear now belonga you! Go ashore!"

The Old Man was dumbfounded, but one glance showed him there was no use arguing and in seconds his quick wits grasped the silver lining.

"Arright," he grinned, "me go shore. Have 'em spell. You gib it plour, tugar, tea, bacca! Me pinish now."

"You finish all right," replied the Skipper grimly. "Arright! By em by me send you one bag tugar, two bag plour, tea, one bokis tobacco. But no more dis time. What's a matter you wantem everyting? You plenty catchem tucker, tobacco longa this boat. You eatem, you sleep. You wake up. You eatem, you sleep. Plenty feller alia time you eatem, you sleepem. You nothing work longa this boat. You alia same gentleman makem this feller holiday boat."

The Old Man burst out laughing. "What's a matter black-feller wantem work?" he demanded. "Holiday more better." A sentiment hilariously received by his downtrodden countrymen.

"You hop into that dinghy and I'll row you ashore myself," roared the Skipper. "Now step lively or I'll throw you in the drink."

For a moment I thought there might be trouble, but the Old Man's instinct warned him that defiance would spoil all chance of receiving the promised presents. So he stepped into the dinghy.

We rounded Point Charles lighthouse and steered west to clear Fish Reef. Soon we were passing Bynoe Harbour and then low-lying Quail Island with its scrubby trees. Thousands of turtle yearly waddle ashore here to lay their eggs. An occasional one among these small, lonely islands is the home of a wanderer of the coast. He would build a hut and garden, growing tropical vegetables and banana palms. Natives would visit him; probably some of them would always be camped upon the island, Man Friday to his Robinson Crusoe. They would bring him odds and ends of flotsam of the sea in exchange for an occasional hand-out of "white man" food-stuffs and tobacco. As the seasons and inclination tempt, he sails away seeking what tortoise-shell or trepang or pearlshell he may pick up. Or puts in a season shooting buffaloes or crocodiles. He sails back to his lonely home as the wet season approaches. He is content with the coming and going of the seasons, with the changing moods of nature, and the nomadic company of the natives. He seeks no other. Nay, he resents the intrusion of white strangers. Some such men, nomads themselves, have lived among the blacks practically all their lives, can't leave them. And it is a fact that such a life grows upon a man, or, rather, upon some men.

Our pleasant cruise nearly ended in shipwreck among treacherous shoals between Quail Island and Fish Reef. Herman swore he knew a short cut; he had sailed through here before. And Jacky also volubly insisted he knew every inch of the passage. If so the short cut would save us hours of sailing and the Skipper, against his better judgment, reluctantly agreed to give it a go. I took the tiller, Herman and Jacky were up for'ard on look-out duty, with the uneasy Skipper popping up now and then from the engine below. All was going well when the Skipper jumped up on the cabin top, gazed around, then yelled:

"Hard over!"

I pushed hard on the tiller and as the bows swung round caught a glimpse of something black through water now suddenly yellow. The ketch missed the reef with barely yards to spare. Jacky and Paddy were staring open-mouthed at the reef as the Skipper threw over the leadline.

"One fathom!" he yelled. "Slow the engine! Push her over!"

I pushed hard on the tiller while Herman jumped for the engine. Slowly the *Lotus* swung round directly in her own wake, with the yellow-green waves chopping all around us.

All us men on the look-out for reefs and yet we were right atop of this one before we saw it. In a matter of seconds we would have crashed upon the reef, the bottom of the ketch would have been ripped open, we would have been floundering in the sea.

In angry energy the Skipper kept swinging the lead. Very gradually the water deepened to one and a half fathoms, then to two. The ketch, built for creeping along shallow waters, luckily drew only four feet. Still, when almost upon the reef, we had a bare two feet of water under our keel.

Guided by the leadline we twisted and turned, slowly nosed a way out into four fathoms deep. With reefs all around us.

"Drop anchor!" called the Skipper. "I'm not fooling around in dangerous waters all night—well swing to it here until daylight."

Glumly we dropped the hook. The wind was rapidly freshening, the sun a red ball swiftly sinking.

"Fancy bouncing on a reef even in this little sea," growled the Skipper. "We would have been food for the sharks by now. I was a blasted fool to allow myself to be talked into entering uncharted waters. I deserve to wear a bib and napkins. Now look here, Herman! You have a little launch of your own. Some day you may be in charge of a larger one. One day you'll take one of these 'short cuts' through uncharted waters and lose your own boat, probably yourself with it, which won't matter. You may sneak through these places once or twice on a high tide, but you'll never remember your exact course. You'll try it again and a lower tide or unexpected current will smash you on a reef. And another thing. Never depend on these downtrodden slaves who 'know every inch of the waters'. They know nothing—all they are used to is a dug-out canoe. They don't care a tinker's cuss about you or your boat. 'Plenty feller water, boss!' they'll tell you. 'Plenty feller. Me been through here plenty time!' Oh, yes! And all they are looking for is a quick anchorage. They know if the boat does strike they can float with the tides and swim ashore."

And the sun flopped down into a crimson sea.

As we settled down in uneasy anchorage to the evening meal on an unpleasantly rocking boat, the Skipper told us story after story of narrow escapes and disaster through men relying too much upon the aboriginal crew for a way through uncharted shoals and reefs and passages.

It certainly comes off sometimes, for coastal aboriginals know many of the local reefs and passages. Where low tide means fairly deep water it may be quite all right. But their knowledge is mostly local and concerns canoes, not vessels that draw from four to ten feet of water. It is not reasonable to expect them to make allowances for a vessel drawing six feet, in shallow waters and on a falling tide.

"Remember, Herman," the Skipper repeated earnestly, "once you lose your boat—it is gone. Nothing will bring it back. All that you once had will be rotting on the bottom of the sea."

The Skipper was very upset. He had a right to be. He took the blame, as he had a right to do also.

All night long we stood to as we swung to anchor in a raging tide, fearing the anchor might drag at any moment, spray stinging our faces, the ketch pitching and tossing to a wailing of wind. All around the vessel were shoals and reefs, occasionally visible in boiling foam through the pitch-black night. The strongest swimmer would have had no hope should the anchor drag. It was a subdued crew who stared at the straining chain as the bows rose and plunged and jerked. With banshees screaming in my ears,

I thought what hell's death it would be to be gathered up and smashed down upon that jagged coral again and again and again. Until a man's flesh was torn to shreds that little fish could eat.

Thankfully we spied the first iron-grey that heralded the coming dawn, a dawn that came so slowly. At last the molten ball in its pink veil rose triumphant and plainly we saw the surging waters around us with patches of churning foam upon many reefs. As the sun rose so the tide came in from the ocean, and gradually the foam patches vanished. Carefully then we felt our way out of this far-flung chessboard of reefs and shoals, now so deceptively innocent, hidden under deep water of tide. Perhaps those irresistible sirens who used to lure the old-time mariners to their doom have been sadly maligned. Probably the real sirens were the black night, the screaming voices of the wind, the cruel reefs lurking just underwater awaiting a ship creeping over uncharted seas.

When at last in deep waters tension relaxed. A passing wariness took its place, me alert at the tiller, Herman at the engine, the boys for'ard on the look-out but more on the lookout for the watery-eyed, very sore Skipper. He would "roar" at the slightest thing now. By and by all hands would relax. Herman and I would wink at one another; the Skipper would go below. The boys would roll their eyes, chuckle, whisper a joke and all hands bar the Skipper would relax and slip back into the old easy-going ways.

Away over the bows a school of heavy, dark fish appeared. It was we who saw them first, not the carefree abos on the look-out.

"Dugong," grunted Paddy.

They were porpoises.

"There," pointed the Skipper dramatically, "you have an illustration of the infallible men of the wilds. They are on look-out duty, but they do not even see a reef that we are right atop of. They are on the look-out again and they do not even see a shoal of porpoises. And when we point them out the men of the wilds declare they are dugong!" And the Skipper spat disgustedly over the side.

We chased the porpoise school with the hope of harpooning one, but they accepted the opportunity to play a game with us, enjoyed the sport. Would appear in one spot, then at the exact moment dive while we sped straight ahead over where they had been. We would glance astern to see them come gracefully to the surface, heading in the opposite direction. Again and again they did this. They ran rings around and around us without the slightest effort, a fascinating exhibition of elusive, perfectly controlled speed, the sun gleaming on the roll and dive of their brown bodies.

"Were chasing a will o' the wisp," said the Skipper irritably. "Head her towards the mainland."

We did so. Swung away and the porpoises then chased us, diving under the boat to come up ahead and run more rings around us.

"They're making goats of us," declared the Skipper. "Man, king of the universe, monarch of all he surveys, just a plaything for porpoises!" And he went grumbling below.

Presently Jacky shouted and pointed to a huge thing lazily swimming towards us. It was like an enormous, purple-black cape in undulating motion upon the sea, glistening in the sunlight. For a moment we thought it held a big white fish in its mouth, but when he came close we saw it was the under white of one of its "wings". Something resembling a bat in shape was this monster of the sea, now swimming effortlessly beside us in a curiosity that was bovine. We let him be. We had no weapon which would have stood a chance against such as he.

"Man," said the Skipper sarcastically, "and a diamond fish can bluff him. Here we are, three he-men, and half a dozen blackboys, and we're scared to tackle a blooming devil-fish. Bah!" Again he spat disgustedly over the rail.

Paddy was standing with eyes large as walnuts, staring at the monster. Almost tremblingly he was handling his largest fish spear. The temptation to hurl it deep into the purple-black mass so close beside us was almost irresistible. But he would only have lost a prized spear.

Time slipped by and the mainland loomed plainly, long stretches of sandy beach like pocket handkerchiefs under the sun, dark rims of trees beside and behind them, then a haze and in the far distance shadowy outline of a range.

A wind sprang up against us. The tide turned. And under power, the *Lotus* slowly battled towards land.

"All the wide seas against us." snarled the Skipper. "All the winds! All the tides! And here we are eating up precious petrol as if we were millionaires. Oh, why was I not born Canute?"

The crew up for'ard chose that moment to start a lively corroboree song, to the Skipper's disgust.

"They're on your side," I explained. "They're calling up the Wind Spirit to lay low the wind."

"Yah!" growled the Skipper. "They're full of wind. Give them a pannikin of metho now and they'd be the wind spirit all right."

A gust shrilled through the rigging and flying spray hissed across the deck. The Skipper went below.

When finally we approached within two miles of the Finnis River mouth the leadline showed only one and a half fathoms below us, just nine feet of water. Between us and shore were little breakers curling white upon miles and miles of shoals.

"Oh, ye deep blue sea," moaned the Skipper, "eating up my petrol. Stop that flaming engine!"

Herman stopped it, and the ketch rolled uncomfortably in the receding tide. As we gazed towards shore there was no sign to suggest that a river mouth lay directly ahead of the bows. There appeared nothing but an unbroken shoreline.

"Take the dinghy," ordered the Skipper to Herman, "and make the passage."

And here was enacted yet another little episode of the almost daily incidents of beachcomber navigation.

Herman and the blackboys tumbled into the dinghy, taking with them bamboo poles and white rags. Theirs was the job to mark, among those shoals, the twistings and windings of the channel which must come from the river mouth some distance out to sea. Here would be the deeper water even in a low tide.

As they pulled away from us Herman swung the leadline, kept swinging it. As it showed shallows so the dinghy edged away, creeping ahead when the line showed deeper water. Thus they slowly crept towards shore. At every few hundred yards they drove a bamboo deep down into the sandy bottom, a white rag flying at its top. These white flags would be a guide to the steersman on the ketch, the channel of deeper water leading to the river mouth.

Several hours went by, the Skipper anxiously watching the sun. Then we saw smoke rising from the shore. Herman was at the river mouth.

But it was nearly sundown before Herman and Jacky came battling back in the dinghy, bouncing like a cork. They had put Paddy ashore to light a smoke to guide us as we came in.

"His luck is right out," said the Skipper grimly, "like the tide. He will stay by his little fire all night. I'm not going to risk this craft in the dark in such dangerous waters with the tide still out."

And I could not blame him, though feeling sorry for Paddy all alone in the night in "foreign" tribal country. Shadows swept over Point Blaze. It was here that Keith Renouf was killed by the blacks only four or five years ago.

Night fell swiftly. The ketch pitched and tossed upon a murmuring, black sea. We ate the evening meal on deck with Jacky gazing apprehensively towards the blackness of shore. He was very disturbed lest a wandering band of myalls sneak on Paddy and spear him and take his kidney fat.

"It's on the cards, too," said the Skipper unfeelingly. "I bet Paddy will keep a brighter look-out tonight than he ever has done aboard this boat."

"Paper-bark men bad!" glowered Jacky.

A subdued, scarlet glow burned like a candle upon the beach. Paddy had lit a small fire, hoping against hope that the beacon would tempt the ketch to try and make the passage.

That fire burned far into the night. Somewhere, a few hundred yards away among the trees, would be Paddy, crouching spears in hand, alternately staring seaward and around him, his ears strained to every sigh of the night.

A lonely vigil.

Crocodile shot on the Logan River in 1905.

XIX

NEW SHOOTING GROUNDS

IT was nine in the morning before we began to move inshore on a high tide. A stiff breeze, the ketch plunging in a choppy sea, Jacky staring from the cabin top for any sign of Paddy.

The Skipper spat overside and the wind blew it back on to his trousers.

"There now," he exclaimed admiringly, "that's the beauty of the wide open spaces. You may spit where you like. You dare not in a drawing-room down South. But here, if you spit in the ocean, another little drop won't do any harm."

"So long as you spit on the right side," grinned Herman.

"Of course, you would notice my little lapse," answered the Skipper.

When it appeared certain that we must run ashore, a break in the treeline showed us the sun shining on the rounded sandbanks of the Finnis, hedged densely with trees. And there was Paddy striding majestically along, a spear over his shoulder with a stingray on the spear prongs, a fat burramundi in his left hand. The Skipper seized my arm and pointed.

"The poor, downtrodden native!" he exclaimed in anguished tones. "Now what can I do for him? What has he got? God's glorious sunshine, the sweet breeze uncontaminated by soot of factories, not a care in the world, perfect health and fifty pounds of fish for breakfast."

"He may be tired of fish," I laughed.

"Tired of fish!" yelled the Skipper. "His fish are very different to our fish! You know their staring eyes in the fish shops at two bob a pound. Oh, what can I do for our helpless brother? Set that prehistoric genius in his naked pelt on a desert island and he immediately begins to live, where a civilized man would perish. What can I do for this poor slave? He already possesses more than a millionaire could buy!"

I laughed to the glorious day and sweet sea breeze, the new land so close where any adventure might lurk. We had followed the guiding flags inshore, and now turned as the flags showed sharply parallel with the mangroves. We swung directly around into the mouth of the river. From within a few hundred yards of the seashore it would be impossible to tell that here was a river mouth. We crept in and anchored in water still as polished glass, beautiful with reflection from the trees. The anchor made a musical splash in this whispering solitude. Two canoes were tethered ashore, but no other sign of natives, except for

Paddy mooching along.

"A pretty little river," I said. "Lonely too. There should be good shooting here."

"Yes," answered the Skipper, 'Tut keep a sharp look-out when ashore. The blacks are not to be trusted. They're hefty, game men too. Not far back from this river they twice determinedly attacked armed police patrols. Remember you'll be in the 'great Australian loneliness' soon as you step out of sight of the *Lotus*.

The loneliness appealed to me. Each day holds keen interest for any man when a little off the beaten path, whether he be on the track of some new cure for disease, or striking colours that may lead to a new goldfield, or feeling he at last has the clue to a new invention, or believes he may locate a new star, or whether he be merely a wanderer setting foot on interesting country.

While we made the ketch shipshape for the shooting to come, Jacky rowed ashore and returned with Paddy, a low-browed, glowering Paddy. Morose indeed, very sulky at having been left ashore all night. Barely mumbling answer to the Skipper's questions, he squatted down for'ard for breakfast.

"Let him get over it," chuckled the Skipper. "He daren't run away now anyway."

The Wangites claimed this country, though there were bands of other tribes amongst them just now. None of our boys were tribesmen of this particular area however.

Herman and Jacky and I rowed ashore, right on to an aboriginal camp, but no one was there. They weren't far away though, for bundles of spears were stacked up in the tree branches. Gazing at the ground we walked slowly around the camp.

"They must have gone up river in their canoes," declared Herman. "There's no fresh tracks leading inland from camp. Some scout will send them 'smoke talk' that we're here. We'll soon see them."

We walked through a maze of trees and came out on a black-soil plain stretching far as the eye could reach, a vista of grey and black for the nomads had burnt the thick grass when hunting. Patches that had escaped the fire were knee-high tangles of coarse grasses and vines. We walked six miles inland under brilliant sunlight and came to a vast maze of bamboo grass that resembled a field ploughed up from the rootings of mobs of wild pigs. They had been searching for yams and bulbs and roots. The plain still stretched to a distant silhouette of low hills. These plains, typical of numerous portions of the long Territory coast, will surely be placed under cultivation of some sort as time goes on. During the wet season they are more or less a morass, but even so the soil must be suitable for growing some tropical products such as rice for instance. The paddyfields of China, Burma and the Dutch East Indies grow enormous crops of foodstuffs under somewhat similar conditions. The soil of those big plains will surely grow vast quantities of foodstuffs in time to come.

Next day Herman took the boys and rowed upstream, shooting across river from bank to bank. In this locality the Skipper would not leave his beloved craft. Wisely so. Men who had savagely attacked armed police patrols were not to be treated with disdain. I rowed ashore, walked through the mangroves and out on to the plain. Then turned down along the coast, walking along the mangrove edge, seeking a creek. From out on the plain came a harsh trumpeting where a silvered line of native companions was dancing under the sun.

The mangroves from here through to the seashore were a mile thick, a maze of saltpans among forest and jungle, vine scrub and mangroves, criss-crossed by innumerable arms of the sea. Away ahead a dense line of mangroves stretched inland, a dull grey-green snake twisting away back into the haze of the plain. A salt-water creek this. Across a brilliant sky clouds like fleecy islands now came drifting, and their shadows momentarily turned the mangroves a dark green. But seaward under sunlight the trees appeared yellow-green, darkening softly as cloud shadows drifted upon them in turn. Away ahead, just like dull quicksilver, a long, shallow arm of water came creeping out of the mangroves and slowly over the plain, a ghostly thing. You splashed in water and looked around you. Then it was everywhere, a film of water creeping over the grass roots. The tide was coming in, creeping up this long, shallow, narrow channel. Where it came out from the man¬groves to spill on to the plain the natives had fenced it across with stakes and branches, leaving an open gateway for fish to come through. When the tide was at the full they would close this gateway and any fish fossicking among the grass inland would be theirs when the tide receded.

I stood listening. From a long distance away came floating the long-drawn-out calls of natives. A hunting party probably.

A muddy gutter led into the mangroves and I followed it seaward. It should develop into an ideal haunt for crocodiles. Gradually it deepened and widened into a narrow creek densely lined with vine jungle, the still, dark pools cluttered with fallen leaves and trees. The air heavy with smell of mud made rich with decaying vegetation. Not a sound in this gloomy place until with a flurry and a splash a crocodile slid down the opposite bank. Quite startled, though expecting that very thing, I kicked myself for not having seen him first. It is a fact that no matter how alert a man may be, he still can be taken by surprise. Just as a wild animal can be taken by surprise. Peering between the hanging vines I saw in places on the opposite bank shelves of greasy mud under the exposed roots of trees, mud beds that might rest giant reptiles from the slime. And crocodiles had been there. Distinctly showing there were claw marks in the runways and yet I had not noticed them.

Grey things were they that rested on the grey mud beds, grey-green was the still water, dull green the jungle, and gloomy grey the scant spaces in between.

When deeper into the timber, silence vanished to the metallic trumpetings of large grey cranes, varied with harsh but occasionally sweet calls from unseen birds, then a babble of squawkings from a colony of tree cranes. A young crocodile slithered from the roots almost at my feet and I wondered what had happened to my sense of sight and caution. Twice again the same thing happened. It is startling when they slither away with a rush at your very feet. And yet you have been expecting that thing to happen.

Hours slipped by. The tide had turned. My feet felt like lead through constant dragging out of the mud, cautious climbing over a slimy maze of roots, while sight and hearing were strained to the uttermost.

At last a burst of sunlight shone ahead and here was where the creek mouth drifted into the sea over a wide area of bare mud. And here, waddling towards the water in plain view, was a crocodile, an enormous thing. Fired—and missed! Four more in quick succession came sliding down into the water. Missed each one. Then a brown snout and walnut eyes rose in midstream, stayed motionless. I took careful aim, only at the last second remembering to lower the sight to avoid the tendency to shoot over the head, and fired. His head and shoulders reared convulsively to the smack of the bullet, then his head splashed down and his tail arose to thrash helplessly. Slowly he sank.

Desperately tired, but relieved to find the hoodoo had gone, I decided to enjoy a smoke. Away across the mud flat, towards the sea, was advancing a line of white-and-black soldiers, slowly, solemnly marching like toys on stilts. A battalion of cranes, all shapes and sizes, all sorts of necks and beaks and attitudes. I wondered whether they thought the world of cranes the most important thing in the world, the gobbling up of shrimp things and shellfish the most important thing to do.

Up into the sky away behind the mangroves rolled a dense volume of black smoke, a hunting fire lit by natives. Must have been those I'd heard out on the plain. Those natives were drawing closer, hunting as they came.

Suddenly a snout tip and eyes arose in the water not fifty feet away. The crocodile gazed directly at me, then vanished without a ripple. I crouched down in the shadow of a tree, rifle across knee, waiting. There may be no sign of these brutes, yet they can be watching a man from only a few yards away. Twenty minutes later and a snout tip and eyes arose in midstream. A crocodile came swimming straight ashore, evidently unaware of the man in the shadows. Suddenly the snout emerged right at the very bank. To the "smack!" of the bullet he fell back with a curiously dismayed shake of the head. He sank. Presently blood came up and floated out in a little brownish cloud. Minutes later and a slow stream of tiny bubbles came gliding up into the middle of the blood patch. The last of his air. Only then I noticed his runway. He had been on the point of coming out on to the mud and could have been shot there, thus saving probing for him later on. I'd reacted like an amateur the whole day long.

Presently a snout arose, well upstream and close inshore. It hovered there, staring. I crouched against the tree trunk, not a move. Neither did he move, while I slowly got cramps. This creek probably had never echoed to the report of a rifle before and the crocodile's curiosity was aroused. Another snout tip appeared, but away downstream. At last the nearer fellow turned and swam about a little. For half an hour he thus fooled about, yet never giving me a chance for a fatal shot. Long-legged cranes stalking their food on the mudbanks came to the water's edge and solemnly regarded him. Several squawked harshly then agitatedly flew to the opposite bank, but one big old grey crane waited there to stare him out. At last, almost imperceptibly, he came gliding towards the bank edge. His snout seemed to slide from the water and he was coming ashore. Such a sinuous, creepy movement, with his snout moving forward close to the mud, his paws creeping forward with a sideways, quaintly stealthy motion. He lay there crescent-shaped, motionless. I fired—and missed! He unwound as if he were a spring and plunged with side twists back into the water.

Feeling mad as a hatter, I trudged straight back to the keteh. Everything had gone wrong this day. I had missed many opportunities. Before reaching the river bank I heard the high-pitched calls of women, yells of piccaninnies at play.

The tribe had returned. By the river a fire glowed. Dark figures were standing and squatting upon the bank opposite the *Lotus*. Through the trees I saw Jacky push straight off with the dinghy, while the natives stared boldly as I walked down to the bank. A fine-looking crowd. Men daubed with scarlet ochre, armed with long, barbed spears, and the far more dangerous shovel-bladed spears. Healthy-looking women and youngsters among them, all of them quite fearless.

Herman had four good skins aboard. He'd shot the crocodiles on the bank. All I had to show was a bad temper and waste of precious cartridges.

Crocodile shot by Ms Krystyna Palowski with one shot in 1955 at Kaumba, in Queensland Gulf country (top). War on the home front 1942 (bottom).

XX

WAGIS, QUEEN OF THE "PUMPKIN"

ONE late afternoon, while sunset was bathing the still waters a rosy hue, a picture appeared like magic. The tip of a little mast, then the bows, then a little cutter seemed to waft through the seaward trees and come gliding up the river mouth. Leading the cutter was a tiny canoe beautifully handled by a young half-caste girl. Behind the cutter came three much larger canoes manned by aboriginal oarsmen who chanted a native water song in deep, melodious voices. In the stern of the cutter sat a big old white man gazing upstream. A tall half-caste Chinee stood by the tiller, and copper-coloured figures stared at us from the crowded vessel's deck. The white man waved a hairy arm and in a bull voice shouted surprised greeting as the cutter glided by. The Skipper waved in reply.

In the now beautiful surroundings the cavalcade fitted the picture. But in daylight that cutter was a most disreputable-looking little vessel. Naturally so, for she had been battered by many seas, by many years. How she could still roam the seas was a mystery. Providence must lend a kindly hand to sea roamers such as these. She still poked her little snout into more gloomy, muddy, tortuous byways of the coast than any other vessel in the far-flung North.

As she anchored a hundred yards away from us her hook and chain rattled out, echoed musically by trees and water while ripples circled rapidly out to lap the banks. The canoes glided up to her and the men leapt aboard to help make all snug and prepare the evening meal.

"Mitchemore," said the Skipper, "in the *Pumpkin*. In such a place as this who'd have thought we were going to have company."

In that lovely sunset and halcyon surroundings what a name for the little craft—the *Pumpkin*!

"What a load he carries," I said. "It's a wonder the cutter doesn't sink under that crowd."

"He daren't let them walk overland," answered the Skipper. "They wouldn't risk the land trip anyhow, for they'd have to run the gauntlet through hostile country. So he carries them and their families aboard the *Pumpkin,* and in the canoes." "Did he pick them up here and there along the coast?" "Yes, over hundreds of miles. Wherever he met a good man. They're all trained men, that crowd. What they don't know about crocodiles and how to catch them isn't worth knowing."

Night enveloped us, like a velvet sheet engulfing all. Camp-fires gleamed ashore; a rosy glow arose from the *Pumpkin's* galley. One by one the stars peeped out. A lubra's laughter echoed across the water. Ashore and on both vessels all were enjoying a welcome meal.

After the evening meal Mitchemore came aboard by canoe. A heavily built, twinkly-eyed, grizzled man of sixty odd. Easy to tell that he lived hard; his face, the stoop of his even now powerful body told it plainly. He was living hard now, on damper and boiled crocodile meat, fish, and a very little jam and watery tea—tea leaves boiled over and over again. At the cheery invitation of the Skipper, he ate slowly but ravenously of our own good fare, putting every mouthful where it would do most good. He lingered luxuriously over his pannikins of tea, strong tea that actually had condensed milk and sugar in it. He sighed, and leaned back. And then came the question. We were waiting for it, saw it coming. In his hoarse, growly voice he didn't suppose we had any trade tobacco to spare!

"Well now, we have!" declared the Skipper. "Now, what do you think of that?"

A slow smile spread over the grizzled face.

"Get two pounds of trade from down below," said the Skipper to Herman.

Herman chuckled, and vanished below.

Trade tobacco! Worth far more than money out in the wilds.

Most of the nondescript crowd aboard the Pumpkin rowed towards the bank to gossip and camp with the tribe ashore. But the dark shadows of a few remained aboard. Occasionally the still night carried their water-borne voices to us.

"I don't trust that crowd ashore too much," said Mitchemore in his slow, hoarse voice, "but my boys know some of them. And it's well to keep the peace. I very seldom allow Wagis ashore at night. Willie will look after the boat—a good boy, Willie."

"He can handle a rifle," said the Skipper.

"He's got the eyes of an owl that see in the night," growled Mitchemore, "and—he's a killer."

Mitchemore, like many men of the far bush, was a listener more than a talker. When he did speak it was in short, slow sentences. And there were no waste words.

We yarned for hours about 'gators and buffaloes, about aboriginals and beachcombers, 'panging (trepang fishing), boats and sail and engines. About life such as these men know it on the lonely coasts, a life unknown except to a handful of sea wanderers. As they yarned old Mitchemore kept wary eyes towards his vessel and the shadowy canoes now drifting out from the river bank. The canoemen were gossiping with those aboard the cutter.

Naturally so; they were eager to barter for, or cadge, or steal, any scrap of precious iron.

The efficient half-caste, Willie, stood on deck to see that no canoeman attempted to come aboard, but old Mitchemore hardly took his eyes off the precious *Pumpkin*, and those fires ashore. The reflections sent scarlet fingers reaching out to both vessels. Should the fires die down as the night grew darker, Mitchemore would hasten aboard lest other canoes drifting downstream rush the cutter. Such things have happened in those waters.

Next morning life commenced lazily. There is no hurry in Aboriginal Land. The first to show aboard the *Pumpkin* was the little half-caste Japanese girl, Wagis. She was soon paddling about in her tiny canoe, her large brown eyes on us. The Skipper called to her to come and get some bread and jam, a great treat. Shyly she responded. She was a copper-coloured little model. Her big brown eyes were solemn and intensely curious until she smiled, when they seemed to twinkle with glee. Her bread and jam vanished quickly, so the Skipper gave her a real breakfast and a few simple presents. She thought it a lot of Christmasses all come at once.

Old Man Mitchemore had adopted Wagis after saving her life. When she was a baby her parents were about to strangle her just when Mitchemore came along. They didn't want her. She was "too much trouble". So he bought the trembling baby, reared her, and she had wandered with him ever since. Life aboard the little craft revolved around her. She was the spirit of the *Pumpkin*.

To lazy calls from men, women and piccanins, Mitchemore's camp-followers came out from shore in their canoes and tied up to the *Pumpkin* with laughing chatter. They'd had a good night ashore and brought half a dozen wild-eyed tribesmen back with them, hoping they could repay hospitality from Mitchemore's scanty stores. The small deck was packed now with brown bodies and black, all sexes and ages. No wonder the old man had to make of his venture a flotilla, with canoes following in the wake of the *Pumpkin*.

The "under below" of that tiny vessel was packed with the little five-horse-power engine, salted crocodile hides and smell, a medley of firearms, cartridges, harpoon poles, native weapons and dillybags, a few stores, and the old bags he slept upon. His prize shooter was Willie, the half-caste Chinee, slim and wiry, coldly alert of eye. But he had several other very good half-caste shooters too, a few hefty aboriginals expert with the crocodile spear and harpoon, while the rest were canoemen and women and skinners. With this variously coloured team Mitchemore had secured a hundred and six good crocodile skins this month.

"It only goes to prove what men who know the game can do," remarked the idly smoking Skipper.

Herman smiled. He was fitting a new string to his guitar.

"Mitchemore must be a good skipper," I said. "He seems to take his shooters where the crocodiles are."

"Don't you believe it," replied the Skipper confidentially. "It's the shooters do it—they whistle up the 'gators and put salt on their tails."

"It's a pity you hadn't thought to bring along some salt," I said.

"Yes," sighed the Skipper, just as Paddy speared a fish to a yell of congratulation from the *Pumpkin*.

This morning, when the *Pumpkin* was ready to weigh anchor, Wagis took the lead in her little canoe, with a solemn little black piccanin perched like a kewpie in the bows. She was very fond of that piccanin. The poddy little chap was her mascot, but she loved her canoe. With native song and joke they hauled up the mudhook and the *Pumpkin* slowly chugged upstream, followed by the canoes. They were bound for a lagoon, shooting wild geese for the day. Our own Jacky and Paddy accompanied them to bring us a share of the spoil. Such a disreputable-looking little old craft she was in daylight, crowded with nondescript humanity, the white man, the half-castes, the aboriginals. The piccanins' laughing voices echoed across the water. Nondescript yes, but how happy they all were.

Day by day we hunted the timid, cunning, inquisitive, hideous, yet gracefully powerful saurians of the coastal waters. Even their runways were a study. The spot chosen was invariably strategic, leading up from a deep pool, with the top of the runway up the bank in such a position as enabled the lurking reptile to hear and ambush any creature approaching from the landward side. At the same time if danger threatened it could slide back straight down into the water and vanish. Sometimes crocodiles favoured a spot where the mud was of the greasy variety, maybe because it would add speed as they slithered down. Although generally difficult to surprise them even in localities where they very rarely, if ever, heard a rifle shot, at times it seemed ridiculously simple. On such occasions they became flurried and in their rush and sideways slither quite often crashed through and over mangrove roots that otherwise they would not even have grazed. If badly startled the crocodile would enter the water with a great splash; otherwise without a sound. Often when surprised thus he would cruise underwater up or downstream, stay submerged a few minutes, then his snout tip and eyes would break surface while he stared around intensely curious to learn what had disturbed him. Curiosity has thus killed many a crocodile. Among the big fellows in particular, each likes to stick to his one area of water, like many wild animals and numer-

numerous birds who also cling to their own feeding grounds, their favourite gully, or mountain crag, or swamp, or beach, or lily-covered lagoon. The crocodile also, as he grows larger and older and surlier, chooses some favourite haunt and this he makes his own. Occasionally a more powerful brute than he comes cruising along, surveys the pleasant surroundings from a cold, nasty eye, then awaits his chance to take possession. For there are bushrangers amongst the crocodiles too. I've witnessed several titanic fights when such a pirate sought to dispossess the rightful owner.

Thus in this wild country, just the same as in waterways nearer civilization, we found many a crocodile claiming his own haunt. Here he makes his private runway. Here, when gorged, he basks on the land, sleeps with "one eye open" and enjoys a spell of open-air life. He knows intimately the locality, the waterholes behind him, the trees all around, and the depths below.

As he surfaces he carefully gazes at the familiar surroundings, sees that all is safe, then waddles ashore. As a rule, while lying on this runway or the bank, his nose is pointing or partly pointing towards the stream so that if alarmed he can slither straight down into the water. But though generally alert, he sleeps sometimes. It is difficult indeed to tell when he is asleep, for he lies just like that when lurking for the unsuspecting. One day I was manoeuvring for a shot at such a brute, which was lying just like a log at the edge of an open forest pool.

To a "thump! thump! thump!" a wallaby came hopping along and hopped right on to the "log". In an instant the tail lashed around and as the wallaby hit the ground a claw stretched out and grabbed him. I fired and the crocodile jerked up convulsively. But the wallaby was too badly hurt; he gasped his life out as I walked across.

That crocodile had come his "log act" right across the faint pad through the grass where the wallabies came to drink. Cunning brutes, swift to strike, ruthless in their strength of jaw and tail and claw.

XXI

EXCITING MOMENTS

THE Finnis was an ideal anchorage for such wanderers as we. Only a narrow, shallow, tidal river walled by trees. Once in the mouth and a small craft was perfectly protected from all the vagaries of the sea. The river just here ran parallel with the coastal fringe but soon turned inland. Creeks meandered into it, while other gloomy waterways edged out from it deep through the mangrove and forest and vine scrub, while yet again other twisting water arms vanished into swamps. Though the Finnis rises in a distant range, it is difficult indeed to follow its course to the sea. Every now and again it spreads and vanishes in swamps, only to pick up its course again and wind away down to the coast. Along the coast itself were numerous salt arms of the sea and tidal creeks that crept into the ocean from plain and forest, jungle patch and mangroves. So that from our safe anchorage and base we could "shoot" many miles of waterways by working on foot inland, or rowing up river and into the creeks by dinghy and canoe.

Each shooting morning Mitchemore's little flotilla would start upstream, with Wagis in her canoe singing as she led the *Pumpkin*. The quiet, efficient Willie would stand by the tiller, Mitchemore would sit on the tiny deck crowded by sundry helpers while the large canoes would follow behind with their hefty harpooners and skinners. The "chug-chug" of the tiny engine, the dip of paddles and native song would echo sweetly along the water until they neared the day's shooting location. Then all would travel silently. When the *Pumpkin* had crept as far as possible up some heavily wooded creek she would tie up to a tree. Willie would take command of the canoes and they would paddle quietly deeper into the mangroves or jungle. Very different now from the carefree sing-song up the river. All hands, men, women, children, quiet as mice, with eyes alight watching the water, the runways, the root-lined hanks. The half-caste shooters gripping their rifles, the spearmen ready should a harpoon be needed. At first sign of a crocodile a warning hiss or cluck of the tongue brought all hands motionless as rifles were raised. To the crack of the rifle, a yell of delight and the canoes surged forward should the crocodile be badly hit.

If the crocodiles were plentiful the canoes would work together. If not they would separate, a shooter in charge of each canoe. Noiselessly paddling, they would poke into any shallow arm that branched out from the creek, pulling themselves along if necessary by roots and overhanging branches as the waterway narrowed. It would eventually come to a deadend deep within the mangroves or scrub. Occasionally such a place instead of petering out might end by widening out into a shallow pool. Should a crocodile be up there he would be cornered, for the canoes would be between him and the deep water of the distant creek. In such an exciting case the canoes would advance abreast, the crews shouting and splashing with paddles and hands, frightening the crocodile ahead of them into still shallower water. They would drive him right on to dry land and he would become an easy prey to their rifles. Sometimes though a big fellow, increasingly alarmed as the water shallowed, would wheel around and charge in a frantic fury to break through to the creek. If the shooters failed to kill him, he would come raving straight on to a bedlam of screams and shouts, bullets and spears. He might break through amid yells of consternation if a canoe were overturned, but would have half a dozen bullets and harpoons in him. He probably would reach deep water only to die.

One day they thus chivvied an eighteen-footer farther and farther on into ever shallowing water. He was a very uneasy, pugnacious brute, becoming increasingly energetic as the water shallowed to barely two feet. Again and again he wheeled back in an attempt to break through, but at the critical moment hesitated at their shouts and splashings. Although again and again he was momentarily above water, they could not get a clear shot at his skull for he kept twisting and turning, rushing backwards and forwards as the canoes inexorably advanced. He had churned the shallows into almost liquid mud and this again camouflaged him and obscured the shooters' aim. Finally the corrugations of his powerful body emerged and a bullet ploughed into his snout.

He wheeled straight around and charged with open jaws, his chest violently churning the water aside. Into a rain of spears he hurtled fair across a canoe to shrieks of the leaping occupants. That spinning canoe, that lashing tail and plunging, clawing body overturned the canoes to either side and the water was alive with shrieking figures splashing for the shore. Except Willie and his fellow shooter, who stood to their knees in water firing at the monster now rushing back to the creek.

Old Mitchemore had averaged three good skins each day for the last three months (not counting the poorer-class skins), which was a good average for his team; for many crocodiles, though badly hit, get swept to sea if shot when the outward tide is running strongly. Others, growing weaker from their wounds, become entangled under submerged trees in deep pools, or crawl into submarine caverns and fail to rise again.

Some wounded crocodiles, after taking to the water, would be forced by the water pressing into the inner body through the wounds, to rise to the surface away downstream. Yet other wounded ones, whose wounds had not entered the body proper, would soon be in misery. Blood-sucking leeches would fasten to the raw wounds. Small crabs and tiny fish would nibble at the exposed flesh. This awful irritation would drive the saurian crazy. Thus are the mighty fallen. Driven nearly frantic, these would dodge us and crawl up the banks to elude their vicious little tormentors, vanishing into the mangroves or jungle either to recover or die.

At low tide we would prod the waterholes for dead bodies, and for live ones too. Mitchemore's boys were past masters at this. When a crocodile was detected, we would lift him, or try to, by means of long bamboo poles on the end of which were strong iron hooks. That is another of the numerous little secrets that count so much in the life of the wild, the detecting of live things underwater by the gentle touch of a spear haft. The aboriginals thus locate and identify crocodile, tortoise and several species of sluggard fish and eel from submerged logs, roots, water-plants, rocks, on sandy, pebbly or hard bottom, they can distinguish shellfish from stones, too. When told about it, and when shown how, the white man with experience can also learn to feel the "touch" of a crocodile, turtle, or other living thing should the bottom be not a mass of water plants. There comes a thrill when first you definitely succeed. You locate something. Then a faint, queer "feel" comes up the spear haft as with gentle prod here, then gentle prod farther along, your hand registers the feeling that it is not hard, unresilient rock bottom down below under the spear haft, nor is it the lifeless, elusive feeling of mud, nor the gritty feeling of gravel. You prod a little more, adding the gentlest pressure, and feel certain it is not the inanimate, soggy sameness of a sodden log. No, this is some definitely solid body that has some faint "give" in it, a vague but definite "live feel". Motionless, unseen, below water, connected to you by a ghostly feeling through the spear haft is a live thing. Experience teaches, develops the "feeling". You thrill indeed when you feel your first big old-man crocodile. Utterly moveless he is, and very uncertain as he too feels that gentle questing touch of the spear.

When treated thus by an expert hand they seldom move. Even in the big swamps, those in which the paper-barks grow, with soggy islets in them thick with pandanus palm and reeds, with the water below encumbered with snags, dense with water-roots and covered on the surface with giant waterlilies I have seen the aboriginals thus locate the crocodile, whether wounded or not wounded.

When we would locate one, half-castes and aboriginals could generally distinguish whether it was alive or dead. But not always. Several times we brought a big "proper dead feller"' to the surface, where he immediately broke into a fury of clashing jaws and lashing tail to the consternation of us in the dinghy or canoe. The shooters always stood with rifle ready when the boys were bringing a crocodile to the surface.

They can be raised fairly easily by men who know how. Mitchemore's men were experts. The hooks are not too sharp, for if the point pierces the tough hide the crocodile will violently object. Generally two men tackle the job, one fore and one aft in the dinghy as they gently grope to get the hooks under the crocodile. Then the bamboo hafts are evenly pulled up, care being taken to bring up the crocodile on an "even keel". He comes up far more easily than would be imagined, for it is much easier to lift a body under water than it would be to lift that same body on land. The crocodile may even help, for at times the boys have declared "him dead feller" only on raising him a few feet to whisper excitedly, "Him plenty feller alive too much!"

They could feel he was rising to the pressure of the hooks, and also could feel his body more buoyant than the dead weight of a carcass. The crocodile under such circumstances lies doggo until he can learn what it is all about. Imagining himself secure at home in the depths, he feels the occasional questing touch of spear or bamboo haft very gently working up along his body. Then comes an interval. After a while, the gentle touch of the blunt hooks groping for a leverage. Feeling a little uncomfortable, he helps the action. The hooks worm their way under him. Then comes a very slow, upward, gentle pull. Fie feels that slow, compelling urge to rise, begins then to arise gently. It is a new experience for him. Nothing similar has happened him before. No experience has taught him what to do. He feels uneasy but still reasonably secure in his natural element. He does not connect what is now happening to him with his enemy, man. His instinctive wariness urges him to lie doggo, warns him not to betray himself by violent action until he sees what it is all about. Should he be dead it is all right. A noose is slipped around him and he is towed ashore to be skinned.

Should he be still alive, trouble occurs immediately he "wakes up" to what is doing. If the water is muddy, he may be brought so close to the surface that there is just time to smash his skull with a bullet.

If there is a doubt about his being dead, or if the water is clear, it is best to pierce him vitally with the steel-headed harpoon. Perhaps he has been located by the long slender bamboo haft. With a vicious grin over his shoulder to us, the tribesman then lifts up the haft and inserts in its hollow end the long, sharp steel spike. Hardly breathing, we watch it go down into the water, guided by the haft. This is an expert's job. The harpoon man may favour a spot at the base of the neck, or that paralysing stroke midway between the two hind legs. Whichever it is he probes down, delicately feels the point exactly on the desired spot. Then, with gritted teeth and using all his weight, he presses hard down.

The saurian plunges away and the tip of the harpoon haft is a frantic periscope. But if the job is well done the saurian is soon part paralysed, or else the water penetrates the wound into his body and sooner or later he must rise.

The hide of a crocodile is very tough. But the steel spike, with sudden pressure and weight driving it, penetrates the hide fairly easily when it is under water.

On occasions we experienced a few swift moments of wildest excitement. In each case the boys swore it was a dead crocodile coming up, so we did not bother to pierce it with the harpoon. The water was clear. As the crocodile came up he saw the canoes and dinghies, the men leaning over. Just before he broke surface he swerved violently up with open jaws and thrashing tail. As his weight hurled itself upon the canoe, the crew leaped overboard. The fury was riddled with bullets and harpoon and spears from the other canoes and dinghies. Hectic while it lasted and the shooters needed nerves of ice. It was a rush and heave of the great body all mixed up with leaping men. But no man was ever shot, or ripped by harpoon.

Little Wagis was in her element when excitement was brewing, her eyes fairly leaping from her head, her body tensed forward, hands gripping the paddle in instant readiness to swerve aside or fly straight into the fray. And when it was over hers was the laugh that led the wild merriment and shouting jokes as men overturned in the excitement swam or climbed to safety. If Mitchemore had ever known, he would never have let her out of sight of the *Pumpkin*. But all hands were careful not to put her away. Willie always kept her away from trouble until right at the point where his leadership might be needed. And right then, with a few swift strokes of her paddle, Wagis would race right up into the trouble.

Of course she'd promise solemnly never, never to do it again.

XXII

MEN OF THE WILDS

THE boys had added a couple of wild myalls to our crew, bush blacks who could not speak a word of English.

"Just a couple more mouths for us to feed," said the Skipper airily, "mouths as big as sharks', bellies as big as elephants'. I've heard of the non-refillable bottle, but give me the aboriginal non-fillable belly."

However, it was all in life as lived along the coasts. The myalls would probably earn their tucker. The tribesmen ashore fully expected some little share of tucker, tobacco and any scraps of precious iron they might barter from us and the crew. Reasonably enough, for after all we were making use of their country and they were justified in expecting something in return. Fragments of iron they prized most. With stone and sand and water and patient labour they shaped and ground this into knives and spearheads incomparably more efficient than stone or bone or shell.

One morning Herman and the boys and I rowed ashore with the two myalls. With a myall and Paddy I was to walk inland, then shoot down along a creek towards the sea. Herman and the others would row along the coast to the creek mouth, and from there shoot up the creek.

We entered the creek, the myall crouching forward as easily and stealthily he led the way. A fine figure of a man in his wild nakedness that showed muscles and sinews trained to every call of the wild. Spears in left hand, wommera in the right, he was a picture of agile wariness. And yet right now he was making more noise than I did because of some peculiar property of the mud just here. With each step it made a soft moaning, sucking sound. The pressure of his step, the grip of the mud, then the cautious withdrawal of his living foot caused it, I suppose. Peering ahead as he walked, yet he missed seeing the first crocodile, a grey monster lying curled head and tail towards water under the leafy mangroves shading a muddy runway. He splashed down into the water like a hurtling log. It is startling. At any moment you expect sight of a brute, but instead comes a grey flurry, a crackling of roots and a huge body has hurtled "smack!" into a deathly quiet pool.

A little farther on and the myall, peering from behind a tree, clucked softly and beckoned. A crocodile was floating downstream right on the surface. He looked large as a whale. The bullet struck him like a hammer blow and he surged forward and down with lashing tail that whipped the pool into a cauldron. Still farther along, and the myall clucked again. Up on the opposite bank where a giant tree had crashed and cleared a path amongst the mangroves a saurian was bathing himself in a shaft of sunlight, a beautiful shot. He spun round in amazement at the shock of the bullet and rolled over and over down the bank. He reached the water and dived, but soon surfaced and swam around and around, rolling over and over to a heaving of white belly, his outstretched paws blindly beating air and water. He became entangled in a fallen tree and tried to bite his way up it, only to roll helplessly again. Then weakly, slowly, he sank. The myall glanced around with a smile of marvellous teeth, his savage eyes gleaming. There would be a giant feast for the tribe when they hauled all this meat up from the depths.

Muffled reports told of Herman, his shots coming gradually closer. This was a good creek. A crocodile bobbed up at the water's edge almost at our feet. He submerged in surprise. But another rose almost at the same spot and to the smack of the bullet plunged half out of the water. He rolled over and dived with a lash of the tail.

And so the shoot went on until we met Herman and his muddy men about midday. We sat upon the mangrove roots and enjoyed the midday meal. In an odour of mud and decaying vegetation and murky water, the aboriginals sent their good fodder to the right place in huge mouthfuls. Every line of their screwed-up faces was rippling with concentrated enjoyment. If only I could enjoy a week's eating like that my skinny frame would put on a stone weight.

We were busy eating when a naked myall appeared right beside us, motionless. A reddish ochre made his body the colour of a Red Indian, a phantom man in the gloom. With a nod of the head and some voiceless sign he greeted the myalls, then squatted down in dignified silence. An alert, savagely intelligent, powerfully built warrior, a tuft of parrot feathers in his forehead band, a beautifully made stone knife in his belt of human hair, a dozen long, cruelly barbed spears. One of a band of travelling nomads he had heard the shooting, cut Herman's tracks, then followed them along. Ten minutes later another myall appeared, a tall, glowering warrior whose savage eyes appeared to glow strangely red in the gloom. This effect came from the vivid circles of scarlet ochre around his eyes. An eerie effect, especially in jungle gloom. I used to wonder whether that particular red ochre contained some trace of phosphorus which faintly reflected on their gleaming eyes. Noiselessly others joined us.

We worked our way back out on to the sunlit plain. And a little party appeared ahead, three warriors, two young lubras, one with a tiny piccanin across her shoulders. Big solemn eyes the youngster had, his chubby fists clinging to the mother's hair. We spread out in single file and soon met a party of twenty others, bucks and lubras but only two piccanins. Girl mothers, they might be fourteen years of age, merry little things. They strode along at that free, easy pace of the wild aboriginal. Herman and I had to step out at the limit to keep up with them. The laughing voices floated back to us, joking at our expense. Truly, here the wild man is king of his own domain.

From away out on the plain came an occasional long-drawn hunting call from tribesmen walking parallel to us. We were walking along the edge of the plain, beside the wall of mangroves stretching for many miles. Presently we came to a large dry claypan, a patch of sun-dried clay bare of grass as a bald crown is of hair. This bald patch extended out from the mangroves for nearly three hundred yards into the plain, and about the same in width. It was a gigantic horseshoe of bare red clay, fronted by the mangroves, otherwise enclosed by the tall dry grass of the plain.

Right against the mangroves the lubras put down their babies and grass dilly-bags with their belongings, then eagerly scattered to collect sturdy sticks—throwing sticks. The men squatted down after a long-drawn cry, answered immediately from away out in the plain.

"It's going to be a hunt," said Herman.

"Yes, we'd best pick a spot where we can dive into the mangroves if the fire comes too hot."

Our own boys were eagerly gathering sticks, for they carried no spears today. Besides, a throwing stick is often handier than a spear at close quarters when the bounding quarry is momentarily visible in the wafting smoke. Every now and then other tribesmen joined us. Away out in the plain a puff of smoke arose, then another and another which, as we watched, joined together in a long, advancing line amid streaks of flame blown towards us by the wind.

Right away to right and left of this but coming towards us appeared two other lines of puffs and flame, all rapidly joining together until soon the fire was in the shape of a fast- advancing horseshoe which finally would descend on the claypan. The only escape for any animal within that horseshoe was to dash straight down through the grass to the claypan.

The main wall of smoke, horribly black and swirling and lit by scarlet tongues, was now rushing upon us with a roar. Above it had appeared like magic hundreds of kites diving down into the smoke, their little yellow eyes bright and cruel. They were feasting on grasshoppers and butterflies and grass- mice and small lizards struggling helplessly in the smoke. The natives with us, chattering excitedly, now spread out in line facing the advancing fire, the men shaking spears and flourishing throwing weapons, the women and youngsters their throwing sticks. Acrid breaths of hot wind now blew over us, long curling cinders of burning grass eerily dissolved high up in the hot currents of air. The fire must die out where the grass ended at the claypan edge, but it was going to be very sultry here for a while. I sat down in the cooler air, for wisps of smoke were smarting the eyes.

Suddenly a yell of laughter as a long black snake came gliding from the grass out on to the bare claypan, frantic to put as much clear ground as possible between the flames and itself. Then a wallaby bounded from the grass going all out. It sat back in the open gasping for breath, beating at its eyes with its forepaws, and then writhed to the ground with two spears through its body. With a sudden awful roar an increase of wind threw a wall of flame towards us and there bounded from the smoking grass a dozen terrified wallabies straight into a hail of throwing sticks, a bedlam of yells. Through the smoke now wafting over the claypan other snakes came wriggling out from the grass, while three large goannas sped out fairly at the gallop. I knew they could run fast, but these unfortunates were fairly scorching the earth. Amid the now close roar of the flames sounded a hoarse grunting, terrified squeals, and out on to the claypan sped a sow with a dozen suckers at her heels. To yells of delight another sow and suckers burst from the grass.

The excited aboriginals leapt towards them hurling spears and sticks. Through smarting eyes I stared, expecting any moment to see man or woman or child transfixed. It was wild excitement of leaping figures through whirling smoke, a medley in which the roar of the fire mingled with the shrieks of women and agonized squealing of speared pigs.

Then a sudden howl of alarm. Shrieking figures leapt aside as from the smoke emerged a demon, a big old boar charging straight through everything, piggish eyes screwed up with rage and pain, two hundred pounds of maddened animal seeking anything into which he could bury his tusks. At amazing speed he came charging straight down over the claypan and on into the mangroves. He would have ripped the entrails from the strongest tribesman had any dared stand in his path.

When the fire burned down to a blackened, smoking mass all the folk spread over the claypan collecting the game, laughing over episodes in the hunt, the lubras in shrill sarcasm over the way the warriors had leapt from the path of the charging boar. The warriors excused themselves by pantomime of how the brave white men had run too, and the shrieks of laughter from the lubras were no compliment to said white men.

It had been a great little hunt. Snakes, lizards, sucking pigs and wallabies littered the claypan. As soon as the earth cooled sufficiently, the lubras would hop out on to the burnt patch to retrieve the half-roasted reptiles and porcupines and other small fry that had not been able to escape the flames.

Aboriginals with turtle eggs on the *Aroetta*, Donald Thomson expedition 1942.

XXIII

WILD WOMEN

ONE evening I was sitting in the tiny cabin for'ard, grudgingly writing up my diary. Since boyhood I'd been a wanderer and looked forward to evening just to rest and gaze up at the stars and dream and smoke. But since I'd taken to book writing, responsibility weighed heavily and any notes not written by day must be written at eventide while events and mind and memory were fresh. Behind my back was the open manhole leading to the big cabin where the Skipper was lazing on his bunk smoking. Herman lay a little aft, my empty bunk opposite the Skipper. Far more pleasant—to be lazing there than writing notes here, cramped up by bulkheads and the anchor chain.

It was a bewitching night, stuff that the universe and men's dreams are made of. Far above the tiny open hatch was deep-blue sky daubed with moveless stars. Not the faintest movement from the ketch; never had I known her so utterly still. No sound either of water lapping the planks, not even the familiar caressing whisper. Then from the immensity of sky drifted the eerie trumpeting of a flight of wild geese. Something inexpressibly wild and free haunted the senses in that vanishing call from the night. And now from the big cabin aft came the Skipper's joke followed by Herman's soft laugh, even their voices muffled and softened by some mystery of the night. Then drifted in across the water the clicking of kylies, the hoarse boom of a didgeridoo, voices melodious in rhythmic song, a lilting corroboree tremulously sweet and musical. I stood up, my head just above the hatch gazing out into a velvet night. Vivid along the river bank were six fires. Two small ones were twinkling, the trees around them lit by the flames. A coil of smoke hovered there, flame lit. There was just a suspicion of grouped figures. The voices now came strongly across the still water.

What if we go ashore," came the Skipper's lazy voice. "Jack will look after the ship."

"Righto," agreed Herman with alacrity.

"We're going ashore, Jack," called the Skipper.

"Righto." And I moved into the big roomy cabin with its luxury of a chart table, a flat board set across two kerosene tins of fresh water. From the open companionway came the diminishing sound of rowlocks. That ceased, its place taken by the clicking of kylies, soft voices chanting some haunting native song. I listened a while. The tune was compelling. Far away up above the open companionway stars were floating in black night.

"Blast the notes," I muttered. "A man's got to stay aboard and scribble on a night like this."

Presently I glanced up at the stars, listening. There had come like a whisper the dip of a canoe blade in water. And silence again.

I glanced at the rifles handy near by. A canoe must be very close outside, but there came not the faintest sound. And then something blotted out the stars. Two litde heads, the thick black hair boyishly cut, side by side two little heads were gazing down. Liquid black eyes stared down into mine. One pair was glistening with laughter, the other pair big and solemn. Laughing Eyes showed a flash of teeth, a questioning, mischievous smile, a soft giggle. Light as a butterfly she was coming down the companionway steps. She stood on the cabin floor, one big smile.

"Me Waldawidgee," she smiled. "This feller one Gillagun." And jerked her chin towards the head above.

"What are you doing here?" I asked sternly.

"Me come," she pouted impishly.

"You'll catch it when the Skipper returns."

She threw back her head and laughed the merriest little laugh. Gillagun stepped over the companion top and sat on the steps above, gazing down into the cabin with her big, serious eyes. They could hardly have been fifteen years but were slender, perfectly formed girl women, girl women of the wilds. Good features, not squat and repulsive but remarkably well formed. Probably because in their ancestry was a little Malay blood, from the proas of Malay wanderers that for centuries have touched the coast. Wildawidgee was more like a laughing schoolgirl than a woman, Gillagun a serious one. Each wore a little loincloth only, tight fitting. I recognized that cloth. It had mysteriously disappeared from aboard. A sharper clicking of the kylies sounded down the companion-way, a stirring lilt in the voices. And Waldawidgee began to dance. Such a dance, like a lily stalk in a whispering breeze swaying there under the cabin roof.

"Good feller!" I encouraged. "You dance proper feller."

She smiled in quick glee, picked up the chanting and started again with increased vim.

She danced amazingly, this untamed, merry girl woman of the wilds. I leaned back and watched her while that hypnotic rhythm floated dreamily through the ship. On arched toes, her girlish hands to shapely hips, she swayed with knees slightly bent to a sinuous, breathless movement. Her boyish head was inclined slightly forward, big eyes staring unseeing at the floor, an indefinable attitude as of listening. There was a suggestion of things unguessed at in all her pulsing body, a tense feeling she was seeking something, striving to capture something. Never had I seen such a dance, neither by white woman or coloured or aboriginal, not even on the "pictures". A quite intriguing experience. I'd wandered for years among the aboriginals, but never dreamed that any of them could dance like this. Perhaps away back in time some disgraced Malay dancer, banished to the proas, may have endowed her ancestry with his forbidden art.

When the Skipper returned with the dinghy he stepped down the companionway and exclaimed:

"Ho! Visitors. Ladies, too. Now you just clear out of this, you little tom-cats!"

But Waldawidgee giggled, laughed; then with hands on hips spun round and round in dizzy exhibition.

"Well, I'm blessed," exclaimed the Skipper. "The Dancing Dervish. Here, Pavlova, you dance your way ashore! Quick feller too!"

"She's a wonderful dancer," I suggested, "I wonder how she'd go to the gramophone."

Eagerly Herman set the gramophone going. The lubras listened all ears and eyes. Then Waldawidgee swayed her body to keep time to the white man's music, her face entranced as she captured the strange rhythm. Delighted at our encour-agement she did wonderfully well, this imp from the woods, dancing to the first civilized music she had ever heard. Perhaps she had heard music in her dreams.

The Skipper tried her with jazz. She took to it with delight and whirled around the cabin to the quickened rhythm. We were staggered. Perhaps far away back in that particular music was some primitive wail that brought response from her.

Perched on the companionway steps Gillagun stared down, listening to this strange music. Her polished skin seemed soft yet firm in the hurricane-lamp light. I wondered what feeling was expressed in her slumbrous eyes.

Eventually the Skipper had his work cut out to get rid of them. He had to spank Waldawidgee's tail up the companion-way steps. Finally, one with a cheeky pout, the other with solemn face that left things unsaid, they were hoisted up on deck and into their canoe. To a defiant stroke of the paddle they melted into the night.

"And that's that!" exclaimed the Skipper. "Now we can turn in. I'll bet the bucks ashore sent those two little she-devils here, but they can jolly well paddle back to camp again. There's enough trouble aboard with the downtrodden slaves without those little wretches adding further complications."

We stood up and prepared for bed. With a yawn the Skipper turned down the hurricane lamp very low and with sundry grunts and groans rolled over on his side to sleep. Herman was already gone to the vale of dreams. All was deathly silence. Just the low murmur of sleeping breaths in the ship, the kylies and that strange corroboree song now silent as the night. I was asleep.

Next morning I yawned, convinced I was dreaming of Waldawidgee the dancer and her mate Gillagun. For there they were curled up like two little black kittens, fast asleep on the cabin floor.

"I'll go hopping to hell!" exclaimed the Skipper.

Herman laughed.

It was a lovely dawn, ushering in a sunlit day with a gay breeze. Wagis was already paddling about in her canoe. A wisp of smoke arose from the Pumpkin where Willie was lighting the galley fire. Lazy calls echoed across the water to waken friends among the tribesmen ashore who were still sound asleep, coiled up in the ashes around the campfires. After breakfast our lady visitors reluctantly canoed ashore when they saw that the Skipper would really throw them overboard if they didn't go. Like spirits in the night they had come aboard again with not the faintest sound, had slept on the cabin floor between our bunks and we knew not one thing about it. With the first breath of dawn they had awakened and, noiseless as mice, pirated every little article that appealed to them and could be hidden within their hair, under their armpits and legs, and within their tiny loincloths.

But the Skipper was a "wake-up". Roaring like an old bull crocodile, he ordered them ashore. He was not above searching them with heavy hand. Waldawidgee flounced sulky tail because at the last moment she could not wheedle a pipe, but the Skipper snatched that tail and withdrew a cool half- pound of Nigger Twist tobacco. Waldawidgee bounded up the companionway steps like a scalded cat.

"And don't dare show your faces aboard again!" roared the Skipper as they leapt into the canoe and pushed off.

Waldawidgee poked a face. She stood up, turned her back and bent down.

"Come aboard again and I'll kiss it with my foot!" roared the Skipper.

But girlish laughter was his aggravating answer.

"There you are," growled the Skipper as he turned upon us. "The

Stone Age flappers of the coast can diddle us at any turn. And yet civilization demands of us that we carry the white man's burden."

With arms raised helplessly to the skies he lumbered below to prepare breakfast.

We had just finished a hearty meal when a stalwart savage with frowning brow canoed over and reported a crocodile basking on a sandbank at a distant creek mouth. He wanted the loan of a rifle to go and shoot it.

"He's got a fat hope," growled the Skipper disgustedly. 'What does the simple savage take us for? Thinks we may be silly enough to lend him a rifle! Like to amuse himself with a few pot shots at us, would he? Even if he did mean to bring it back there'd be no crocodile—he'd simply claim a stick of tobacco for his alleged trouble."

And so it proved, as we learned from Mitchemore's boys later in the day. The aboriginal is by no means simple as he seems.

XXIV

WHERE ALL THINGS EAT TO LIVE

A MORNING came when Mitchemore's crowd cruised away on the hunt. Herman took our boys and rowed upstream.

"I'll try around the river mouth," I suggested to the Skipper.

"Right. I'm not leaving this boat one moment. There'd be nothing left if I did." And he glanced ashore where now each day seemed to be adding to the number of natives coming in from the hills.

Behind a lone mangrove nearest the sparkling sea I took up a strategic position, beside the channel that led out to sea. On the seaward side there was now a huge mud flat. Across it marched a host of birds in whites and greys, browns and blacks. Rich feeding grounds those flats when the tide is out. Incredible the life in that mud, secrets of nature undreamed of. A world can exist in a spoonful of mud—a microbe world uncountable, insect life, invisible eggs and babies of things that will grow into we know not what. Some may be born to live in the depths, some to crawl out and live upon the land, some to live both in water and upon land, some even to fly. That mud. may even hold chemicals, or the kaolins or ochres that man can transform into paint. It may quite possibly contain gas too, or mineral, or some ingredient of a cement. If it were old, old mud it might now be rock containing a voiceless story of ages long past, of petrified fern or fish, animal or bird or lizard, even of man.

And now away across this one mud flat were trillions of live things of all species and sizes and shapes and colours and habits. Many are engaged in the one fierce object, to fight and eat one another. Of the more visible things, the flat was now alive with the ever restless hoppy fish with the ever restless sail. It was a dreamy kind of day.

Suddenly a crocodile appeared some hundreds of yards farther out towards the channel mouth. An inexperienced man would not have glanced at it again. A man would hardly have noticed an almost submerged stick drifting almost imper-ceptibly towards shore. Thus he swam, moving just a shade faster than tide or current, which might have been against him. Just the snout tip and eyes and bony ridge of "forehead", like a barely floating stick. He propelled himself by unseen movement from the tip of his tail. At the shore edge he rested with his snout on the mud, but there was only the domed tip around his eyes visible. He appeared now exactly like half a coconut shell stranded at the waters edge. No one walking along the channel edge would have dreamed he was a fourteen-foot crocodile. Only the most alert crocodile hunter might have guessed so from a hundred yards' distance. And thus the brute remained for nearly two hours.

Out in midstream the full length of a crocodile appeared. They come with uncanny suddenness.

This brute's snout tip was visible, his eyes and forehead and the serrations all down his back and along his long, flexible tail. Momentarily he would submerge until only his eyes and snout tip were visible. Then up would bob the serrations along his back, hut no more. He was just too far away for me to risk a shot at his cunning little brain, for a miss might spoil a chance should a big fellow decide to come ashore. Presently five of the brutes were visible gently swimming across the channel mouth. All morning some were visible, constantly cruising from one bank to the other across the channel mouth just where it empties into the sea. They were intercepting fish coming in or swimming out to sea. They do this most cunningly. Should a fish dodge one it must run the gauntlet of another and yet another. Now and again an unseen disturbance caused violent upheaval of the water as one in hot pursuit chased a fish below. Very occasionally a fish frantically broke surface only to be rushed by a saurian farther downstream. When two big fellows met under below chasing the same fish the shallows fairly boiled. This was only when they were actually chasing fish. Their surface cruising was almost imperceptible, but could swerve into instant speed when necessary.

Apparently none were inclined to come ashore, or come farther up the channel from their strategic position, until this phase of their fishing was over. The hunter must remain motionless in quiet patience.

The tide was now right out, the sea edge a mile distant from the glistening mud flat teeming with life. Many birds of different sizes were scattered all over it, running, or hopping, or stalking, or crouching, or standing motionless, as in their different ways they captured their prey. Countless numbers of "sausages" hopped and scurried everywhere; grotesque little things were these sea-land-and-mud fish, hopping about their burrows while chasing food and enjoying the sunlight and few hours' safety from the voracious things of the sea. Presently they would be forced to hop down into their dug-outs when the waters came creeping back, bringing enemies who with poking snout and tooth would claw down after them. Then woe betide any amongst them who had been too lazy to dig their foxholes deep enough.

Millions of other energetic things were moving on that glistening, slowly bubbling mud flat. Tiny crabs smaller than a threepenny-bit in teeming battalions all quickly manoeuvring about and around one another, all in feverish energy taking toll of every minute of freedom and sunlight, all fiercely seeking and eating infinitesimal things that also got their life from the mud. These crablets had two claws, one a tiny thing constantly picking up and lifting things to the mouth, the other a large white one protectingly held across the mouth and fiercely champing. Those countless thousands of moving white dots were the fighting claws. Every now and again a tiny crablet would pick on another and, sidling up to him, make a jab instantly parried by the opponent's fighting claw. I singled one out and watched him. Though beaten off in half a dozen fights, he was still seeking a weaker victim when my interest waned.

Among these tiny crabs were countless other things. A man would never notice such pinpoints of life were he not sitting in such places hour after hour, watching them while waiting for larger game. Among the crabs were grey things like tiny flies; and ant things that scurried; and crawly and wriggly things; hairy and spiky and snaky things; leggy and finny things; and gaping, motionless things that vanished as if a lid had been drawn over them; and absurd hoppy things barely visible to the eye. All fiercely busy popping in and out of holes as danger approached or receded.

Occasionally a long-legged bird would come with a dazzling run, but in a flash his prey would have vanished. A thousand crabs or hoppy things disappeared in the twinkling of an eye. The bird would crouch with neck outstretched in tense readi-ness, his ruby eye fairly alight with eagerness to snatch and eat. Should some incautious thing peep from its burrow a second too soon, the bird was on to it like a flash. The bird would jerk its bill in the air and the prey was swallowed on the instant. Or it might miss and snatch only a beakful of mud. In ruffled anger it would snap its beak from side to side to cleanse it. All this time it was threatened by a circle of thousands of champing claws and goggling eyes, for only those things within radius of the bird's reach would pop down. With a stately, contemptuous step the bird would stride on while many things retreated warily before it, sidling around it always just out of reach. The bird would be marking out a new victim and estimating its distance, judging the time for another swift run. But all the funny things around it were estimating too and when it moved—they vanished!

Not all the birds hunted like that. Some hunted slowly and methodically. Others hunted by playing a waiting game.

The crocodiles were still enjoying good fishing across the channel mouth. A dozen of the brutes were visible now, but not one near enough to offer chance of a fatal shot. Away behind was the quiet hush of the mangroves, out in front a mile across the mud flats the murmur of the dreamy sea.

Around the roots of my hide-out tree there stuck up many "cobbler's pegs". From a round hole sidled a dull-green crab, fully the size of a two-shilling piece. Gazing slyly up, he stared for a while, then considering I was not worth bothering about commenced the serious business of dining. His were two dainty claws, the pincers of which were delicately curved and pointed. With the tips of these he fastidiously "feathered" the mud, then unhurriedly and daintily brought food to his lips. He worked both claws constantly hut unhurriedly. A little hoppy fish came wobbling along, one of the small variety. He sidled to the rounded lip of the crab's hole and regarded the occupier steadfastly from big, protruding, stupid eyes. Occasionally it turned its bovine head towards me, but was much more interested in the crab. Obviously he admired that crab, real hero worship. The crab carried on with his job as if used to this homage. They may have been gossiping, discussing the glorious morning and freshness of the food, discussing their neighbours in this great mud world of theirs.

"Queer mates," I thought. And just then the hoppy fish nosedived down the hole. So, they shared the same compartment.

Two large crocodiles came cruising downstream but submerged and went past me underwater, to reappear with the others at the channel mouth. Annoying brutes. The first brute of all, he of the coconut head, was still visible away out at the water's edge. A crane was now regarding him solemnly. That lucky crane had chased its prey right to the edge. That is how the lurking crocodile secures an occasional tit-bit. The crane running after its prospective victim loses caution as its prey scurries closer to the water. One flip of the crocodile's tail and the crane is spinning out and over to fall into an open mouth. But this crane had stopped in the nick of time, staring straight down at that ugly, almost submerged snout, staring as if mesmerized.

Two more fish hoppers came hopping inquiringly to peep at my toes. Their silly-looking heads quizzed sideways and up and down as they hopped around the toes, curious to know what manner of fish these were. One of these inquisitive fellows was fully four inches long, his bull-shaped head with the foolish bulbs of eyes, his glistening round body so like a poodle spaniel's, his quaint tail a sharp point sticking out behind like the bowsprit of a boat.

And all over the mudbank were many birds, from giant jabirus to cranes of all sizes, herons, ibis, waders, pelicans, cormorants, seagulls and sea snipe and many others. Fish and sharks and turtle, seasnakes and crocodiles in the water; fish hawks swooping from above; countless things in and on the flats; and a man sitting there—all intensely concentrated on taking life.

And then a big, ugly snout broke water quite close. The dirty grey head rose as the snout wiggled up on the mud. The bulk of a big old-man crocodile was half-slithering, half waddling up on the mud. A monstrous thing snakily waddling straight towards the tree as if confident that nothing in life could match his strength and ferocity and cunning. Until we grow wiser we humans think very much the same about ourselves, until we realize that a tiny microbe can bring us low. To the smack of the bullet he roared once harshly as his great bulk catapulted in a series of thrashings, in vain struggling to throw himself back to the water.

Goodness knows what his weight was. He was seventeen feet long with a barrel like a bullock, but one ounce of lead ended his life.

The Skipper would have been much more pleased had the result been two fellows about ten feet long each, for the medium skins are the best. But men, like crocodiles and birds and fish and crabs, cannot always pick their victims in Crocodile Land.

XXV

LIFE OF THE WILD

BUT other unsuspected things, large things, can be hidden in mud too. In a number of these creeks, and in arms of the sea, the tide goes right out in places, leaving only the muddy channel. There is nothing around but the gloom of the mangroves, or jungle-vine scrub. Where the water has been there is a slimy, twisting roadway of soft mud, opalescent at times with the colours of decaying vegetable gases. Mysterious, with every here and there slow-rising bubbles that bulge in a film of slime before they explode, or quietly subside. It may be gas rising, or air from some living thing down there. Occasionally there may sound the "Plop!" "Plop!" of falling mangrove pods. Otherwise, an eerie silence.

But—invisible there may be a huge old crocodile who has buried himself in the slurry. His belly so full of fish that he has been too lazy to drift with the tide back into the deeper waterholes, or to the river. In his soft couch in the liquid slurry he will sleep while awaiting the turning of the tide. Often we have examined such poisonous pools of slimy, liquid mud. The aboriginals enter into them, walk carefully in a line, prodding with their spear hafts as cautiously they step ahead. Then—a hiss or a cluck. A spear haft has prodded some living thing, a log that is not a log.

We got a number of crocodiles like this, buried deep in mud. No visible sign of life, nothing but a noisome mudhole. Only experience and the wary probing of the spear can detect them. They would not move unless prodded too sharply by the point of a harpoon. I used to wonder what these crocodiles thought, what uneasy feeling at the prod of spear or harpoon. They would know the water was gone, that they were marooned in a bed of mud. Every questing prod of the spear must have sent a chill of fear through and through them.

With eyes that talked, the aboriginal would signal to his mates. We would gather round. The spear would prod farther up to detect the shoulders, the neck, the skull. The aboriginal's eyes would gleam. His spear would gently rest upon the skull. The others would step softly in. The harpoon men would gently prod down to rest their points on a vital spot. At a signal of their eyes they would thrust, while leaping upward so that the weight of their bodies would deeply imbed the harpoon. The agonized jaws would rise with a gurgling, muddy bellow as the tail swept up and the aboriginals leapt away. But the rifles would crack and a coughing, writhing thing would be lashing in the mud.

Thus we shot out creek after creek. And Mitchemore shot out creek after creek. Like our Skipper he did no shooting. His full-time job was to look after his cutter, the *Pumpkin,* and arrange that his chief half-caste shooter kept a ceaseless eye on the little girl, Wagis. For not only was there the ever present danger of some Tarzan warrior seizing and running away with her, but she was always into the thick of everything as well. Paddling her tiny canoe, she would seek to he the leader into the most gloomy creeks, into the maze of the creeper-entangled swamps. One lash of a crocodile's tail and Wagis and her toy canoe would be no more.

But we aboard the *Lotus* knew it was not the crocodile old Mitchemore feared most. It was wild men.

Back on the river at sunset, smoke was lazily arising from the native cooking fires. The *Pumpkin* was just gliding to anchorage, her canoes pulling ashore with the men shouting to the tribesmen details of the day's adventures. Hilarious, it seemed. Mitchemore told us later that the cause of the mirth was a tribesman overbalancing as he thrust with the harpoon. The next second he was in the water with a crocodile at his heels. It was only Willie firing a bullet straight down the open jaws that saved the man. Thus he lived to laugh at his own escape in corroboree many a time. Aboard the ketch the Skipper was preparing the sundown meal. Herman was climbing aboard with six good skins.

"Just as well there's one shooter aboard can help to keep the tucker bags filled," remarked the Skipper.

Six good skins for one shooter and those aboriginals in a day was very good indeed. A record. Old Mitchemore with all his crowd was only averaging three good skins a day. Of course many of the brutes could not be recovered. Then again, there was much time lost in cruising along the coast from river to river, and from creek to creek.

Suddenly a violent harangue broke out from the *Pumpkin's* deck, the shrill voice of an old gin in screeching invective yowling out to the camp across the river. She was calling dawdlers from the *Pumpkin* to come aboard for the evening meal, yelling bloodthirsty threats if they didn't hurry. That old lubra was an unusual character amongst natives. She was a wanderer from tribe to tribe. They would have killed her years ago but that they had some superstitious dread of her. She had failed to hold two husbands; both abandoned her because she "goes blind". Years ago, wandering and alone and in terror of the night, she had boarded Mitchemore's craft just at sundown, and had been with him ever since. She was a capital lubra aboard ship, looking after things and bossing everyone, old Mitchemore included. Willie alone escaped her domination. She had proved invaluable to Mitchemore and he knew he would never lose her because she never roamed at night, while for her the little old *Pumpkin* was an ever safe haven from the terrors of darkness. With the regularity of clockwork her sight quickly faded towards sundown. She lost her sight exactly as the sun set, and regained it an hour before sunrise. She always rose then and commenced getting breakfast ready, another invaluable help in getting a start for the day because aboriginal workers are notorious for sleeping in. Just before sundown the old gin became very fretful and hurried the others up to finish their tasks so that she could be safely camped before her sight failed. And that was what she was doing now, hurrying up her wayward charges and waking the river about it.

Just as we were about to sit down to the evening meal two little black heads popped over the companionway.

"Get to hell out of this!" roared the Skipper.

But Waldawidgee giggled and next instant was down the steps and smilingly standing in the cabin.

"I thought I told you not to come aboard again," roared the Skipper.

"Brother belonga we he bringem us," answered Walda-widgee aggrievedly.

"Oh, your brothers brought you, did they?" said the Skipper suspiciously. He poked his head out of the hatch and called to the crew and half a dozen tribesmen for'ard. Yes, their brothers had brought the girls aboard, so the crew swore. They pointed to the brothers, three husky natives squatting down gorging rice and fish.

"Ou ai!" nodded the "brothers".

"I don't believe a word of it," growled the Skipper as he stepped back into the cabin. "However, we'll give them a feed now they're aboard. Must preserve the *entente cordiale*. Here's a bar of soap, you dirty little wretches. Now go up for'ard and wash yourselves, you grubby pigs."

We could hear Waldawidgee making a joke of it, laughing with the crew as Jacky showed them how to use the soap, screeching when it got into her eyes. Then came the hilarious roar as Jacky doused her lathered head in the bucket. Gillagun took it much more seriously, seemed to like playing with the unfamiliar lather. They came back down into the cabin wreathed in smiles.

"And very little else," growled the Skipper. "Squat down there on that bag and don't come one inch nearer us. There's your kai-kai."

Seriously then they squatted down over a huge bowl of rice, half a wild goose, johnny-cakes, and tinned butter and jam. With amazing speed they ate with their fingers until the Skipper handed them a spoon.

"Pigs!" he said disgustedly. "This is the way to eat rice."

Waldawidgee tried, and near swallowed the spoon. To her choking gasps Gillagun almost split her sides in laughter, her first laugh and a good one. The Skipper gave up in disgust.

"Barbarians," he growled, "gorge yourselves till you bust. And I hope you bite your fingers."

I almost thought they would burst.

"Just look at their stomachs!" exclaimed the Skipper. "You could crack a flea on them."

When they could eat no more they stretched their already distended stomachs with tea drunk from a jam tin.

Waldawidgee at last with a contented sigh slowly eased back on the cabin floor, hands tenderly on her stomach. Regarding us with half-closed eyes, she giggled dreamily. Gillagun followed her example with her big eyes half closed and a smile instead of a giggle.

The Skipper lit the hurricane lamp.

"If you were to tread on their tummies now," he declared, "they'd explode like a cannon."

He rolled a cigarette, the two regarding him with dreamy speculation. As he lit the cigarette Waldawidgee came to life. With one easy movement she had risen, stepped across the cabin, taken the cigarette from the Skipper's lips, transferred it to her own, puffed, and had climbed into his bunk. She put her arms behind her head and dangled one small leg over the bunk. She puffed again.

"Hussy!" exclaimed the Skipper.

With a smile Herman made Gillagun a cigarette. She enjoyed it.

The Skipper got the "gun" and sprayed the first of the early evening cockroaches. The lubras laughed hilariously.

"Laugh! You little hussies, laugh!" admonished the Skipper as he made a flying squirt at a hurrying cockroach on the cabin roof. "It's you should be sprayed with insecticide, not the 'roaches. You should be ashamed of yourself if you had any moral sense at all, which you have not. Here you are on a dark night down below in a ship's cabin with three bad men and you are enjoying it as if you were having the time of your life. You are the white man's burden all right; what civilization is going to do with the likes of you I'm sure I don't know."

Waldawidgee giggled. Gillagun smiled as she gazed seriously at our three faces in turn. I was looking at her finger. She held it out instantly—the top joint of her first finger on the right hand was missing.

"Her mother bit it off when she was a baby," explained Herman. "It is a custom with a number of tribes around here."

Waldawidgee leaned across and calmly took a fresh cigarette from my lips. She blew a cloud of smoke at the Skipper and he lectured her on manners to her keen delight. She arranged the blankets on his bunk, put the pillow under her and treated us to some tomboyish gymnastics. She was indescribably funny and we enjoyed it. Gillagun no doubt wished she could join in as hilariously carefree. Waldawidgee's personality was amazing. She took possession of the ship as she had of the Skipper's bunk, laughing away his serious remonstrances. She tried on his big straw hat and joined in the laugh as it flopped down over her ears. She threw it to the floor. Then jumped up and stretched her tiny figure in all its becoming lines. Twining her arms around the Skipper's neck, she laid her cheek on his chest.

"Well, I'll go hopping to hell!" exclaimed the Skipper.

She giggled, drew him to his bunk and climbed upon his knee. She giggled again, laid her head upon his shoulder and pretended to go to sleep. The Skipper put her across his knee and spanked her, then lifted her up the companionway to the deck.

"Get to hell out of this!" he ordered.

But his back was no sooner turned than she was back down into the cabin, laughing.

"I never believed in reincarnation before," said the Skipper, "but if this practised little minx is not some reincarnation of an Eastern dancing girl then I'll eat my hat."

She smiled mystifyingly, stretched herself like a sleepy kitten, slowly relaxed. Her smile said, "What next?"

"Whoever would have thought to see that in a lubra?" said the Skipper. 'Well, I'm going to pack them ashore now and they can take their surly brothers with them, whether they like it or no. And there's to be no strangers camping up on deck with the crew tonight. There's too many myall bushmen drifting in to that camp ashore for my liking."

XXVI

DANGEROUS NIGHTS

ONE afternoon the Skipper was poring over charts while Herman was tinkering with the engine. The crew had rowed away to spear fish. A canoe came gliding alongside full of painted tribesmen, who held up big green and purplish crabs. I could see no weapons in the canoe, but they might have tomahawks fastened to the bottom of the canoe with clay. Another canoe came, loaded with barramundi. Each man demanded payment in tobacco despite the fact that our own boys would return with plenty of fish.

I left them arguing with the Skipper, took the rifle and rowed ashore, dallying a while until the Skipper got rid of the persistent tribesmen. Warily walking through the mangroves fringing the river bank, I lifted the rifle towards a black snout but immediately saw it was only a dead hawk floating downstream. Cautiously gazing up and down a slimy runway I crossed it and stepped into the mangroves. Instantly I wheeled around, with the rifle muzzle poking into the belly of Big Jimmy. I'd expected a charging crocodile but not this— he would have been a dead man had it not been my habit never to walk with a rifle cocked. I cursed him with beating heart, his big, red-painted body standing there among the leaves with the rifle muzzle pressed against him. Motioning him to walk ahead of me, I prowled on, but presently heard the busy "phut-phut-phut-phut"of Mitchemore's tiny engine.

"Pumpkin," growled Big Jimmy.

We turned back then, for the craft would have scared any basking crocodiles. Soon the laughing voices of lubras, the song of men, the howl of a piccaninny came to us through the trees as the battered little vessel phutted by. After a noiseless walk we came out of the mangroves on to the small beach. The *Pumpkin* had anchored a hundred yards upstream ahead of the *Lotus*. The crew of the *Pumpkin* were calling to friends ashore, and in the midst of their din Mitchemore was shouting something across to the Skipper. With the little black kewpie of a piccanin aboard her tiny canoe, Wagis paddled downstream towards the river mouth. I rowed aboard, took a kerosene tin full of crabs ashore to cook them—and did a very foolish thing. Left the rifle aboard. Four of the bucks strolled from their camp and all started gathering twigs after I'd make a fire. I told them I did not want them, but they stood and squatted around. When the crabs were cooked I lifted the tin off, poured out the water and walked towards the dinghy. Immediately then a big, hook-nosed native sprang in my way.

"Me wantem pay longa spear-em pish!" he demanded.

"Captain pay you. Get out!" I replied, and pushed past him.

Before I reached the dinghy an old woman shrilled a suggestion to the warrior. He came at the run and again barred my way.

"Me wantem rifle belonga Mitchemore!" he demanded "Shootem alligator. Mitchemore givem me."

"Mitchemore would not promise you my rifle," I snapped. "Get out of it."

There was a definite aggressiveness in his bearing; he was a powerful, athletic brute. He imagined the rifle was in the dinghy and he could bluff the loan of it. I pushed past him again, feeling glad both vessels were in plain view not a hundred yards out in midstream. When I rowed back to the *Lotus* Mitchemore was aboard, looking worried.

"What did that man want?" he asked.

"He demanded payment for fish he said he speared for the Skipper. Then he demanded a rifle. Said you promised him one.

"That fellow is dangerous," growled Mitchemore. "Only a while back he killed a man on the sandspit. Chopped him to pieces with a tomahawk."

Then the Skipper opened a tirade because I'd gone ashore unarmed.

"You reckon these natives are harmless," he stormed. "So they are until they catch you alone without a gun," and he settled down to quite a tongue thrashing.

Both men were uneasy, as also were Herman and Willie.

I was sorry, for this was an ideal camp for shooting. To me the tribesmen, providing a man took ordinary precautions, were quite all right; but both these men thought more of their boats than they did, I believe, of their lives. Their boats were their livelihood and their homes. They would be bankrupt and lost without them.

That night there were two large batches of campfires, one lot on each bank of the river, both vessels in between. Very unusual, such large fires. These natives were of two tribal groups and, although apparently friendly, something was brewing between them. Mitchemore's natives while ashore had picked up a hint here and there, but whether we were involved or not we could not tell. When it got properly dark, canoes began to paddle from one bank to the other, passing across stream like shadows.

Smoking idly up on deck I knew what was in Mitchemore's and the Skipper's minds. A very lonely spot. Two vessels, to the native mind crammed with riches. In the black of night a sudden rush of canoes from both banks, a leap aboard and "They'd do it," growled the Skipper, "only they know there are plenty of rifles aboard and we know how to use them."

"You're a thought-reader," I said.

"I've been years at this game," he replied, "years of prowling along the coast. It's the natives' minds I try to read."

Mitchemore suddenly jumped up and shouted, "Look out there longa alligator!"

We strained our eyes to the bank and Mitchemore sighed in relief as Wagis's tiny canoe emerged from the shadows.

"I heard a splash," he growled. "That little fool Wagis has been bathing by the bank."

"Risky," shrugged the Skipper.

"Of course, but what can you do with a fool of a girl who believes a crocodile won't take her. The crocodile is her totem."

"There's worse than crocodiles," hinted the Skipper.

"I know, but Willie keeps a look-out. He's been with me sixteen years and I've learned to trust him. Wagis has been with me fourteen years now. They know the natives, know the language, but all the same I daren't leave her out of mine or Willie's sight lest a native take her."

On both banks of the river a wild corroboree song broke out, swelled to steady volume. We sat on deck, smoking and listening. This was a different corroboree from the hunting songs of the nights before. There seemed a vibrant threat in that savage rhythm coming from the stamping feet of painted warriors, in deep grunts hoarsely shouted, in the hollow drumming of the lubras. A shrill, inciting menace in those women's voices.

"A war corroboree," grunted Mitchemore. "I'm going aboard. Good night."

"Good night," answered the Skipper. "I think I'll turn in too."

The next day we took it easy. Tired of inaction, in the afternoon I rowed ashore intent on a shot at an old-man crocodile that habitually dozed on a sandbank in a creek nearby. Had hardly stepped ashore when a powerful savage stepped from the mangroves.

"Tabac!" he demanded with outstretched paw.

Half a dozen of his band came to grin each side of me. Hefty, cheeky bucks these fellows, smelling of grease and stale war paint, their naked bodies a glowing red, polished so by powder from a burnt ant-bed. They were myalls of a fighting tribe, a stamp of men I've always admired. No cringing aboriginals these fellows.

I stepped back, swung the rifle unobtrusively between me and that hairy paw threateningly close to my throat, and glanced swiftly to see if the Skipper was watching. He was. He swung a rifle across his knee as the big fellow's mates tried to edge behind me and the dinghy.

I lost no time in getting aboard. The big buck was Moodoorish, the man who had killed young Renouf at Point Blaze a few miles away.

Next morning Mitchemore weighed anchor and left with the tide en route for Darwin, well satisfied with his last month's bag—a hundred and six hides. As the tiny vessel drew away, the river echoed to the long-drawn farewells of the natives. Little Wagis waved to us from the stern, standing beside her toy canoe. We up-anchored in the afternoon, with a few natives aboard who craved a "lift". Among them were Waldawidgee and Gillagun and their alleged brothers and friends returning to their tribe at the Daly River, farther west along the coast. They also would show us fresh water when our tanks needed filling.

We were out to sea again and rounded Point Blaze heading west, the coast a stretch of sandy beaches, mangroves and scrub jungle. It was blowing hard at sunset when the anxious Skipper just made the wide, shallow inlet of what proved to be a gloomy creek. It was exposed to the sea and here we pitched and tossed all that black night in a howl of wind.

From out the darkness a log seemed to glide to the rolling deck and two little black shadows leaped aboard as the canoe fell away. It just happened. I called to the Skipper and he jumped up on deck staring at one tiny lubra who appeared to be a child of eight, the other but a few years older.

"Get to the devil out of this," roared the Skipper. "Hi!" he yelled to the shadowy canoe, "come back alonga here! Take him this feller girl back longa shore!"

But the canoe had drifted away into the blackness, not understanding or unwilling to understand. The Skipper made Jacky shout out, but the wind shrieked in derision.

"These flaming natives are taking my ship for a tourist craft," fumed the Skipper, "and me for a blasted fool. Why didn't you block them from coming aboard, you black malingerer," he yelled at Jacky. "I've a flaming good mind to make you row them ashore again!"

But it would have meant a long, hazardous pull, with the return trip pitch dark against a howling wind and tide. A sulky crew indeed would have been forced to man the dinghy.

Even so they would he scared to land. Uneasy at the thought of tribesmen awaiting them ashore, tribesmen too who would be insulted at us thus unceremoniously bundling their women ashore without a load of presents.

Waldawidgee put her arms around the tiny lubra and fondled her.

"Quarquor sister belonga me," she smiled up at the Skipper. "Come alonga Daly we feller, see mother belonga us."

"Sister my eye!" growled the Skipper. "She's no more your sister than those hulking louts for'ard are your brothers."

Wrathfully he went below.

And in a moment we were all there, except the crew for'ard. Waldawidgee brought her smiling "sister" and the other girl, A-but. Young Quarquor immediately made herself at home. Claimed a cigarette with a flip of the fingers and, puffing away, calmly proceeded to examine everything in the cabin.

"Why not take the whole blooming ship while you're at it," growled the Skipper.

Quarquor smiled with a flash of dazzling teeth and appropriated his comb.

"Drop that!" howled the Skipper and he snatched it from her. She grimaced, turned her lack and showed him a glossily naked little backside.

Bright-eyed, she walked down the long cabin towards the fo'c'sle bulkhead. In the little dark hole leading to the fo'c'sle cabin she knelt, the yellow-white soles of her feet strangely plain under the glow of the hurricane lamp. Across those soles were the long, dirt-black scars and cuts where stone and shell and thorn had ripped her. The bare feet of this child could carry her with ease where the feet of a white man would fail. She stepped into the little dark cabin, stared at the fo'c'sle bunks, the blankets and clothes, the litter of paint pots and coiled-up anchor chains and rope within the fo'c'sle head. We could see her poking about like a ship's rat. She reached first for the tobacco tin which was my ash tray. Adroitly she transferred the cigarette butts to the sure pocket of her hair. The pipe scrapings she rolled into a nicotine-saturated ball and rammed behind her ear. She treated every ash tray thus, then searched with eyes and poking fingers into every cranny of the bulkheads, the ship's ribs, anywhere where a cigarette might have been laid.

"That little devil knows her way about a ship," growled the Skipper as the laughing little lubra came crawling back and into the big cabin.

She was the tiniest lubra I'd ever seen. No child at all, just another child woman. The Skipper nicknamed her "The Diminutive". She may have been a sister of Waldawidgee's; she certainly possessed abundance of her confidence and cheek.

"Little hell-cats," said the Skipper uneasily. "The sooner I land this harem the better I'll be pleased."

"There's a stiff breeze blowing in the right direction out¬side. We'll be off the Daly tomorrow evening," I sympathized.

"Can't be too soon," he mumbled. "This crowd are in league with the crew above."

As usual he was thinking of the boat, of the things that might happen. There were a number of Larrakia men ashore whom our boys knew, but there were many Mulluk-Mulluk, Pongo-Pongo, and Dillik-Dillik also, while the myalls amongst them were some crowd down from the distant hills. Our boys were scared of these.

All the natives in the back country ashore, including the wanderers from the hills, would soon be what we vaguely call "civilized". For their tribal boundaries are already broken. Constantly bands are travelling through tribal country even to Darwin, to make contact with the "white man town". It is a pity. I'd like to see Arnhem Land, and another last wild area west of the Daly, another in the Kimberleys north of the King Leopold Ranges, and a big area west of the Centre left entirely to the primitive people and their animals and birds.

Certainly there was something very suspicious about these young girls. They had prepared for an expected night's entertainment. Their bodies shone with the healthy gloss of the native girl after a vigorous bath. No taint of human or goanna fat upon their lithe young bodies, no wild animal smell as a lubra freshly risen from the campfire ashes would surely possess. Good features, despite thick nose and lips, markedly different from the lubras of the interior, and from the great majority along the coast too. Their fresh, boyish-looking heads were clean, their short cropped hair thick and crisp.

The air became heavy from cigarette smoke and warm breaths.

The Skipper sat frowning, almost impossible to send the girls ashore now. Black night, a howling wind, a tide against us. Nor would we order them up on deck to be at the mercy of the crew and tribesmen for'ard. At last he threw Gillagun a blanket. She pulled it over her. With dream-filled eyes she seemed to sink into its folds, then slowly coiled up upon the cabin floor. He threw the Diminutive a blanket. It flopped around her head. She drew it around her in delight. Her little possum head gazed around once, then disappeared as shecoiled up beside her "sister". Waldawidgee reached out plump arms and drew her blanket around her with a caressing twist of the body, framing her blue-black hair. Her childishly smiling face peeped from the blanket folds. She yawned, half laughed, stretched lingeringly, then disappeared as she snuggled up beside the others. In three minutes all were fast asleep.

"And that's that," said the Skipper decisively.

"The innocents slumber," I remarked.

"Innocents be damned!" exploded the Skipper. "Here we have all the ingredients for a first-class bloody massacre. A bit more copy for the papers this time if it came off, for an Australian author would be chopped up in it."

Herman yawned. So did I.

156

"All right," growled the Skipper, "turn in if that's all you are interested. But sleep lightly."

He reached to the rack and took down a rifle, loaded the magazine. With the weapon beside his bunk he lay down fully clothed, staring up at the white-painted cabin top.

We sailed soon after dawn. There was a big sea outside, but a strong following wind fairly raced us along. We entered the broad mouth of the Daly just at sundown. Here the river appeared to be about tree miles across, a small sea of muddy water rippling in waves, thrashed in places by tortuous currents. Low-lying shores, densely fringed with mangroves. We ran up river about a mile where a densely wooded island divided the river into two channels, one deep and one shallow. The river soon narrowed to a short mile across with the mud-banks only a few feet above high water. Under the misty stars we anchored at Duck Point and the crew and most of their friends lost no time in going ashore, hastened by the Skipper's threats. We had found them out in a number of outrageous lies during the day and the Skipper was very wroth.

"Come aboard early morning time," he yelled at the departing dinghy, "and bring your swags with you or I'll break your necks. Good riddance to bad rubbish," he growled to me. "For the most worthless creature in creation recommend me to the Australian aboriginal."

"You don't seem to be able to do without them," I laughed.

"Who can - in this land of sin and sorrow?" he demanded.

Through a canopy of filmy cloud, star specks beamed down upon the tiny craft. The banks were two hazy black walls between which a dark expanse of water was rushing out to sea with fiercely murmurous sound. It was wonderful to listen to in the hushed silence of night. You gradually breathed in some vague sense of the mighty power encompassing this atom of woodwork straining at the anchor chain, the vastness of this hissing, sucking, shining strength racing out to sea. If a man slipped overboard he would swiftly drown in the night.

XXVII

THE CREW IN DISGRACE

MORNING broke mistily, with a land breeze that whipped spray from the waves. The tide was just going out. Hopeless to attempt moving against it. We could see it now. By night it was one mighty, eerie sound; now we could see it in hissing, tossing, twisting might furiously racing the one way, armies of urgently hurrying little waves. I wondered what power would be generated if but portion of that immeasurable force could be harnessed. Some day we will do that with all our tidal rivers. All around our coast we will have stations relaying into the continent this inexhaustible source of cheap power.

"There are the slaves," nodded the Skipper, and we saw their dark figures on the bank away upstream, preparing to launch the dinghy. "Nice and punctual, aren't they," added the Skipper sarcastically. "It's breakfast time. I was half hoping some of the Daly River boys would have cut their throats by now. But no such luck!"

"They're not such a bad crowd," I said.

"As good as any other," admitted the Skipper grudgingly, "which isn't saying much. Here they come. They wouldn't be so smart if they had to pull the dinghy."

They came racing down to the ketch, Paddy steering. No need to use the oars for the current was carrying the dinghy as if it were cork. Paddy, a delighted grin on his ugly face, steered beautifully. They dashed straight down beside the ketch and snatched the rail.

"Just as well they didn't miss," smiled Herman, "though the Skipper would have laughed if they'd gone spinning downstream."

The grinning crew leaped aboard and secured the dinghy astern. Hurrying for'ard they squatted down to breakfast as if they had not dined for a week. After which they calmly curled up on the cabin top and fell fast asleep.

"I thought they went ashore last night to sleep," I nodded.

Herman laughed. "Why should they waste time sleeping ashore, when they can sleep on the boat."

Somehow I couldn't blame the crew. In their place perhaps I would have done the same.

Suddenly a blackfellow stepped in full view from the trees ashore on the west bank of the river. The head and shoulders of another appeared among the bushes behind. As the Skipper came on deck more black heads appeared among the trees. The first man walked out on the bare bank and waved a green branch. We waved in reply. The two closest to him stepped out and waved their arms. They had no spears. They yelled something, then a dozen black figures spilled out from the trees. Behind them appeared others climbing trees to peer out across the river. Their faces were grotesque, painted around by a broad circle of white ochre. Red and white bars were painted across their chests.

We woke the crew. They stared sleepily towards shore, somewhat uneasily. The natives shouted and began making arm, hand and body signs. Paddy answered in a shouted, long-drawn sentence. The figures leaped back and vanished.

"Do you know what he said?" asked Herman.

"No!" snapped the Skipper. "What was it?"

"He said, 'If you want tobacco there's plenty of it up on the bank in my swag.' "

"I thought I told you to bring your swags aboard with you!" roared the Skipper. "And what do you mean by thieving my tobacco for those myalls?"

But the crew remained sulkily silent. Herman only knew a word or two of this lingo, but he had guessed correctly. The Skipper was furious. It seemed natural enough to me. The crew had to "pay their way" ashore, otherwise they would not have been welcomed.

I trained the glasses on the trees. There was only a thick fringe of them, with an open plain behind. Presently the figures began to reappear, walking and running up behind the trees. I saw now through the glasses that they all carried spears. When in among the trees they dropped the spears and walked out on to the open bank.

One man waved Paddy's swag, shouting triumphantly. I wondered why Paddy had not hidden the tobacco and other presents the crew may have stolen to appease the tribesmen, then simply brought his swag aboard. His little lapse would not have been found out then. Renewed yelling broke out from the shore. I noticed that Waldawidgee and Gillagun, Quarquor and A-but stared silently towards the tribesmen. These men were not of their tribe. Probably a hunting party from the wild lands farther west. Out there in the Fitzmaurice River country the abo. boys are pretty tough.

"I bet we couldn't land them now if we tried," nodded the Skipper grimly, indicating the lubras.

The faces of the young girls certainly were a study. Silently they gazed towards the painted figures. The Skipper laughed and pointing over the water asked Waldawidgee would she like us to land her among her friends. Vigorously she shook her head. The crew laughed loutishly and were immediately roared upon by the Skipper. He was sore over that thieving of the tobacco. It had been so neatly done right under our noses.

"Those flaming hell-cats did it," stormed the Skipper. "Only that it's impossible now to row them ashore I'd land them into the arms of that menagerie and let 'em he tom to pieces."

The boys last night must have quietly rowed to the west bank, left the tobacco and whatever presents they had purloined, then returned to the east bank. No doubt some tribesmen ashore had advised it would be just as well to keep "sweet" with the crowd on the west bank.

Very interesting country away to the west, Aboriginal Land. It stretches past the gloomy Fitzmaurice right on to the rugged Victoria. Roughly about centre are the far-flung swamps and plains of the Mod country, and away back inland an unmapped tangle of ranges. It is all "wild man's" country. A large area of it was Nemarluk's in particular. Not far west was Treachery Bay where Nemarluk's Red Band attacked the crew of the lugger *Ouida*, killed those who failed to escape, then looted the vessel. That started the Big Chief on a wild and woolly three years' adventure, constantly chased by the police patrols. I've always admired Nemarluk. Alas, he died of a broken heart in Darwin Jail.

It was in the tangled maze of the Fitzmaurice country that Tiger's mob cruelly murdered Stephens and Cook. A much less likable type of virile primitive was Tiger, a low-browed killer.

It's wild country away out there, plenty of wild men. And now some marauding band of them had come prowling to the west bank of the Daly. Silently our passengers stared across at the naked warriors, wearing bone daggers in their human-hair belts, tufted cockatoo feathers in their headbands. And in among the trees were plenty of shovel-headed spears. I'd seen them with the glasses.

As the tide went down it left two long, glistening lines of mudbank extending up the river. Along both banks every here and there in plain view now was a basking crocodile. At the first shot the tribesmen ashore vanished. But here was not a good place for shooting. The wounded crocodiles writhed back into the water in most cases and were lost in deep channel or hole. There was very little chance of recovering them in this broad and channelled tide-swept portion of the river.

At midday we chugged upstream seeking a more favourable shooting ground and a landing for our passengers. We anchored at eventide but the passengers begged to stay aboard until morning.

"They're afraid that hunting party may be around," explained Herman.

After the evening meal we went below. Reluctantly I forced myself to sit down and write up notes. Always the hardest work of the day, this writing notes of the simple little incidents to defeat a vagrant memory. I finished them, sighed and leaned back. As I lit a cigarette I glanced around the cabin. Presently the imp that pesters my hand again won the day, or rather night. And I wrote again. Here it is, from the notes:

"A very quiet night outside, no movement of the vessel, no sound of lapping water, only the gramophone music filling the big cabin alight under the steadily burning hurricane lamp. The Skipper is stretched out on his bunk dreaming up at the cabin roof. Herman is master of ceremonies at the gramophone, sitting there listening, quietly changing the records. The lubras are sprawled dreamily on the cabin floor, the Diminutive a chocolate cameo of a baby girl with big black eyes gazing up at the cabin roof. Those eyes at times seem to be swimming under reflection from the lamp. A-but, with firm young arms clasped under her head, is staring at the gramophone, her wild tangle of hair a thick mop. Gillagun stares too. She seems to be all eyes, so moveless she barely appears to be breathing. Waldawidgee is in one of her moody turns. She lies coiled on her side as a restless kitten might lie, her legs doubled up, boyish head pillowed on ebony arm. Her skin is healthy and glossy and young-looking. Still and silent as a mouse she listens intently, her big, liquid eyes wide open, glistening under the lamplight. She has a good forehead. Her eyes are not deep-set. Her chin, neck, shoulders and breasts are little models, as are her perfect teeth. Her short cropped hair is a deep, purple-black. She, and the three others too are far and away more interesting-looking than the great majority of aboriginal girls. But this dancer is something right out of the box. Prehistoric little girl woman though she is, true daughter of Eve from the dawn of time, she is not nearly so lacking in intelligence, no, not by a very long way, as the anthropoid-ape theory of science would have us believe. I admire her too for her crafty little ways—the clever little schemes she has treated us to while on the boat. Much deeper-laid tricks than in sneaking all the tobacco and cigarette butts, nails, fragments of iron, looking glass, any little thing she could lay her agile fingers upon and smuggle up to her tribesmen on deck. Engaged in active intrigue with them too. Why shouldn't she be?

"Herman has put on a famous Edison record, last word in modernity. The little dancer is listening, drinking it all in, this girl who chants by the campfires of a hundred thousand years ago. From the gramophone a world-famous artiste is singing to some great accompanist. Surely that singer never dreamed how sweet her song would sound upon this lonely river whose turbulent waters have stilled to a death-like listening. That singer never dreamed of the entranced audience that is here, never imagined she would ever sing to a Stone Age audience. Not even the croon of a corroboree song from those above, for the crew and the rugged visaged tribesmen listen silent as the night while here below the four lubras scarcely seem to be breathing. The little dancer's ear is towards the music, her velvet black face in rapt attention, her big eyes open wide as if seeking the singer behind the voice. What manner of woman does she imagine bears that voice?

"The record stops. Herman sighs, lights a cigarette. After a while he reaches for the records and hands the dancer the stub of his cigarette. She accepts automatically, puffs dreamily away. The gramophone blares a jazz tune. She sits up, puffs her cigarette, stares at the Skipper, Herman and me in turn. She steps to the cabin floor and begins to dance.

"A living girl from prehistoric times; yes, but I wish I could show her dance to the world, give the world her dance on the pictures as the world gives our singers to the records.

"She goes back to the wild tomorrow."

XXVIII

THE TRAPPER TRAPPED

AS a change from this cruising and shooting (that lazy cruising along a lonely coast, poking into unnamed waterways to hike inland to chance meeting the untamed folk and animals and birds of the wild never grew monotonous to me), we'll farewell the *Lotus* as she sails back to Darwin while we seek the crocodile by other means.

Trapping is one way. But it is very difficult, needs great skill, cunning and patience, and can only successfully he accomplished by men to whom the study of things of the wild is a joy. Probably there are not more than a dozen highly skilled crocodile trappers in Australia. The main reason of course is because there is so little demand for live crocodiles. They are such awkward pets. But the zoos of the world, and private collectors, order a few now and then.

The trapper first finds his quarry, notes the runway. The crocodile returns to this again and again. For one style of trap there must be a decent-sized tree handy. No sapling will do because the strength of an enraged crocodile will smash a sapling or pull it up by the roots. That tree must take the strength of the crocodile. To a limb is lashed a pulley-block with steel rope running through it to the ground. The rope is fitted as a running noose. The idea is to entice the crocodile to "lasso" himself. When he crawls through the noose and seizes the bait he really pulls a trigger which tightens the lasso around his shoulders. And then he is in a fix, very similar to a steer that has been roped. Only this is a much stronger rope and, instead of being held by man and horse, is "held" by a tree.

Now a crocodile is a cunning fellow who does not put his head in a noose for nothing. So a bait is used, wallaby or goat so dead that the aroma reaches a considerable distance. A goat in such a state is a delicacy almost irresistible to a crocodile. The bait is placed at the foot of the tree in such a position that the crocodile must come straight to it, and through the noose, to get at it. Sometimes a rough fence of stakes, an enclosed pathway, is built up to the tree to ensure that the crocodile approaches the trap correctly. A cord is tied to the bait. The other end of the cord leads up the tree and is tied to a bag of sand which is attached to the cable and pulley-block. The cord really acts as a trigger. When the bait is pulled the cord is pulled too and down falls the sandbag weight, jerking tight the noose around the crocodile.

On the instant, hell breaks loose. The crocodile throws himself back and the cable tightens deep around his shoulders. He lashes out with claws and tail and the cable quivers under the strain. Realizing he is caught, he rears up and roars as he flails the mud and tears at everything within reach. Clouts of mud spatter trees and water. The great jaws smash a sapling as a man would snap a stick. The crocodile hurls himself backward, hurls himself forward, twists around and around in a wallow of mud while the terrible jaws clash together and the claws rip air and mud and roots with the awful energy of a maniac thing. Soon he has torn and wallowed a great hole in the mud and ripped everything within the radius that the rope holds him in. In despairing rage his jaws tear at the steel rope and he whirls himself around and around and around it until he has tied himself in a knot. He reverses in baffled fury. Although he is taken at such a terrible disadvantage he has been known at times to break even a steel rope.

A somewhat similar trap, simple but effective, is the pole and bar. The pole is a strong upright of timber firmly embedded in the ground. It may be the trunk of a tree. Balanced upon the tip of this, held by a bolt in the centre, is a long, strong beam of timber. Under the end nearest the water is affixed a rope. One end of the rope rests on the ground in the form of a slipknot. The other end leads towards the butt of the pole. At this end of the rope is fixed the bait, in such a way that when the bait is pulled a hook is released, allowing a heavy weight to act on the other end of the beam. The crocodile must crawl through the noose before he can grab the bait. The hook is then released and the beam flies up under the action of the weight. As one end of the beam thumps down and the other flies up the noose tightens around the crocodile and the weight of beam and attached weight jerks him off his paws and half suspends him in mid-air. He then is nearly helpless, a writhing, furious thing.

Traps vary in construction, according to the choice of the trapper and as to whether he wishes to take the crocodile in as undamaged a physical condition as possible, or whether he merely wishes to hold him long enough to shoot him. A trap may be built to resemble a long, narrow box, huge and very strong. Once in there with the trapdoor closed, a crocodile really is boxed in. And yet a large crocodile when in frantic despair is possessed of such a fury of strength that he may even escape from the most carefully made and strongest of these traps.

Such an experience befell Frank Pover of Wyndham, East Kimberley, just across the border from where we left the *Lotus*. Pover is a noted crocodile trapper. This particular old-man crocodile escaped five times, smashing the trap each time. It was a grand duel between man and beast, a triumph in the patience and study and nature-craft necessary to entice a cunning old-man crocodile into a trap five different times. But the crocodile won in the end.

This crocodile was twenty-six feet nine inches long. It was measured by the simple expedient of measuring that length of its tail which protruded from one trap before it got away. The trap was twenty feet long; the length of tail which protruded was six feet nine inches. The strength of such a monster when crazily enraged is unbelievable. This trap was very carefully and strongly built of nine-by-two kauri planks, ten feet high; it was more of a long narrow room than a box. The bait could only be reached by the saurian crawling right into this "room" and reaching the bait with paw or snout at the farthest end. When he did so a trigger was released and down crashed a trapdoor behind him. He was thus boxed in. That sliding door, suspended from a forty-foot rope, weighed four hundredweight. So there was not only weight and bulk but great strength in the door itself. But the fury caged inside turned into a writhing tornado of berserk energy and under the terrific strain one by one those strong planks began to creak, give way, snap apart. He fought his way out of five such traps; broke five three-inch brand-new manila ropes. And any seaman could tell you the strength of such a rope. The last Pover saw of him he was surging out into the Cambridge Gulf, taking three-quarters of a ton of timber on a rope with him.

Generally these long box traps are open at the top, but not always. A trap may be arranged so that the crocodile enters at high tide, when it is underwater. When the tide recedes, a stick is poked in under the mud and a rope manipulated around and behind the captive's shoulders, and another around the tail. Then a pulley knot is fastened around the snout and the helpless, furious captive is pulled out by leverage.

Trapping crocodiles is by no means as easy as it seems to the casual onlooker. Lots of men have found this out as did a visitor to Wyndham quite some time ago. He was a travelled man and under the incentive of a few spots in the local hotel was telling the boys just what he had done to 'gators in other parts of the world. The boys listened, encouraged him, had a few more, then gravely suggested he meet Frank Pover and make a wager he could handle 'gators just as well as Frank could. After one or two more the visitor was perfectly agreeable and just about that time Pover strolled in. He smiled at the challenge, but would not accept. He is a very quiet man. However, the visitor insisted and at last Pover drawled, 'Well, look here. I expect to catch a 'gator in the trap tonight. I don't expect you to handle him as you say you can, but I'll drop a ten-pound note near him and if you can pick up that note it is yours." And the proposal was immediately accepted.

Sure enough next morning a decent-sized crocodile was caught in the trap. It was away out on the marsh edge, near the stream, the broad, muddy waters of the Gulf. While walking out across the marsh, the two men almost walked upon a crocodile lurking up a little side creek. The visitor registered a nasty scare and Pover immediately knew that his companion knew nothing about crocodiles. They walked out to the mangroves and, standing side by side nearly to their knees in mud, Pover pointed out over the trapped crocodile to the eyes and nose of another just visible above the surface.

"There's his mate," he said.

The visitor slipped his hand in his pocket, nervously glancing over his shoulder. He was evidently scared that the crocodile they'd disturbed in the creek might crawl up and take them in the rear. To a violent explosion both men sprang aside.

"My God!" exclaimed the visitor. "I believe I'm shot!"

"To hell you are!" gasped Pover. "It's me!"

His thigh had been right against the pocket of the other man and for a moment he thought the bullet had hit him. He felt his legs. To his intense relief no bones were broken.

"Let's have a look at you," he demanded.

He pulled up the visitor's shorts and there was a big hole in the thigh with a long, rapidly bulging line of flesh running right down to the knee where the bullet had lodged. That line was already turning black.

" A nice mess you've made of yourself," said Pover. "Why didn't you tell me you had a gun? You stay right here while I run and get the doctor."

But to get across that muddy marsh and up to the township and a doctor meant time. When Pover returned with transport, the wounded man was crawling back to the road. The thought of that crocodile in the creek haunted him. Old Doc Adams surveyed him grimly. A good doctor, but a tough old boy was Adams.

"You're not dead," he growled and ran his finger along the bullet track. "This is going to be a probing job. When did your bowels act last?"

"When the gun went off!" answered the visitor sulkily.

As a memento Pover later mailed him a pair of the crocodile's tusks set up in a brooch.

XXIX

THE FLYING PLAGUE

WYNDHAM was a quaint little township isolated from everywhere in the wet season. It came into being as a port to the inland during the wild and woolly days of the Kimberley gold rush at Hall's Creek in 1885. It has long since subsided to a tiny, almost forgotten township. It comes to life though during six months of the year just after the wet season, when work starts at the meatworks. It is then that the big mobs of cattle come slowly in from the ranges throughout the rugged back country. It is the last trip of the cattle. They leave the meatworks as frozen beef en route for overseas markets. When the season is over steamers take the meatworkers back home to Perth, the big plant falls silent and Wyndham again slips back to some two hundred people in quiet isolation.

Through a maze of hilly country the broad Cambridge Gulf works its way some forty miles. It is wild country. The brown waters swirl past a number of islands; one is De Rougemont's Isle. Lashed by the rise and fall of great tides, still the Gulf can shelter deep-sea vessels. Wyndham nestles down towards the end of the Gulf with the water lapping its doorstep, while directly behind the town towers the black, barren bulk of the Bastion Range. This is a gloomy black wall on cloudy days, but melts into browns and purples under shafts of sunlight. The township has a few little bungalows, half a dozen cottages. There is a "white" store, a dozen Chinese stores, the two-storied Wyndham Hotel, the police station and jail yard walled by tall iron sheets, the little school, the tiny post office. A mile farther on across a marsh looms the bulk of the meatworks, a steamer at the wharf if the season is "on", a hive of industry. Otherwise that area is deserted.

Away around the Bastion is another great dry marsh area on which is the airfield, near the road which leads into the back country—the rich Ord River district, and the tangle of hills and valleys reaching back into the interior and east away into the Territory, and away west to the rugged West Kimberley coast. These lands are now sparsely settled, with million-acre cattle stations. A day will come when numbers of the watercourses will be dammed and the land carry many more people. But now the pioneer stations are few and far between. In fact to the west is Aboriginal Land, where the only white men are the wandering dingo poisoner and the dozen pioneers, occupiers of lonely huts.

One evening I went for a walk down past the little hospital to see old Paddy Rominy. Chinese youngsters were playing in the street squealing insults to one another as "Ching Chong Chinaman!" And being shrilly abused by their parents. The evening was quiet and beautiful, the big marsh like black velvet merging into the night. Away downstream the meat- works and wharf were a blaze of electric lights; there came the distant grind of electrically driven engines. Rising sheer behind the town the Bastion loomed as a shadow against the sky.

Little Paddy Rominy was an old-time teamster who had always paid his way through life. After many years in the back country he had been brought back very ill to Wyndham. He thought he would know no one now, would have no friends.

The boys had rallied around him. Almost forgotten debts of years ago were paid. He was cared for as he had never been since his mother kissed him good-bye long, long ago. He found he had not only friends but treatment in his sickness, and money as well.

He was quietly happy. And he was going back to his beloved "show" tomorrow, for he had been prospecting for gold far back in the sun-baked hills towards the desert fringe. Old Paddy was a bit bowed now, and very thin and weak from the after effects of fever. His grey hair was scanty too, as was his bristly little moustache and little goatee beard. But his bushy, sandy eyebrows shaded eyes alive with quiet purpose. As he talked in his slow, quiet way I found myself trying to guess at what colour his eyes were. They gazed so directly, compelling attention. They seemed to be between blue and grey; but I could not be sure, for they seemed to alter as he spoke with quiet faith of his plans and the work he hoped to do.

Paddy was leaving a sickbed much too soon, but the grim back country was calling him with irresistible urge. To many a bushman our back country, aye and the harshest of it, can draw a man back with invisible bonds stronger than the fairest siren.

Paddy's "show" was out at the Willy Willy. That particular area is round about Mount Dockrell away south towards the desert edge. Deathly lonely, hard country out there—very hard. Lonely men there have been killed by the blacks. Others set out from camp never to return. Some have perished of thirst. The records of the Mounted Police at Hall's Creek carry many a grim story of that country out near the desert fringe.

The Kimberleys have a very healthy climate, but that year saw by far the worst outbreak of fever ever known. It was a particularly virulent variety and wiped out hundreds of aboriginals, while almost all the whites caught it in some form or other. A few died in their saddles, just rolled off to mother earth. Several dropped by their donkey wagons. The old hands think they're all right so long as they can climb into the saddle.

"I'll be all right as soon as I get on the old horse," more than one fever-stricken victim mumbled to me. Numbers rode, or drove their teams, until a morning dawned when they could no longer stagger upright. Only then were they forced to lie down. Almost all suffered relapses by getting up and "across the old horse" too soon.

Under the brilliant sun the rumble of the meatworks could not drown the screeching of thousands of cockatoos. Its buildings appeared to be roofed with snow, the yards a moving whiteness where the birds strutted about pulling up the grass roots, rooting for seed that had slipped down into cracks in the earth. The noisy birds get fresh water and salt at the yards as well. It is "Christinas" for the cockatoos during the busy meat season. Crowds of them were now playing on the wireless masts, blondining down the wire stays with monkeyish glee to the disgust of Jack Christie, the wireless man.

"I'm a bird-lover, Jack," he snorted, "but those cunning, mischievous wretches out there would try the patience of Job."

A little while back the cockatoos had got the little wireless station in a "jam", for their ceaseless play and "Catherine wheeling" down the wires had twisted them. With the result that an irate ship at sea demanded to know what the hell the wireless man was doing, mixing his metres and wave lengths in the maddest of wireless jamborees.

Not far from the comfortable little wireless cabin raged the hurly-burly of thousands of beasts being urged up the great ramp towards the noisy building which they would leave as meat. I stepped out into a living hailstorm—uncountable millions of flying grasshoppers. It was misery at times, for they kept banging into a man's face and head. When walking back to the town I saw they were upon the ground two inches thick in places, miles upon miles of resting grasshoppers. Clouds were constantly descending and constantly rising, with other clouds ceaselessly flying overhead—clouds of grasshoppers. They were coming over the Gulf from the coast. Goodness knows where they originally came from. Perhaps from eggs laid along the coast, for they surely could not have come across the sea. The northern coastline was only a few miles distant. They were flying directly south to get inland.

I wondered how they would climb the Bastion. That huge barrier would be mighty Alps to their toiling myriads. I walked along its base, across the bare, flat marsh. High up the hoppers were flying, a twinkling mist of whirring wings, right into the barrier that towered above. I drew in towards the range and started to ascend where a rocky road came straight down over a divide. Would instinct lead the 'hoppers to this lowest point over the range, as common sense had led man?

When only a little way up I drew into the midst of the ever-vanishing ever coming clouds. They were flying slowly, laboriously; like the tired movements of a man after a long and exhausting walk. Their wings revolved just as rapidly but, plain to see, with considerable loss of power. Their thick, torpedo-shaped bodies whirring past looked heavy, their legs well tucked up under. Looking straight up to the sky I could still see them there, myriad little flecks of light under the sun. Their countless passing wings produced a laboured chirruping like the sighing of a wind. A continuous fluttering whirr arose as I advanced and I saw that every stone of the millions of stones was a brown mass of tired, motionless grasshoppers. Far up the rocky road to the tip of the Bastion all was paved in brown that whirred up with the crackling of an advancing bushfire. These were the tired ones, those that had fallen temporarily by the way. I halted and turned around for a spell, looking down and out over the marsh towards the Gulf. The air was a shimmer of beating wings flying high over the barren marsh in this determined attempt to cross the Bastion. All flying high as they possibly could, the lucky ones thickly massed in the air to many hundreds of feet in height.

There was something terrifying in the purposeful, steady, ceaseless flight of these insects. Their numbers seemed as inexhaustible as the sands of the shore over which they had flown. I climbed steadily and the hillsides of the divide closed in. Here the sound of their wing beats was concentrated to a steady sighing that rose again and again into a rapid whirring, almost to a moaning sound. This was because of little puffs of wind coming in over the marsh to sweep up the hillside towards the divide, thus lending new power and life to the 'hoppers. They responded with a clashing of wings and an immediate rising in height. Their ceaseless struggle was not only to keep flying and maintain height, but to rise still higher and higher to get over the Bastion. I paused again and noticed that all the coarse grass tufts that littered the hill-sides were a mass of brown; the stunted trees were massed with brown instead of leaves.

What power these 'hoppers have, to eat to death in a few hours the stunted trees that for years had defied the rock and heat of the Bastion, the winds and the hottest of seasons. The buck spinifex grass, the grass that defies the desert itself, to be eaten to withered stalks. What would these countless hosts do to the shrubs of the valleys and the tender grasses of the inland plains.

I climbed high enough to see up above the crest of

the Bastion. Twinkling for a hundred feet above it were the triumphant wings of 'hoppers. Hill crest after hill crest all twinkling under myriad wings beating in the last final flutter as now down below they saw their Land of Canaan, the green forests and scrubs and plains, the hills and valleys spreading far away.

Flocks of kite hawks flew lazily through and through the 'hoppers, but their eating power lessened the numbers no more than the wind blowing away a wisp of sand from the seashore. Many other birds had gathered from far and wide to the feast. But now, perched full and replete on stones, they took no notice of the winged meals that flew so steadily past. Near the crest I turned, and looked away down the Bastion back towards the Gulf. All the air below was a glitter of wings. Away down there by the Bastion base they were rising up far as the eye could penetrate. Slowly, steadily, ceaselessly climbing.

It was interesting to pick out one some distance below and watch his steady, laborious progress, the ceaseless beat of his wings in that great upward climb. He would sway now and then, regain control and climb steadily upward. Suddenly his wings would flash and he would rise rapidly with the whirr of millions of others responding to a wind puff. And if you could watch him long enough among the evenly advancing horde, he would come climbing steadily on and appear to be sinking fast. He would now struggle on six feet above the ground, but be would still come on. Rising with the slope, he would fly past and over with rapidly moving wings, his legs well tucked up, his body looking very heavy and tired. But—he had won.

XXX

FIGHT FOR LIFE

IT was the "Kimberley Rush", that remarkable, feverish gold stampede of a thousand unwritten stories, which originally started Wyndham. The shiploads of diggers from two and three thousand miles away, from as far away as New Zealand, had to find a disembarkation point somewhere. So they landed just on that spot on the wild shores of Cambridge Gulf. And from there trekked inland. And so Wyndham was horn.

After the rush Wyndham was forgotten for years. It would have reverted to the wild bush but for the great cattle treks that came drifting in from the other States. But the cattle-men took up their million-acre stations and Wyndham struggled into the position of a strategic port that had come to stay. And then the Overland Telegraph Line came creeping up from south to north. Wyndham hung on to a two-thousand-mile thread of wire for news of the outside world—a miracle wire. The passing years eventually brought wireless and the fortnightly mail plane. In the whirligig of modern progress we have no time to think what those things meant to a tiny handful of forgotten people at the end of a continent.

For the policing of the back country a jail grew up with the port, by far the majority of its guests being coloured folk. The frontier jail was run on efficient, if occasionally happy-go-lucky lines. When the patrols were absent in the back country, probably hundreds of miles away, and the sergeant back at Wyndham would be busy at the police station, or away on some urgent duty inland, the jail might then be in charge of a white prisoner, if one luckily happened to be in durance vile. His then the job to keep an eye on the coloured prisoners, see they did their jobs, see that they got their food, and make himself generally useful. At such times the temporary jail-keeper always acted up to the trust reposed in him. But there have been some funny incidents. There was the young "guest" who awaited His Majesty's pleasure on the little matter of a horse. Passengers from an unexpected steamer visited the jail. They were admitted by the courteous young man, who showed them the sights while reeling off a vivid and blood-curdling commentary on the inmates. While being entertained, the visitors noticed a tall, long-legged man with stern mien, in shirt and trousers, come striding across the yard.

"And who is he?" inquired a visitor.

"Oh, he's a prisoner doing time he richly deserves," replied the guide. "He'd swing if justice was done. He's a particularly generous man. If ever you meet him outside give him a wide berth."

That evening at the local hostelry the visitors were intro-duced to the sergeant. They glanced in puzzled fashion at the tall, uniformed, long-legged man of stem mien. Then a lady smiled.

"Oh, sergeant, such a nice young man this afternoon showed us all round the jail."

"Oh hell, did he!" growled the sergeant.

"Yes," proceeded the lady with the innocent eyes, "and he pointed out an awful desperado walking across the yard. He looked like you, sergeant, but of course we only saw his back. The young man said the criminal should swing!"

"Oh, did he!" snarled the sergeant. "Just wait till I lay hands on him!"

Another bright young fellow was a magician with the banjo. When in town he used to play at the local dances. On this particular occasion the mere fact that he was temporarily a guest of His Majesty was not going to be allowed to spoil the dance. So the doctor, who was resident magistrate, called at the jail and asked him to play for the dance that night out at the Six Mile. To which the prisoner delightedly agreed. The sergeant and constable had ridden away on an outside case for the day, and the prisoner's job was to supervise the coloured prisoners. So when sunset came he fed them, locked them in their quarters, locked up the jail and with banjo under his arm gaily whistled his way to the doctor's house, where he donned his best suit. In no time they were to the car and out to the Six Mile.

The dance went merrily from the start, but a bushie had blown in that day and started to knock down his cheque. He was a lively little customer, and by the time the dance was in full swing he was livelier still. He mixed with the guests until his horseplay became a little too rough. So the doctor advised him to "ease off". The exuberant one resented this and hopping into a fighting attitude, abused the doctor. The doctor answered sharply. Thereupon the fightable one thumped the doctor, who struck back and knocked him out.

The men carried him out to the back veranda, threw a bucket of water over him, and left him to sleep it off.

He partly did, to awake in a disgruntled daze and reel back into the dance room and abuse all and sundry. Then he imagined he was a wild hull on the loose. He lowered his head and, bellowing, charged the dancers. He scattered them too, but they fell upon the rip-roaring cattle-buster and brought him under a heap to the floor. The doctor promptly arrested him. They carried the dazed drunk out to the car and threw him in. The doctor, with a guest, decided to take him where he could cool off in congenial company.

"You'd better come too," said the doctor to the banjo-player. "You know the ropes at the jail. We'll lock this silly galoot up and be back at the dance within half an hour."

So to a laughing cheer they buzzed away into the night, the musician twanging his banjo and chuckling to himself.

"I'm hanged if I know how they're going to lock him up," he laughed to the hood of the car. "I've got the keys of the jail, and they are in my old trousers in the doctor's house." The car whisked into town and the doctor pulled up at the police station. But to their knocking there was no answer—the sergeant apparently had not returned. Meanwhile the banjo kept accompaniment to a plaintive melody, the player grinning at the thought of what a lovely row was brewing when the sergeant came along and found he could not get into his own jail.

By this time the unruly one in the car, somewhat sobered by his drive, waited until all hands were busy trying to locate someone at the station. Then he bolted. They yelled and sprang after him, but he managed to gain the jetty and racing along it dived straight over.

They paused in horror for the Gulf is alive with crocodiles.

"Come out of that, you silly fool," yelled the doctor.

"If you want me, come in and get me, you bastards," yelled back the swimmer.

"For Heaven's sake, come ashore, man," shouted the doctor. "The crocodiles will get you!"

"You come and get me," was the sarcastic reply.

They turned and ran back along the jetty.

"My God, what a mess!" groaned the doctor. "The crocodiles will tear him to pieces."

They jumped off the jetty and ran out on the marsh to the water's edge. He was still there, paddling along with the tide. He greeted them with a derisive yell, inviting them to "come in and get your feet wet".

"It won't do you any harm," he yelled. "You've not had a bath since your mother took your napkins off—you dirty — !"

They walked along level with the swimmer, expecting gaping jaws to close upon him at any moment. To their shouts of entreaty he called back delighted abuse.

The doctor thought quickly. Along the shore there are bottles in places, dead marines. They collected a few of these and grouped mysteriously together. Then the doctor shouted out, "All right, you silly baboon, if you want to stay there — then stay there!"

Then the party sat down on the foreshore with clink of glasses and low-voiced laughter. In the loony darkness they indulged in a mimic jag, their nerves strained for the shriek of the fool out there when the crocodile grabbed him. Meanwhile he, now forgotten and lonely, trod water. Listening he heard the popping of corks, the gurgle of liquid, the low tones of some intently listened to story, followed by the sudden laughter. Again he heard the popping as of a cork.

Presently he came swimming in, right to the shore. In a burst of good fellowship they called to him to "come and have one".

He did.

They grabbed him.

"You stupid, flaming imbecile!" swore the doctor as he half strangled him. 'You've kept us in suspense for an hour. Now take this! And this and this!"

The banjo-player was so relieved at the lucky escape that he told straight away where the keys of the jail were. Moreover, he helped to throw the unruly one into his new quarters.

In due course the culprit stood before the court. The doctor was the magistrate. The man was charged with riotous behaviour on the foreshore.

He brought a month.

Although the great Gulf swarms with crocodiles, aboriginals occasionally swim across — very occasionally. A grisly risk, as anyone can see even from the street of the township. For nearly always there are two or three ugly snouts drifting past the jetty with the tide. Cynical are they of civilization. But the few crocodiles visible from the jetty are no indication of the numbers that swarm in the forty-mile Gulf with its hills and cliff's and low-lying lands empty of white men.

However, there are reasons why a few natives occasionally do cross those wide, brown, often turbulent waters. One reason is the saving of a day's walk or more. And a stronger reason is faith in one of their age-old beliefs.

The men who do cross claim the crocodile as totem. A man of this totem believes that the crocodile will recognize him, and will not harm him. For the spirit of the crocodile and his own spirit are brothers, just as his totem friends are brothers all belonging to the one totem family. Similarly, a man whose totem is the shark believes he can safely swim in shark-infested waters.

Even so, these "crocodile men" do not tempt their totem brothers too often. When they do they swim in company, crossing with the tide. Generally each man hangs on to a log, on each end of which is lashed a cross stick which acts as support for his long bundle of spears. Or he clings lightly to a long, forked sapling which is swiftly carried on with the tide. The favourite is the forked sapling, for it is light and travels faster while supporting the swimmer. Across the fork is generally laid a strip of bark. This supports a few heavy throwing sticks, but particularly the spearheads of the spears, protecting the weapons from the water. The hafts of the weapons lie down along the pole, or log as the case may be.

The swimmers wade into the water, each man with a hand at the end of his sapling. Soon they are swimming. The tide catches them, and presently they are carried away out in the Gulf.

Should an ominous snout rise and survey them they shout in recognition, with a wave of the arm calling a totem greeting which they believe the crocodile understands. If the brute changes direction and effortlessly follows them they shout to him, "Go away!" Your wife wants you!" "Clear out!" "Go about your business!" while vigorously waving him away.

This action is by no means so ineffectively childish as we would believe. For the waving arms and splashing are clearly directed at him, the shouts are the voices of mankind of whom he is instinctively wary. These men although in the water obviously recognize him and do not appear to be afraid of him. The understanding checks violent action, slows him down to caution.

If he still follows and draws slowly closer they howl angry abuse, threatening him with dire penalties. Should he draw dangerously close they hurl sticks at him. They do this with a twist of the wrist that splashes the stick with a sharp smack before the crocodile's snout, while the stick whizzes on and if it does not strike the partially submerged head it ricochets across the water in a series of smart splashings. There is no mistaking the vicious threat in such a well-thrown stick. The unfamiliar sound also puzzles the undecided monster. His actions are regulated now to a considerable extent by how long it is since he has dined.

Should he still come on, they know now he is either a very hungry one or a very evil one. Which to them will mean the same thing.

While keeping an eye on the brute they swim grimly now, each man with one hand pushing the end of his pole. And now their legs kick out with an action that volleys sharp, metallic sounds underwater. Clapping of cupped hands through the water surface conveys a still greater sound effect.

A shout!

"He comes!"

They seize spears and leap around as he swirls in among them. Open jaws and terrible fangs, a huge body breaking up the water amongst rolling logs and stabbing spears and plunging human bodies that fairly leap from the water.

He is gone.

His anticipated prey is not nearly so easy as we would imagine. They had drawn together for mutual protection. Each man's left hand is on the sapling which not only lends him support but is leverage when he leaps clean up out of the water. The sapling also is a weapon to help parry or divert or confuse a rush. Those expert swimmers are no helpless victims. As the crocodile rushes in he is faced by prepared men delivering spear thrusts deadly dangerous. In each thrust is the experience of a lifetime of survival of the fittest, concentrated in this one moment. Each man may have but one chance, this one thrust which must mean life or death. A horrible death.

They thrust for the eye, or straight down the open throat.

The crocodile feels the blinding stab of the spears. His chosen victim has leapt clear of the swirling water and bouncing logs and grim stabbing figures. With a convulsive surge of body and tail he vanishes while each man has snatched another spear. Then with a push at the logs they swim again for life.

If the crocodile has not been badly wounded he may return later. Effortlessly he follows the elusive swimmers, but at a safe distance.

With the strong tide behind them and by their own exertions they fairly shoot through the water, drawing nearer and nearer the shore. With shouts and ribald remarks given point by a throwing stick now and then they keep the crocodile at a distance as long as they can, confusing him before he can make up his mind to attack again. If he does make up his mind, he attacks much more cunningly. Vanishes. They swim for life, close together, ready. Suddenly he swirls up from below. But they have leapt high out of the water and again spears are thrusting for his eye and throat, while his claws rip into logs instead of the soft bodies of men. He certainly is hurt, while his prey is a miracle of evasion. One man has actually leapt astride him and is wrenching back a forepaw in an amazingly agonizing way. The crocodile lashes out with his tail and dives.

They swim again for life.

Generally they win to safety.

Should a crocodile seize a man, that man fights until he escapes or dies. As he is dragged below he gouges with his thumbs at the crocodile's eyes. I have known cases where aboriginals, though badly mauled, have thus escaped and lived to tell the tale.

Such an escape, though miraculous enough, seems ordinary compared to the escape of the aboriginal swimmer "Treacle", far away on the north-east coast. Treacle, while diving for pearlshell in the Coral Sea, dived right into the mouth of a tiger shark. The great jaws closed on him, engulfing his head to the shoulders. Treacle gouged frantically for the shark's eyes and managed to screw his thumbs into them. The shark coughed him out and swirled away. Treacle, though very badly hurt, lived to exhibit his scars for "a shilling per look" to the steamer passengers that called at Thursday Island.

Should the worst happen and a crocodile totem man be dragged under and eaten, the tribesmen explain it by the fact that some act of his, for instance such as having eaten forbidden totem food, or a secret love affair with some forbidden totem girl, has deeply offended the totem spirit. For, over every totem group there rules the totem spirit. And in this case it has been the totem spirit of the crocodile totem that has been deeply offended by the crocodile man breaking some age-old law of the totem.

White men would stand no chance against crocodiles while swimming in such waters as the Gulf, yet the aboriginal generally manages to pull through. It seems almost unbelievable to us, but it is really a question of environment and a lifetime's understanding of the subject.

The rise of the tide in Cambridge Gulf is up to twenty-three feet. Some day Australia will harness the power in that enormous volume of turbulent water. The tide generally runs at the rate of five knots. The local aboriginal with his knowledge of watercraft can make the tide carry him considerably faster than this. And he makes full use of knowledge and tide when an undecided crocodile is trailing almost at his heels.

When fighting in his own environment against nature that he fully understands, it takes a lot indeed to kill the Australian aboriginal. Nor does age count so much. Old Quart-pot and his faithful spouse Lily had seen many a summer go by before they accompanied Sergeant Buckland to Katanning. They had become very attached to the kindly sergeant and now he was transferred to the south. They refused to leave his household. But in Katanning they found they were foreigners in Aboriginal land.

Local tribesmen would have none of them. The country, the conditions and environment were very different from their own beloved tribal lands. Lonely outcasts, they began to pine for the breezes of the Kimberleys, for the hills and the grim, black gorges, for the sea breeze and turbulent, muddy waters of the Gulf.

The sergeant knew the symptoms and helped them all he could. In a kindly way he suggested they say farewell and make for home.

Joyfully they departed.

Their route covered two thousand five hundred miles. Over plain country and mulga, then over desert—and a fearful desert it is. Then over the vast expanse of the spinifex, and a final desert strip, then into grim, low hills peopled by savage men. And on into the beloved hills of the Kimberleys.

Through the country of numerous hostile tribes they travelled, often by night, hunting scanty food as they trudged on and on. And at last they won through almost to Wyndham, into the ambush of a killer and his gang. They drove five spears into Quart-pot, left him for dead.

But friendly natives pulled out the spears, plastered the wounds with clay and ashes and bird's feathers. Carried old Quart-pot the last few miles back to Wyndham and the white doctor. He had grit, had old Quart-pot, and his none too young wife trudging with bowed back beside him, her eyes telling him to live, his eyes lifting from hers to the shadows of his beloved hills.

He lived.

Crocodile shot in a canefield near Ayr, North Queensland in 1917.

XXXI

THE PATROLS RIDE OUT

THE little police station at Wyndham is overshadowed by its famous jail. Even nature has conspired, most effectively, to draw attention to the jail, for the great bastion looms straight up over it. This sombre mountain barrier looms hundreds of feet straight up from the back wall of the jail and frowns down on the courtyard that has echoed to the hoofs of thousands of incoming and outgoing patrols. The big yard is fenced in by a ten-foot-high iron fence. Inside are the stables and cells. Horses famous in the pioneering history of the rugged back country have been stabled there. Many a "character", especially black, brown, and brindle, has exercised in the big yard. And many a blacktracker, more dangerous by far than any bloodhound, has saddled his horse there, with shaggy eyes aglow with lust of the coming manhunt.

And the Mounted men, expert bushmen and riders. They need to be, for their patrols take them into unexplored country, into the most rugged and isolated comer of all Australia, for months at a time thrown on their own company and resources.

When seeking quarry they had to carry on as best they could when their supplies cut out, and in unmapped country which was a wilderness of gorges and peaks, their quarry elusive as a shadow upon a rock.

Lonely vigils at night. Listening to the horses out in the darkness, apprehensive of the neigh of pain, the blind stampede as a shower of spears came from the night. It was lonely enough by day when the Mounted man's only human company was the blacktracker's. But he had a job to do and it was up to him to carry it out.

Yarning with Sergeant Flinders in the little police station I often wished that the records of this and the other half- dozen police outposts of the Kimberleys had been preserved as a vivid picture of Australian frontier history for the generations to come. It would have made fascinating reading and study when conditions of life and the country itself have changed from the conditions known to our fathers and ourselves.

The Kimberleys is one of the least known yet most intriguing areas in Australia. The history of its frowning coasts really starts in the brave days of venturesome Chinese junks, and of the old-time ships of the Portuguese, Dutch and Spaniards. We know this from old-world archives, and more directly from such relics as bronze carronades and ancient coins and ships' bells exposed by storms, the only traces of nameless ships that perished on that cliff-bound coast. There may have been adventurers before these, perhaps the Phoenicians; even the Egyptians, because the Stone Age men still wear crescent-shaped ornaments of pearlshell, while an occasional custom or rock painting, and the symbolic lay-out of stonework design beside their sacred grounds are hauntingly reminiscent of ancient Egypt. In the little police station of Wyndham many an historic patrol has been planned. The long chase after such notorious native outlaws as "Pigeon", "Captain", Lillimara, men who could use a rifle and who shot to kill. It took three years of ceaseless patrol work, of false trail and alarm and doubling back, of ambush and skirmish and running fight, to round up that gang. They operated distant from here, secure in the caves among the limestone ranges of the West Kimberleys, and it was the West Kimberley Mounteds who bore the brunt of the work. When the long, long chase was ended a number of white men as well as tribesmen had died violent deaths.

Another famous chase was that after "Major" and "Banjo" and their henchmen, native outlaws who also could use the rifle. Men such as these when cornered shot it out with the patrols, slipping away in the night, elusive as shadows. This chase led through the wild valleys of the East Kimberleys far south into the desert. The outlaws would be "here today, gone tomorrow". On foot, they travelled a hundred miles in twenty-four hours when needs must. And none better than they at losing" their tracks. The isolated settlers slept with loaded rifles beside them, doors and windows barricaded and barred. When at last cornered, Major shot it out to the finish.

Many a patrol harried native killers and cattle-spearers innumerable, varied with the ordinary work of seeking lost men or unravelling the bush tragedies inseparable from pioneering lands. Variation too in "grounding" the bumboats that sneaked away among the hills and took the rocky trail that winds down through the ranges to Hall's Creek. Here was the location of the gold rush, some two hundred miles inland through wild but beautiful country. The bumboats were teams of horses (sometimes camels) packed with alleged rum and various brands of firewater. Wherever they went there was trouble—wild fights, crazed men taking to the bush in the horrors, or forays from or against the blacks. Both in the now Northern Territory and the Kimberleys these hum- boats roamed. Wonderful how they did it over such great areas of unexplored country. The resource and initiative of the "skippers" made the job of the Mounted Police all the more difficult.

Besides doing a notable amount of exploring themselves, the patrols at times were called upon to help explorers who came by land and sea. There were yearly visits to the isolated settlers, making sure all was well with them, as they do today. They were called upon in the search for castaways whose ships had foundered along the tide-ripped coast. Long rides too, when word would drift in of some bloodthirsty fight or massacre between coastal tribes and Malay or Jap whose vessel had encroached upon native waters. Some historic patrols too in search of lost airmen—Kingsford Smith and Ulm, Bertram and Klausman, and others. Many and varied are the jobs of the Mounteds of the Kimberleys.

And in addition to hazards in the back-country patrols, tragedy can happen in the little port itself. One night a young policeman was seen on the jetty. He just vanished. Some time later a crocodile was shot at Brackish Lagoon, off the Ord. When opened up its insides were found to contain buttons and fragments of a uniform.

Not even that much was recovered of meatworker Billy Howe. Next morning the mission launch caught a glimpse of his torso floating in the Gulf. Then that too vanished.

Court day in the isolated little port, though conducted with all due decorum, had an atmosphere tinged by the environment. This was due to local conditions, great isolation, and the fact of all in the tiny little community knowing one another. As a rule the local doctor was generally resident magistrate, and very good magistrates they made. They had to, to understand the local colour.

For instance, a good man and citizen was summonsed by a long-suffering storekeeper for the overdue sum of £3 17s. 6d. The accused was an aggrieved and indignant man, who swore he had long since paid the storekeeper. Very much on his dignity, he had never been in court before and took his presence there as a personal affront. To aggravate the case he could not grasp the court procedure at all. Very restless under discipline, finally he blurted at the bespectacled storekeeper,
"Oh, you four-eyed old bastards, I don't owe you that money at all!"
The R.M. solemnly fined him five pounds for contempt of court.

"How can it be a fiver!" shouted the accused. "Strike me pink, it's growing like the hairs on a cow's tail! It's only £3 17s. 6d."

The R.M. called upon the sergeant to explain.

"You are not fined for the stores allegedly owing," he pointed out. "You are fined for contempt of court, for calling Mr Flinders a four-eyed old bastard."

"And so he is!" declared the accused with emphasis.

It all ended by the storekeeper paying the fiver for the man, as a loan. He is still waiting for repayment.

The way of the evil-doer is hard, as a certain shrewd black-boy found when he very neatly broke into old Mon Way's shop and stole sundry boxes of cigarettes. Next morning the old Chinaman sat quietly smoking, calling upon his mind to tell him who had stolen the cigarettes.

Then he ambled along to the police station and accused a certain blackboy.

Boxes of cigarettes were found in the blackboy's camp. In due course he came up before the court. He swore he had come by those cigarettes lawfully, and his case appeared good.

"Are these your cigarettes?" the sergeant demanded of Mon Way.

"Yes, some belong me."

"How you know?"

"I look see," answered old Mon and put on his big horn-rimmed glasses. He opened all the packets, laid the cigarettes side by side, bent over them and rolled them over, peering carefully. Then he held up a cigarette towards the R.M.

"This one mine!" he declared.

"This one not mine!" he said as he held up another cigarette.

Then he carefully sorted the cigarettes into two heaps, laid his hand on the larger pile and declared:

"These cigarettes belong me."

"But how do you know those cigarettes belong you?" demanded the R.M.

"Look see!" answered old Mon Way and held up a cigarette, pointing out a few minute pin-holes. "These cigarette been in my shop long time—weevil eat him. I no sell him. No white man buy."

And on all the cigarettes claimed by Mon Way were the telltale weevil-stains.

The aboriginal brought a month.

Afghans and Chinamen (and other folk too as is well known), because of different creeds and beliefs, take the oath in symbolic acts different from ours. Thus the Chinaman instead of taking the oath on the Bible will probably swear by the chopping off of a fowl's head. As was customary, an old Chinaman charged at Wyndham was asked, "Well, John, what do you wish to swear by? Chop him off fowl's head?"

"No. Me Clistian now. Me swear by Clistian."

"Oh, and so you are a Christian?"

"Yes."

"And what were you before you were a Christian?"

"Me a Methodist."

The trackers are tough men when out on patrol. Charlie the police boy developed a painful boil on his thumb, so he held it on a log and chopped it off with a tomahawk.

"Finish him!" he said grimly as he held up the bleeding stump. "No more that boil been hurtem me now!"

Mounted Constable Marshall had ridden for hundreds of miles seeking a horse. It was not the fact that the horse was a good one that had urged the Mounted man on trail after weary trail. It was the fact that this particular horse had disappeared from the police paddock. This cheeky challenge to authority must have only one ending. But the constable had failed to trace the horse. Worried but determined not to return to Wyndham without the horse, he was now boiling the billy out in the farthest bush.

"White man he come!" said the tracker suddenly.

Marshall listened, staring out amongst the timber. Yes, the sound of approaching hoofs—in a lonely spot a hundred miles from the nearest station.

Up rode a white man driving his mules. He hitched his horse to a tree some little distance away, and strolled up.

"Hullo, Long-uns," he grinned to the policeman. "Who'd ha' thought of meeting you!"

"Hullo, Blue," answered Marshall. "I wasn't expecting company myself. Where did you spring from?"

"I'm helping Toby Moran with a mob of cattle to Wyndham."

"Well, you'd better have some dinner—billy is just boiled."

As he lifted off the billy he glanced towards the horse, looked harder.

"That's a good sort of horse, Blue."

"Not bad."

"Where'd you get him?"

"He belongs to Toby Moran. He's a Rosewood horse."

Marshall strolled casually towards the horse. After a moment's hesitation the hard-bitten character by the fire followed him.

It was a Rosewood brand true enough, so well faked that it appeared to have been there quite a long time. Marshall gazed silently for a moment, then he called the tracker to bring some water.

"I'll show you something, Blue," he said genially. "Just a little matter of neglected education."

With a trick that experts have, Marshall wet the brand. Then with deft fingers smoothed the hair.

"Look!" he invited.

Under the Rosewood brand now showed the faint but unmistakable outline of the police brand.

"Hell!" said Blue.

"You're my man," said Marshall.

"I suppose so," admitted Blue disgustedly, "I deserve to be."

Away back behind the Bastion the dusty road leads inland. Here is a great grey marsh, hard and dry and a wonderful speedway, level as a billiard table for miles and miles. On many a summer's day there is a wondrous mirage here. A phantom lake between a fast-widening valley, with little islands mistily floating above the lake. At times those islands appear to dance, to vanish only to reappear slowly again. In reality those "islands" are distant hills where birds sing on crag and crest.

Away at the back of the Bastion among low hills is the Six Mile. There used to be nearly a dozen pubs here in the old days. It was a favourite camping ground for the diggers coming from and going to Wyndham. There is only the Six Mile now, and it is still a favourite with the characters who roll in from the back country to "put in the wet". For it is a homely place in the wet season. Perhaps of the countless practical jokes played there, one of the best was at the expense of Tony. Tony was an aggressive little cuss when he had a few aboard, and was not above swinging his weight about. The opportunity came when Big Abdul went berserk. Big Abdul was one of the camel drivers, a huge, black-bearded, fierce-looking Afghan. Previously he quarrelled with Tony and threatened to slit his throat from ear to ear and drink his blood. So little Tony (and others too) were relieved when word came through that the big 'Ghan had gone mad, but had been overpowered and locked up to await shipment to the madhouse.

One evening, while Tony was imbibing at the bar of the Six Mile, one of the boys casually answered the phone.

"Hullo! ... Yes, who's speaking? ... Who? ... Oh, the sergeant. Yes, sergeant? ... What! The 'Ghan escaped—Big Atxlul, the mad 'Ghan! ... Yes. By Jove, that's bad. ... Yes. We'll look out. ... What! He's coming this way? ... Who? ... Tony Thomson, you mean? ... Yes, he's here with us now. ... Warn him? Abdul is after him? ... By Jove! Yes, we'll warn him all right—we'll look after Tony. ... Right! We'll keep a sharp look-out. Good-bye, sergeant. Thanks for giving us the warning."

He hung up. With a low whistle he stared around at Tony. The bar was deathly quiet. All hands were staring at Tony.

Next morning at the breakfast table came a sudden hush as a tall bearded Afghan strode into the room, murder glaring from his eye. They stared at a long, curved sword stuck down the front of his belt. His fierce eyes swept the room. His hand clawed the sword-hilt as he fixed Tony with a baleful glare. With a gleam of tigerish teeth he crept gloatingly around the table.

Tony was staring as a helpless bird might stare at a snake. His small form seemed to shrink yet more as slowly he arose, pushing his chair aside.

The mad 'Ghan was almost upon him. Tony stepped back step for step before the leering 'Ghan. Then Tony felt the wall behind him and shuddered as he leapt away. But the 'Ghan had leapt too, barring his way, creeping again upon him. In deathly silence again Tony stepped back. Again the 'Ghan forced him to the wall. Again Tony leapt away and again the 'Ghan checkmated him. And this time he forced him into a comer.

Tony stood trembling. The 'Ghan's face distorted fiendishly as he towered over his victim, his clawed fingers slowly closing around the sword-hilt. He jerked it half out of the scabbard and Tony's shoulders hunched violently to the vicious ring of the steel. With a fearful yell the 'Ghan flashed up the weapon as suddenly three men jumped beside him with threatening guns. In hysterical rage the 'Ghan was forced backwards towards the door and as he got there all hands sprang up from the table and rushed him. With a howl he leapt back and ran along the veranda, jumped the steps and raced for the bush with all hands yelling in pursuit.

Only Tony was left alone with Mrs Me Adam. She was leaning back against the wall helpless, tears welling from her eyes.

"That's always the way," growled Tony as he staggered back to the breakfast table. "When anything goes wrong, you women always go into screaming hysterics, always lose your head. Learn to keep your head. Shut up, woman! Come and sit here. I'm here. There's nothing to be afraid of."

Just then came a thundering crash on the back veranda and the 'Ghan stood framed in the back doorway. In one leap Tony was at the front door and across the veranda and leaping down the steps took to the bush.

XXXII

NALGEE

IT is a lovely Kimberley morning. Blue sky, fresh air, shadowed valley and sunlit hill. There is a rejuvenating atmosphere of freedom, of "plenty of time", of spaciousness, over all the Kimberleys. You know you can travel about for weeks and months if you wish to, and each night camp in a fresh place, and each morning ride on into new scenes of the virgin bush.

On this lovely morning we had a road to follow. You can count the roads in the Kimberleys on one hand. And—there are no fences.

The road runs for nine miles across the flat, dry marsh. Then it begins to climb up along the level of the hills, the roadside cutting on the left hand, the King River straight down to the right. Hedged by hills and mangrove and forest trees, the winding blue river is very pretty at high tide. But at low it is merely a string of pools with banks of slimy black mud. The river vanishes among the hills. We climb on, with the Cockburn Range dominating all. It rises straight up in layers of cliffs, a picturesque valley of winding curves. Mount Cockburn changes in purples and blues as if the colours were wafted upon it by some drifting breeze.

At twenty miles we stop, for here is Road's End. It is No-man's Land out farther. That untamed distance calls to us, but—we are seeking crocodiles.

Here are several cottages and sheds. This is the pumping station which supplies Wyndham with water. Away below is a tree-lined waterhole stretching for a mile towards sandstone cliffs that suggest the mouth of a valley. This deep hole of crystal clear water has never been known to run dry. The engine shed is perched on the bank of the waterhole, hills rising sharply behind it. The engine runs on suction gas produced from charcoal, and does a good job. Johnstone River crocodiles are playing in the deep emerald green away below. There would be a scurry if a big fellow came along, for the estuarine crocodile occasionally cruises upriver to feast in these deep, pleasant holes. At such times the little fellows hurriedly vacate the pools. Some five miles farther upstream is a longer and deeper hole where fish laze in sun-kissed water when not chased by the crocodiles.

Andy Cardwell is the "boss" of this tiny settlement. One of the old hands in the days of Menzies and Cue, Andy is a thin little chap liked by all who know him. His wife, a quiet, pleasant-faced little woman, feels the loneliness. She is pining, I feel, for her children, two thousand miles away in Perth. "Skip" Outridge helps Andy with the engines and being a wireless fiend "talks" to Jack Christie, twenty miles away at the meatworks, twice daily. Bill Flinders and Old Jimmy Baines complete this happy family. Old Jimmy is one of the pioneers, a quiet, little old chap with scanty hair, a broad forehead, dreamy eyes. He is known far and wide as a man who all his life has helped anyone he could as often as he could, and kept his own counsel about it. In the early days he stocked Kaeeda for the K.P.C. when the natives were bad indeed. Jimmy knew the bad lands on the desert fringe when death stalked the lonely rider both day and night.

Old Jimmy now "rides" the pipeline. Rides along it, and if there be any breaks repairs them with help of the man who rides towards him from the Wyndham side. This patrol is vitally important, for, although man believes himself to be very great, he soon would perish without one of the simplest miracles of nature—water.

Sometimes in the evening a fancy struck me that sunset and Jimmy Baines symbolized those grim, yet lovely Kimberley hills. The kindly little old man had battled through life in a country primitive as its sons, the Stone Age men. Throughout many years his heart had responded to the joy of the birds, battled on to win out against the grimness of despair. He had won out. His battling days were over and his eventide sweet with understanding.

That rugged old Cockburn Range, worn down to but a shadow of its towering youth, now stood sombre as the Sphinx, draped in shades of purples and blues merging into rose. The colours took on a velvety texture as the sun slowly sank.

Down at the Big Pool at nights all was deathly quiet. Then—a swirling of water—silence. Water swirling again as if a torpedo were shooting through it—the echoing clap of a giant tail!

The big old-men 'gators, the estuarine crocodiles, had come upriver to harry the little crocodiles in their happy feeding grounds. Woe betide any animal that came to those silvered pools to drink tonight.

We knew what Jimmy was thinking, sitting there silent when that ominous sound came swirling up from below. Some little time before, Billy Weaver, the blind miner, had entrusted to Jimmy his bush race-horse, Nalgee, of which Jimmy was very fond. Even in his blindness Billy Weaver could not resist the call of gold and it had come recently, and of all-places, from away down in Central Australia, near Tennant's Creek. Billy and his family had packed their outfit and commenced the long, hard trek through bush and mulga, spinifex and sand towards the heart of the Centre. Nalgee had been left behind in care of the man who Weaver knew would look after him so very well. Taking the horse with him was out of the question, for, out from the Tennant, water would be nearly as valuable as gold. And grass for horses would he very scarce at times.

Jimmy Baines chose Nalgee's home on the sweet grass that frames the beauty of Big Pool. This pool, away upstream, is difficult of access to the estuarine crocodiles. Even when they get there the way is barred by a rocky bar that extends like a wall right across the river. And here man and horse cemented a friendship known so often between man and horse in the bush.

Nalgee would come whinnying to him when, in early morning, Jimmy would come to see that all was well. And in the evening, after work, Jimmy would come again and rub the horse down and tend to him in those little ways that build confidence and willingness and endurance into a horse. Jimmy soon had Nalgee in great fettle. The trusting brown eyes of the horse were alight with life, his coat shone glossy as the best-cared-for horses in any big city racing stables. In his rippling muscles was a promise of speed. A gallop around the green basin set in a circle of hills was his delight. Just to show Jimmy how he felt he would roll and kick with those delighted grunts that tell of well-being.

The crocodile must have watched the horse for days; even watched the man's daily visits. One afternoon late the crocodile got the horse. As Nalgee bent to drink, a monstrous snout surged up and the bulk of the crocodile was clawing around his neck as Nalgee reared aside with a piercing scream. Nalgee fought in a frenzy of rearing body and pawing, lashing hoofs, actually dragged the crocodile out of the water as his own blood stained Sandy Beach. With a frantic pawing he reared, dragging the great weight with him. Then he crashed down on it with his chest and broke free.

In the distant cottage Jimmy heard the first agonized scream—then stifled screams. For a moment he thought Nalgee must be rolling and playing. Then he came running.

Nalgee was down to it then. His bloody neck was raw flesh, his shoulder a terrible gash, ripped clean open. His entrails were hanging out.

Jimmy's friends shook sorry heads. They quietly suggested shooting the horse to put him out of his misery. His case was hopeless.

But Jimmy was silent. Those pitiful brown eyes that pleaded. While the men watched over the horse he hurried to the cottage, returned with bucket and packing needle and thread. He washed the grass and twigs and sand from the horse's entrails and carefully poked them back into place. Then sewed up the stomach. Washed the shoulder and sewed that up too. He stayed by the horse night and day until it could hobble about again.

Meanwhile he mixed strychnine in a cunning bait and, keeping the taint of human hands from it, craftily fastened it to the right tree over-leaning the pool so that the water would just touch the meat. Thus Jimmy poisoned that crocodile, and laid other baits and got three more.

Nalgee's wounds healed up, miraculous as it seemed. But his shoulder continued to trouble him. Apparently he was crippled for life.

The boys nicknamed Nalgee "Alligator". MacDonald, a government veterinary surgeon visiting Wyndham, came to hear of him. He drove out to the pumping station and examined the horse. Thereafter he took a keen interest in him, opened the shoulder again, and made a thorough job of curing the horse.

When the yearly bush meetings came along again, Nalgee ran second in a flying handicap. Then won the Shorts Handicap in Hall's Creek.

Since then he has won in both Wyndham and Hall's Creek.

Nalgee truly was blessed by the Goddess of Fortune. So also after many battling years was Billy Weaver, the blind miner. Returning through Central Australia soon after this trip on which these notes were written, I stayed a while at the then "wild and woolly" newly discovered goldfield at Tennant's Creek, and visited Billy Weaver in his big, cool, spinifex-built camp. And Billy had pitched his camp right on one of the rich gold mines among the hungry, brown hills. Surely he is the only blind man in the world who has found a gold mine.

One morning there by the King River we were smoking under the Prisoner's Tree when Jimmy suddenly jumped up and killed a venomous-looking brown snake. I hadn't even seen the thing.

"I did not know you were so quick on your pins, Jimmy," I remarked.

"I detest crocodiles," he answered in his gentle, dreamy voice. "And sharks, and poisonous snakes."

"Ever been bitten?"

"Yes. By a tiger snake, too. At Bamboo Creek. Fell asleep, head pillowed on hand. Woke up with a tiger snake hanging on to a finger. It felt exactly like a vicious, continued pinch from a pair of strong, sharp thumbnails. The cursed thing held on too. I'd never dreamed what beastly things snakes' eyes can be. Violently I slung it off. There was no pain then, but very soon a great longing for sleep. I've never longed in all my life for anything as I longed to be allowed to go to sleep. My mates forced me to swallow half a bottle of whisky. It had no effect at all. They cut the wound, but luckily did not put any dry Condy's into it. The doctor said later that dry Condy's might have stopped the wound, whereas the idea is to make it bleed. A friend struck me smartly left and right across the face. Hardly felt it.

Hardly knew what they were doing. I wanted to fall asleep. They made me swallow mustard and other stuff. But it did not make me very sick. They pulled me up and started to walk me, but I could not hear what they were saying. They walked me around and around the camp all night, slapping my face every time my head dropped to my chest. Just after daylight I was getting a bit better. It felt then exactly as if a bandage was pressed across both shoulders and was drawn tightly across the chest. Three days later the doctor said this feeling was wonderfully lucky. It was the first action of the blood working its way through the veins in proper circulation again. Had they not walked me about and thrashed me to keep awake it would have meant the end. But it was a lovely feeling, that longing to go to sleep."

The "Prisoner's Tree", sometimes called the "Hillgrove Lock-up", is a big old bottle tree. What its age might be would be hard to guess. There is a big hollow space inside the grotesque trunk. A tiny doorway has long since been cut into the trunk. Inside the shell is as gnarled and wrinkled as the face of a very, very old man. All deep, twisting ridges and rough corrugations. High up where the branches begin on the outside gleam several air-holes, where shafts of light filter in. It is like a little room with a tall, narrow dome. In the days of the Kimberley rush the diggers passing this way used the tree as a safe deposit for provisions during the night against native stealers. Occasionally since it has been used to cage native prisoners for the night when a patrol riding in from the wild lands camped here on the last stage to Wyndham.

XXXIII

THE STONE AGE WILL PASS AWAY

RIGHT west of here, and south-west, the Wild Lands lie. Hills and valleys that grow more rugged until they merge in the tangled fastnesses towards the nor'-west coast. Not many miles north-west is the Forrest River Mission, on the Forrest River winding towards the Gulf between its cliffs.

Inland from the mission is Aboriginal Land. Away up this valley and far over it, nearly three hundred miles away, is a cattle run belonging to Scotty Salmon and Scotty Menmuir. It is now practically abandoned. Battlers with a few hundred head of cattle out in that wilderness, with no transportation, they have toiled against very heavy odds in that untamed country, amongst Stone Age men not averse to varying their diet by a little cattle-spearing. From Wyndham along this route they bring their stores over hill and valley, swamp and river, to their frontier station. But it looks as if conditions have very nearly beaten them.

Yet there are always other men to battle on. Young Martin has started a place, a ranch our American cousins would call it, only sixty miles away from here. Spewah, he names it. It is not far from Siddon's place. Siddon was in the Fifth Light Horse Regiment with me. We fought throughout Gallipoli and Palestine. After the war he started a place away out there in the wilderness. He battled very hard, supported by his game little wife. In the great loneliness she had a baby too. But the country beat them at last. The loneliness, the conditions, the wildness, lack of transport, the primitive all around them. Their only civilization was the tiny port of Wyndham so far away. Wyndham, isolated itself during the wet season, and two thousand miles from Perth.

There are no estuarine crocodiles out there, not until you come to the cliff-bound coast and its fiords and rock-walled rivers. But in the lands in between, in swamp and lagoon and river waterhole framed by towering cliffs there live the fresh-water crocodiles, they who do not venture out into the sea.

While on a previous trip through that intriguing country I often watched the tribesmen spear or catch this crocodile. By the way, he does not look so little when he grows to a length of six feet and is struggling viciously for life in his native element. But the sons of the wild can beat him and make him appear stupidly foolish; the primitive man knows his holts.

The fresh-water crocodile does not look all round and upwards as we do. He looks along the surface of the water when swimming. So that he is at the mercy of a motionless, silent spearman who may happen to be above him. The hunters crawl out on to trees or branches which over-lean the water, and wait. Their mates, stationed around the lagoon, clap stones together underwater and this sends the crocodiles scurrying. Generally they come to the surface and sooner or later one or more will swim under a leaning tree. Then down fly the spears.

Nor is there always need to prepare an ambush. I've watched a lone huntsman step out from the trees at a lagoon edge. One glance and he sees a crocodile basking on the surface under a leaning tree. The hunter vanishes. A few moments and, invisible from the water, he appears behind the tree, begins to climb. Creepily reminiscent of the movement of a black snake, he worms his way out over the water. His spear probably is held with the point-end down under his armpit, the haft pressed against his side. If the limb is slender the hunter seems to make his body slender too. The spear-end may be gripped in his mouth, the long haft under his body which is pressed close to the tree. If any warning reflection falls upon the water, the crocodile would take alarm. When directly above the prey or at the best angle the tree allows him, he cautiously edges up his spear along the trunk. Gripping it he leans over and aims. His spear arm rises. Then down hisses the spear.

He does not miss.

Probably the crocodile is not vitally hit. No matter. In a day or two he will be floating belly up. Until then there is many a good meal to be won from the lagoon.

If the keen eye of the hunter notices by the air bubbles or fine uprising of silt that a crocodile has been lying on the sand or mud underwater, he casually swims out and marks the spot with a bamboo thrust down into the bottom. Next day, or the day after, the crocodile will again be lying in his favourite underwater possy.

The hunter and his mate swim underwater up behind the crocodile. If the water is clear they see him, even though his body merges so well into the bottom, or mud, or weeds upon which he may be lying. If not, the stick is there to guide them to his approximate position. Immediately they see him they glide along the bottom. A touch of the fingertips does it. Should the water be discoloured or if he has really buried himself among the weeds, then near the stick they grope with sensitive fingertips, reaching ahead and out all around them. They touch the crocodile. He feels the light, reassuring, caressing touch. He seldom moves. You can tickle the belly of a fish that way and he likes it. A fairy-like touch along the crocodile's back. He feels another on the back at the shoulders. A light groping down both sides, and suddenly his paws are wrenched up and jerked agonizingly across his neck and across his hindquarters over the butt of the tail. He feels himself lifted up, carried forward helplessly. The hunters swim, then wade with him to the bank, laughing. He is terror-stricken but helpless. He can neither snap with his jaws, rend with his claws, nor lash with his tail. He is doomed.

Hidden away below in deep lagoons are many mysterious things. We never dream they exist. Our eyes see only the broad expanse of the waterlily leaves, and sometimes acres of big flowers, the masses of water-grasses, the ducks and wild geese and tree-shadows. The life contained in a lagoon is really a seething world. But we cannot linger longer in that fascinating world.

Here and there, in water gloom going away in under the bank, is actually a cave. In other places the bank is undermined sometimes to such an extent that just there it is really a verdantly covered veranda.

Such cool recesses are congregating places for the crocodiles. Here they often gather together and indulge in crocodile gossip, telling all the news of the lagoon. Where the best fish are feeding now, and when they saw the last sign of their dreaded enemy, the black huntsman, and what the tortoise said to the water-rat. They criticize the chatter of the ducks and the pygmy geese, and chuckle about the old-man swan who in a huff has withdrawn to the farthermost end of the lagoon after the latest quarrel with his wife. Most of all do they love to gossip of food, and scandal among themselves.

At least so my Stone Age friends have assured me during half a lifetime amongst them. They have taught me so many undreamed-of facts, and verifiable facts of other denizens of the wild, that from my heart I could not contradict them when they have assured me that crocodiles talk with one another.

Over the bank just above a cavern the black hunters glide. Vanish in noiseless ripples. As they sink down, one or two men bend over and swim straight inside the cavern with a speedy kicking of flying arms and legs. The startled crocodiles rush out. The terrified young ones rush blindly into hands which snatch out and cling around their long, thin, pointed snouts.

I have seen men at times come shooting to the surface with a young crocodile thus grasped in either hand.

It is a failing of human nature that many of us think we know all about a subject after we have studied it a while. When we find difficulty in increasing our knowledge about any particular subject we are liable to tell ourselves we have become masters of it. But we can master no subject. Any subject on earth is far too big for any one man's lifetime.

I thought I knew a lot about crocodiles, but these "simple" children of nature taught me that I had hardly begun to learn. They laughed delightedly, making jokes at my expense. I was staring at a crocodile. He was almost at my feet, yet I could not see him. I stared at the shallow water, so crystal clear. There were pebbles down there that shone like diamonds. I could see the eyes of a little fish that was swimming past. But a five-foot crocodile—no!

They looked down at him again and laughed uproariously. I followed their glances, but could not see him. Then a tribesman stabbed downwards and a crocodile writhed up, splashing my feet with green slime. Just in a little patch of the green slime you see in every swamp or waterhole or lagoon. He was there right on the surface, buried in the slime. When camouflaged so perfectly they rarely move either to sound or sight, no matter how close you may be.

This slime is not only an impenetrable camouflage; it is one of nature's wonders as a trap for prey. Water-birds on long legs come treading through it seeking their prey. Frogs, turtle, crayfish, water-rats, water-snakes seek food there.

And—walk straight into the crocodile's jaws.

The crocodiles are just as clever in deep water where patches of yellow and russet water-grass sometimes float on the surface like drifting seaweed. A crocodile floats in the middle of that weed, its fronds draped all around him, the yellow and russet merging with his slaty-grey to brownish body and yellowish white belly, in perfect concealment. Any fish or turtle that comes to nibble at that grass, any fairy-winged water-bird that settles upon it in search of insects, meets with an upward surge of open jaws gleaming with needle-sharp teeth.

Thus also they lie in wait under the broad lily leaves that look so innocent in their flat greenness upon the water, massed with beautiful flowers. Upon these broad leaves spidery-legged birds skip from leaf to leaf and flower to flower. While water-rats hop across on airy feet.

And just under the leaf the crocodile is lurking.

But time moves on. Just flows by in the destinies of men as it does for crocodiles and for all things. We are back again at Wyndham, back where the sleepy township nestles on the shores of the great, muddy Gulf. Time flows on for Wyndham, just from the wet to the dry. But—it will not be always so.

Around this fertile corner of the nor'-west there are some four hundred thousand square miles with only one person, white or coloured, to every eighty square miles. And nearly all live close to a little forgotten port or two.

And away behind Wyndham, but to the east side, there is one river alone, the Ord, which runs through two hundred miles of country, much of it fertile plains. And away back in that river, where the cliffs are a beauty of purple and gold in the rising and setting of the sun, there is a great gorge. And this gorge will eventually be dammed.

And the water will irrigate the plains.

And alas! the Stone Age man will fade away. And there will come mighty herds of cattle. And plains that for a thousand years have known only the trumpeting of the brolga, the howl of the dingo, the cackle of wild fowl and the lonely passing of wild geese in the night will soon be green under cultivation. And where rose the smoke from the wild man's corroboree grounds will rise the smoke from many a homestead chimney. Aye, and from virile towns too.

Time marches on—time waits for no man.

XXXIV

THE BLOOD HOLE

(Notes from the Diary)

EVENING.

All afternoon have been sitting by the Blood Hole. Mangroves to the brown water's edge; thick mud. Near a vaguely glimpsed opening in the mangroves little mullet swim close inshore, timid of enemies.

Cockatoos are screeching, fluttering like big white flowers on the green mangrove tops. Out on the broad waters is anchored the one resident vessel of Wyndham, the pilot launch. Away across the Gulf stand green and brown the trees and hills of the westward side from which strike back the rays of the afternoon sun to gleam into the Blood Hole. Uncanny reflection. From away back behind the mangroves comes the dull sound of the meatworks machinery.

Clinging to the muddy water edge where the tide laps that leaf-shadowed opening in the mangroves is an arresting, dull, brickish-red scum. It looks vaguely unhealthy, repulsive. It is blood—for the blood drain from the meatworks trickles into here. And now, the volume of the irresistibly rising tide holds the heavy fluid edged to the mud, whence it tries to spread as a great wide stain overwhelming the brown.

The lifeblood from hundreds of slaughtered cattle daily empties here, and even the waters of Cambridge Gulf cannot wash it entirely away.

All is quiet. The busy sound of the meatworks comes sub-dued through the trees. A little crab is burrowing in the mud.

Something appears, quite silently—the knobby head of a crocodile.

But only the vague knobby top of it, like floating seed pods upon the water. The tip of the snout is there now, the horny ridges of the eyes, cruel eyes, deep set. It rises a fraction more and the serrations along the top of the tail appear. Even so, it is barely visible. No one would see it unless expecting it. Its cold eyes are surveying things; it hears the noises of the earth, the screech of cockatoos, the faint clang of a hammer at the meatworks, the distant rattle of a bucket from the launch. In deathly stillness it surveys the shoreline; it knows a rifleman may be lurking there. It sinks.

Twenty minutes dream by. Something appears quite sud-denly away out on the water, where the placid calm is now broken by a knobby head, a long serrated tail. The snout is turned inshore. The tail lazily moves keeping the ugly body headed shorewards. Another rises beside it. They gaze towards the mangroves. Nothing moves, not a sign of life. With a lash of tail they chase one another around and around in slow enjoyment. A cockatoo screeches harshly—they vanish.

Time dreamed by again. The earth seemed quietly breathing the smell of water upon mangrove mud. Suddenly they appeared again. Three this time, just the pods of their snouts and eyes. Presently they rose, plainly visible, reassured by the death-like stillness, absence of movement. They lazily paddled and floated around the edge of the Blood Hole. With a quick swirl one chased the other. They clove through the water, a sudden display of unexpected agility so different from their calm floating of a moment before. The third lifted his big head high out of the water with his snout pointing to heaven. Again he lifted out of the water as if swallowing lazily. The chased one made a detour and came gliding back to the bank, wary of the one that had chased him away. The third, only his snout exposed, came swimming to the bank. He came waddling ashore, slowly, his snout pressing in the mud like the bill of a gobbling duck, his stubby forepaws hunched well in under, his back twisting like a twisty lizard. A horrible thing of the mud he looked.

Now the tide begins to run out and the blood follows it. The never dying stain grows gradually redder. Through the flabby flap in their gullet the big fellows force air with a grunting, gurgling sound as they jerk their snouts clear of the water. They laze in the blood drain with horrid mouths open while slimy fragments of gristle and refuse come drifting down to them. This refuse of the great slaughter they dreamily sift in their open mouths. When the hideous jaws are clogged full they lift horrid heads to the sky with a slow, jerking swallow.

Two hours drift by; the sun is sinking; half a dozen crocodiles have risen to stare towards the shore. With the falling of the water the blood is coming thicker. Mudbanks have crept into vision as the water recedes. Suddenly something brightly pink glows under the water twenty feet out from the shoreline. It has grown to the size of a submerged blanket coloured with the pinkness of a rosy sunset. Just as fast as the tides recedes so does this pink blanket spread and grow. It is blood. Very slowly it turns russet. It must be coming from some drain outlet under the water. Every moment it spreads more strongly as the waters recede. Another crocodile comes up, gazing shoreward. He stays longer. He knows the sun is going down, darkness is coming. The russet turns to blood red, undiluted now as it creeps out from the muddy edge, gurgling after the receding water. It travels now with an uncanny swiftness. Its long, crimson, pencil-like feelers creep along the mud edge and thence into the mouth of that slimy inlet.

Sunset has come. A gorgeous sunset, a rosy flash of pink. It bathes the horrid snouts of many crocodiles. As the pink fades to eventide they are right in among the darkening pink dribbling out from the shore. One coughs harshly; there sounds the lash of a tail. Night has come.

Evening.

This morning was calm; high tide; the water high over the outlet of the blood drain, lapping in among the mangroves. The cloud in the water a rich pink. Very still was that cloud, for the tide that held it back was stationary. Under the just-risen sun the mangrove shadows on the water were in cameo. A cockatoo screeched. On the outskirts of the cloud the water assumed a yellowish tinge and through this appeared long ribbons of darkish brown, many of them stretching right back among the mangroves. A crocodile lay almost motionless in the centre of the pink cloud, his snout tip, his eyes, his serrated tail a brown-grey blob bathed in that rich pink.

Almost imperceptibly the cloud began to spread as at a breath from the turn of the tide. As the tide moved, slowly the cloud crept in, drifting shorewards. Now visible gently floating through it were crimson clots of blood, like rich red plums. These were what the crocodiles lay open-mouthed for, to strain between their fangs. One had his mouth nearly full now. His head, jaws partly open, partly rises from the water. He "blows" with a hoarse, throaty rattle. Then swallows. Then sinks again.

The edge of the pink cloud now drifted down deep into the water; as it swayed in tenuous movement these edges spread like the fleecy drapery of clouds. A silver garfish swam with sinuous movement through the pink. A lane opened out behind him, a criss-crossy lane that came rolling lazily in again. Thick, barely moving, slow walls of pink. The cloud edges, drifting ever more as the tide gradually gained way, now swayed to ever more beautiful cloud effects, drifting and gathering strength and floating away as a cloud might under a blood-red sun; only this cloud did not fade away—it was ever replenished.

Evening.

Not even the bellow escapes at Wyndham. Death falls too swiftly. As the goaded cattle stumble up their Bridge of Sighs, each beast is met at the top by the man with the hammer. It drops with awful swiftness. In twelve minutes it is frozen beef—lightning speed.

No wonder the crocodiles are fat.

Waste blood of thirty-three thousand bullocks gurgles down the blood drain.

But nothing is wasted.

Down at the Blood Hole the crocodiles wait. Fat fellows, greasy, slimy, slit-eyed, heavy-jowled.

ION IDRIESS
From ETT IMPRINT

Flynn of the Inland

The Desert Column

The Red Chief

Nemarluk

Horrie the Wog Dog

Prospecting for Gold

Drums of Mer

Madman's Island

The Yellow Joss

Forty Fathoms Deep Lasseter's
Last Ride

Sniping

Shoot to Kill

Guerrilla Tactics

Trapping the Jap

Lurking Death

The Scout

The Wild White Man of Badu

Gold Dust and Ashes

Headhunters of the Coral Sea

Gouger of the Bulletin

Ion Idriess: The Last Interview

Man Tracks

Men of the Jungle

Outlaws of the Leopolds Over
the Range

Tracks of Destiny

The Opium Smugglers

In Crocodile Land

Our Flying Aces

www.ingramcontent.com/pod-product-compliance
Lightning Source LLC
Chambersburg PA
CBHW021228090426
42740CB00006B/441